VICTORIA'S MADMEN

REVOLUTION AND ALIENATION

CLIVE BLOOM

palgrave
macmillan

First published 2013 by
PALGRAVE MACMILLAN

Palgrave Macmillan in the UK is an imprint of Macmillan Publishers Limited, registered in England, company number 785998, of Houndmills, Basingstoke, Hampshire RG21 6XS.

Palgrave Macmillan in the US is a division of St Martin's Press LLC, 175 Fifth Avenue, New York, NY 10010.

Palgrave Macmillan is the global academic imprint of the above companies and has companies and representatives throughout the world.

Palgrave® and Macmillan® are registered trademarks in the United States, the United Kingdom, Europe and other countries.

ISBN 978–0–230–31382–8

This book is printed on paper suitable for recycling and made from fully managed and sustained forest sources. Logging, pulping and manufacturing processes are expected to conform to the environmental regulations of the country of origin.

A catalogue record for this book is available from the British Library.

A catalog record for this book is available from the Library of Congress.

Frontispiece image: Queen Victoria, published in 1887 by Charles Knight with the title 'Her Majesty's Gracious Smile'

Typeset by MPS Limited, Chennai, India.

To my family as yet unborn, makers of the future

CONTENTS

ACKNOWLEDGEMENTS

Thanks are due to the following: Paul Ford at the Walsall Local History Centre and Jennifer Thompson at Walsall Central Library and Museum; Barrie N. Roberts, local historian, Walsall; the archivists at the Greenwich Local History Museum; Nancy Langfeldt and the librarians at the Bishopsgate Institute; Jo Parker, Tim Foster and Gary Heals at the Vestry House Museum, Walthamstow; Robert Thwaite and Renata Pillay, Bruce Castle Museum, Haringey Council; Colin Gale of the Bethlem Royal Hospital Archives and Museum Service; Catherine Coulthard at the City of London Police; Alice Tyrell at Notre Dame University; Nick Hamilton at Resonance FM; Malcolm Hopkins and William Hudson at Housmans Bookshop; Clive Bettington; Donald Rumbelow; Philip Ruff and Helen Rappaport, who worked on the Siege of Sidney Street exhibition at the Museum of London in Docklands with me; and finally, Michael Strang, Ruth Ireland, Jon Lloyd, Jennifer McCall and Clare Mence, who 'encouraged' the last push.

The portrait of Queen Victoria (frontispiece) is reproduced by kind permission of the GL Archive/Alamy.

Information on the revolutionary movements described in Chapter 9 was first published in a greatly shortened form in the Jewish East End Society's special Siege of Sidney Street edition (23 November 2010). My thanks to Clive Bettington for permission to reprint. The description of the actual siege of Sidney Street in Chapter 19 first appeared in the *BBC History Magazine* (2011). My thanks to the editor David Musgrove for permission to reprint the article here. The story of William Courtney in Chapter 6 first appeared in *Riotous Revolutionaries: A History of Britain's Fight for a Republic* (2007). My thanks to the History Press for permission to reprint the section in a new context. The section on socialist churches and Arthur Conan Doyle in Chapter 5 and thereafter first appeared in a greatly abridged version as 'The Legacy of Sherlock

Holmes' in Catherine Wynne and Sabine Varnacker (eds), *Sherlock Holmes and Conan Doyle: Multi-Media Afterlives* (Palgrave Macmillan, 2012). Some small sections of Chapters 3, 4 and 5 first appeared as 'Angels in the Architecture' in Peter Buse and Andrew Stott (eds), *Ghosts: Deconstruction, Psychoanalysis, History* (Palgrave, 1999), whilst the opening few paragraphs of Chapter 15 first appeared in *Gothic Histories* (Continuum, 2009).

In another moment Alice was through the glass.

Lewis Carroll, *Through the Looking-Glass: and what Alice found there*

ONE
MANYPEEPLIA UPSIDOWNIA

In the sewers something stirs. The Victorian age appears to us so stable and so assured, and yet voices from subterranean depths proclaimed strange futures from deep in the labyrinth; Victoria Imperatrix: an empress of a world of strange shadows. This is the story of those Victorian political, personal and cultural struggles from which the modern world emerged and here are those Victorian individuals whose often strange ideas created the atmosphere of changing times. This book concentrates on two neglected aspects of Victorian Britain – personal alienation and social revolution – and how these forces had a profound affect both on the conduct of individuals and on the very idea of the society that these individuals inhabited.

Above all, this is the story of a number of extraordinary men and women, some of whom are remembered (but whose more extreme ideas are marginalised as aberrations) and some of whom are now all but forgotten and were literally considered mad by most, if not all, of their contemporaries and whose mainly utopian ideals were pursued against the prevailing norms of the day: Victorians against the Victorian age. This community of dreamers included social visionaries, artists, politicians and seekers of spiritual enlightenment, all of whom were considered out-of-step, eccentric, downright dangerous or morally corrupt during their lifetime.

The Victorian age has long been seen by historians as one far more diverse in every respect than earlier commentators liked to think. The monolith of steam and class conflict, antimacassars and aspidistras has long since given way to a more subtly nuanced picture. Indeed, Philipp Blom has pointed out that:

> To most people who lived around 1900 this nostalgic view with its emphasis on solidity and grace would have come as a surprise.

Nevertheless, this newer Victorian landscape is also oddly traditional, inasmuch as the sense of the period has still been partially created by the leading voices of the age rather than those in partial or complete shadow.

It is true that historians have backdated the period called the 'Victorian Age' before Victoria's accession to her uncle's William IV's reign in which the Reform Act of 1832 frames the 'true' beginning of the Victorian period: 'Victorianism before Victoria'. This period is itself seen as being followed by a 'middle' period symbolised by Victorian prosperity and the Great Exhibition, and then a 'late' period where things reach their apotheosis. Such periodisation also sees the century as divided into three economic and constitutionally different periods, leading from individualism to collectivism.

Such discussions of periodisation and meaning were often framed in the nineteenth century by the expression 'spirit of the age', a phrase invented in the eighteenth century by David Hume but endlessly repeated by writers such as William Hazlitt, John Stuart Mill, Edward Bulwer Lytton and Thomas Carlyle. For Mill, the period was one of 'transition' and 'intellectual anarchy', where the old ways had been outgrown but new ways were not yet available, whilst for Carlyle, it was an age caught between scepticism and belief, and for Bulwer Lytton, it was an age of bleak utilitarianism, the age of romanticism having passed with the death of Lord Byron. Benjamin Disraeli saw the age as one of social and economic strife divided between 'two nations', yet these two nations were not entirely made up just of divergent classes, but also of divergent and irreconcilable thought processes.

Indeed, the nineteenth century might be divided between three groups: those who represented the old Georgian decadence; the young Turks eager for reform; and a third group who felt an allegiance to the world of their grandparents or great-grandparents, but who were forced to exist in the world of reforming moralism and priggishness. In the end, the young Turks won and created the lasting view of the age. Those other few who existed in the cracks between the old order and the new Victorianism were, I contend, the makers of the future, its habits and social outlook, but were ignored in their day as cranks.

Here are Victorian revolutionary thinkers and the sometimes bizarre ideas held by those whose politics or lifestyles grated against the mainstream thought of their times and the attitudes of their contemporaries. Some were shunned as mad, some were actually sent to asylums, some became gurus for a new generation, while others dreamt their fantasies in print and in secret. William Morris in his utopian novel *News from Nowhere* (1890) speaks of 'the unlucky nineteenth century', his heroes those who opposed the crass utilitarian progress of his age and instead formed an 'alternative history' of the century, made up from those who were 'artist[s] ... genius[es] and ... revolutionist[s]'. Such revolutionary thinkers and their radical tendencies spill uneasily into the Edwardian period and beyond.

The story includes celebrities such as Oscar Wilde and T.E. Lawrence; writers such as H.G. Wells, Arthur Conan Doyle, Edward Bulwer-Lytton and the lesser known Edward Fawcett; the many revolutionaries and radicals of the times from Karl Marx, Annie Besant, Charles Bradlaugh, Dan Chatterton, Beatrice Webb and Eleanor Marx to the dubious charms of Oswald Mosley; the messiahs 'Octavia' and 'Jezreel'; the occultist Aleister Crowley and his Scarlet Woman; murderers like Richard Dadd and Jack the Ripper; early town planners and ecologists such as Ebenezer Howard, John Hargrave, Harold Booth and Archibald Belaney; Indian nationalists and anti-imperialists such as Mohandas Gandhi, Shapurji Saklatvala and Vinayak Savarkar; the Latvian anarchists who killed three policemen in the East End of London; the Green Shirts of the Kibbo Kift and many more: ideas and people tumble into the twentieth century with new and dangerous ideas developed in the mental laboratory of the Victorian age.

In the nineteenth century the unrealised self and the unrealised state where the infinite potential of the future was to be found existed as much inside one's head as outside in the world, and where revolutionaries thought they either embodied the future in their own person or were bringing it about by preaching the gospel of what they had witnessed in the politics they embraced. Such visions were their visions, often hallucinatory, but intended to liberate the individual and set society free. This is the story of extremes of thought, action and mind, chosen by people living at breaking point within their social position, personal history and culture in nineteenth- and early twentieth-century Britain; men and women motivated by certainties granted to them by outward logic or inner illumination, travelling light, as it were, stripped of those Victorian certainties that provided the social, emotional and intellectual foundations they wished to destroy. They had no guiding god, nor maps beyond those which they imagined and through which they travelled as a visionary company and as the salvation of the world.

Within the supposedly stable world of Victorian ideals lurked their opposites and in that grand antithesis was created the age that would follow and would obliterate the apparently solid foundations of the past. We are, of course, the products of what went before, but the attempt to denigrate or actually obliterate our Victorian foundations, as was the case with town planners, the media, films, thinkers and academics up to the 1970s makes for problematic history. We are, as Matthew Sweet pointed out in his book *Inventing the Victorians*, the inheritors of a world that we consider at best embarrassing and at worst something to be denied altogether. Sweet's argument – that we are nearer to the Victorian sense of the world than we like to think – is convincing, but my point is that we are also nearer that part of the Victorian age that the very Victorians refused to countenance.

It is these countervailing tendencies of the nineteenth century that became the orthodoxies of the twentieth century. As Blom has pointed out:

> Modernity did not rise virgin-born from the trenches of the Somme. Well before 1914, it had already taken a firm hold … The War acted not as a creator, but as a catalyst, forcing old structures to collapse more quickly and new identities to assert themselves more readily.

The peculiar Victorian 'essence' is for many of us still one of coal steam, factories, imperial adventures, spices, fog and antimacassar oil, gas light, workhouses, uniformed servants, middle-class propriety and colourful musical halls. On the one hand, Victoria gave her name to an era, but on the other to a sensibility and an emotion: Victorian and Victorianism. Yet even during her lifetime, the terms were being confused and confounded.

As much as 'Victorian' designates the period from Victoria's accession in 1837 to her death in 1901, conjuring in its wake everything from the London of Dickens to the bridges of Isambard Kingdom Brunel, so later Victorianism also seems to designate a claustrophobic attitude of mind hardly conducive to anything other than a narrow consensus and conformity of thought.

Thus, we might talk of a neglected Victorianism: Victorianism after Victoria, not the conservative world of dull conformist values and black-frocked uniformity, but a period extending into the future of the First World War and beyond, in which the roots of systems which had begun deep in the nineteenth century, but had never been allowed to grow, finally took shape above the surface and ushered in the modern world.

Victorianism therefore has a multiplicity of meanings stretching from the most conventional to the republican revolutionary. We now think of Victorianism in terms of its conformity, its imperialism and its industrialisation, but the term might equally cover those who embraced revolution, communism or the occult. It was only in the last few decades of the twentieth century that historians looked further than the stereotype of Victorian Britain, but often this was merely to discover the salacious and prick the pompous image of imperial complacency.

Victorianism has a wide embrace and a long life, a life that in many respects did not finish until the 1960s when those born in the previous century finally died and their ideas faltered and were extinguished, but whose legacy was passed on in feminism, anti-imperialism, occultism, environmentalism and bohemianism, and again caught the imagination of a generation bored with inertia and complacency. Above all, Victorianism is about the life of ideas and how these flourished beyond the nineteenth century and became the language of counter-cultural modernity.

It is this 'alternative' Victorianism that is so elusive and so fascinating, a set of conditions of thought far more wild, adventurous and non-conformist than might be expected from reading traditional histories. Indeed, a period scandalised by its own wayward children and their strange ideas is hardly likely to advertise its aberrations. The very term 'Victorianism' created the grounds for a number of visionary thinkers born into but emotionally divergent from the very age in which they lived, many of whom found their rightful place in the historical movement of ideas long after the specific circumstances of their own lives were forgotten. This was far more than simple futurology or wish fulfilment; it was the notion of a new era and a new spiritual dispensation – of the new person of the future rising from the ashes of a defunct, corrupt civilisation. It was a vision of a New Jerusalem, created by those 'strong enough to build up the world again … [a] world brought to its second birth', as William Morris believed.

Central to many was the problem of faith, as the evangelism of eighteenth-century non-conformism gave way to a more diffuse sense of spiritual well-being and purpose: socialism and women's suffrage, patriotism and conservatism, painting and architecture were all soaked in evangelism, and the obsession with occultism and esoteric lifestyle was a direct result of evangelism's restless search for spiritual guidance.

When Arthur Sullivan wrote the hymn 'The Lost Chord' in 1877, it proved to be an instant favourite with the public. Containing the lines 'all perplexèd meanings [turned]/Into one perfect peace', the lyrics appealed to those looking for certainties that were no longer available and could no longer be couched in the language of Christian faith. This desire for certainty and quietude was repeated later in sentimental but nevertheless powerfully emotional musical hall anthems such as 'The Holy City: Jerusalem' written by Stephen Adams in 1892:

> New earth there seemed to be.
> I saw the Holy City
> Beside the tideless sea.
> The light of God was on its streets,
> The gates were open wide,
> It was the new Jerusalem
> That would not pass away.

For most thinking Victorians, the period hung between the problems of doubt and belief, science and the spirit, social reform or revolution, and these in turn led to a certain dynamic. The 'new Jerusalem' was waiting to be built in the future and the new world would be ushered in over the wreck of old beliefs. This wreck, left after the destruction of old certainties, would lead some to explore the edge of insanity as others might explore the world in search of new physical discoveries. The inward life became more and more attractive to those whose inclinations did not send them into far distant deserts, jungles or mountains. The world was all inside your head. This realisation would effectively allow the future to be born from the margins of Victorian consciousness rather than from imperial action.

It would be ridiculous to argue that the tales in this book offer a completely alternative story to mainstream Victorian history. For too long, however, these particular voices have been muffled in contempt, disregard or unthinking adulation, but they do speak to a different and complementary Victorianism no less rich than the story of the age's main achievements and interesting principally in their implications for a future which came to self-realisation in the twentieth century. This tale of conflicted existential heroes and heroines is no less a myth, but it is different because it was the myth of self-determination propagated by those actually involved.

The challenges to Victorian conformity came from every direction, not least of which was Darwinism, but the challenges to the age outlined in this book were so extreme that they existed at the outer limits of the admissible and often embraced only one true believer. Many of the emergent ideas, especially those of a religious nature or those of cooperative socialism, stood in direct contrast to Darwinian progress – some of a political bent (like socialist democracy, communism and anarchism) could not exist without its prognoses.

The Victorian period as defined here was above all a period exemplified by its 'isms'; the times marked by a search for a way of life different from that inherited from the past which those very 'isms' embodied. At the margins, antithetical systems arose, took root, gestated and waited to be born. Ideas heralded coming times and the new person whose modernity was expressed by adherence to one or a combination of the following: anarchism, hedonism and individualism, bohemianism and avant-gardism; collectivism, syndicalism, suffragetism, communism and socialism; vegetarianism, nudism and sun worship; Zionism and anti-semitism; Islamism; medievalism, Christian gothicism, atheism and secularism; spiritualism, theology and social Darwinism; demon worship;

free love and drug addiction; fairies and woodcraft – all of these were powerful ideologies at one time or another. All the ideologies loudly preached the idea of the future as the possibility of the seeds that existed hidden inside the nineteenth century. You chose your necessary ideological poison and consequently your damnation or salvation.

The aim of all this motion, all this expenditure of energy, largely ignored by those at the centre of government or at the top of society, was to create the one event or crisis that would bring the past to a halt and usher in the future; to defy the past with its policemen, magistrates and established ways of tradition and history, and to combat these with the promissory note of times to come. In this future world all would be well, everyone healed, the soul at rest at last. Yet the event, whether a bomb exploding, a pistol pointed, a book written, a canvass covered or a speech made, also defied the future, demanded that it conform to the will of individual perception that was being expressed at the time. What was the future world to be?

The new world order was to be a radical break from all that went before it. The stable world of Victorian proprieties was to be shaken to its foundations. Nothing less would do. Nineteen years after the death of Queen Victoria, the writer Gerald Gould could predict in the nascent Communist Party of Great Britain that 'there is going to be a revolution in Great Britain'. It was an extraordinary prediction and one almost unthinkable before 1900, except by a huddle of fanatical cultists of one sort or another. The First World War, the Great War as it was, was not the decisive break with the past, but the culmination of imperial rivalries as well as revolutionary forces and the release of those pent-up revolutionary movements that had gestated throughout the previous century.

The break may be seen in the new modernism that rapidly emerged in the early years of the twentieth century. As Owen Hattersley reminds us, the movement in painting, literature, dance, music and cultural habits generally 'had no interest in the continuity of … civilisation and the uninterrupted parade of progress'. Instead, the old 'encrustation' of the past was ditched for the functional 'bare concrete' of experience. An apparent 'rupture' occurred which itself was meant to be an absolute break with the past in order to bury that past with its dream of a 'parade of progress' once and for all.

The struggle of political ideas and personal and social revolutionary ideals belongs to concerns and events which had their roots in a period when Victoria was still a child and her uncles were on the throne, but then often only found themselves fulfilled 63 years later on her death when her son and grandson reigned. In this respect, Victorianism represents both an affirmation and rejection. It is contained in the progressive possibilities of a future age of imagined politics and societies as well as a belief in the overwhelming power of the self to make society new in the first place.

Secularism was the 'religion' of the intellectual mid-Victorian. 'I suggest', wrote Beatrice Webb in *My Apprenticeship* in 1926, that 'it was during the middle decades of the nineteenth century [that] the impulse of self-subordinating service was transferred, consciously and overtly, from God to man'. For William Morris, it was this triumph of the 'religion of humanity' which would eventually release humankind from its subordination to heaven and hell, allow beauty to flourish and 'the world' to live in harmony with its creatures. For him, this new world was to be a rebuke to utilitarianism, but at the same time the very product of its way of thinking. Sociology was to be the new religion of the humanist.

Everything from now on would apparently be settled by science and scientific methods alone. Herbert Spencer was the guru of this new religiosity, and sociological study (mostly of the poor) was its liturgy. The 'great unwashed' would no longer be the recipients of charity, for now they would be the laboratory of the new society. The quest for a set of ideas of the self and an ideal politics in which that self might thrive (and which in itself would be the end of traditional politics) seemed to be ever on the brink of fulfilment, the new secular Jerusalem on a horizon ever nearer. The explorer, Darwinian and secularist Winwood Reade put the case in a work that would become the handbook of every atheist utopian. *The Martyrdom of Man* was published in 1872 to the applause of all those who had signed up to the Victorian counter-culture:

But the God of Light, the Spirit of Knowledge, the Divine Intellect, is gradually spreading over the planet, and upwards to the skies … Earth, which is now a purgatory, will be made a paradise, not by idle prayers and

supplications, but by the efforts of man himself ... Not only will man subdue
the forces of evil that are without; he will subdue those that are within. He
will repress the base instincts and propensities which he has inherited from
the animals below him; he will obey the laws written in his heart; he will
worship the divinity that is within him ... Disease will be extirpated; the
causes of decay will be removed; immortality will be invented. And then the
earth being small, mankind will emigrate into space and will cross airless
Saharas which separate planet from planet, and sun from sun. The earth
will become a Holy Land which will be visited by pilgrims from all the
quarters of the universe. Finally, men will master the forces of nature; they
will become themselves architects of systems, manufacturers of worlds. Man
will then be perfect; he will be a creator; he will therefore be what the vulgar
worship as God.

And yet Jerusalem was not built quite as expected by the followers
of Reade; men who included Cecil Rhodes, H.G. Wells, George
Bernard Shaw or Arthur Conan Doyle all looked for a substitute faith
in imperialism, science, anarchist politics or spiritualism. This was a
declaration of spiritual war against 'traditional' believers such as William
Gladstone, who roundly condemned the flow of 'irreligious works', but
who was powerless to stop them and the contrariness induced by their
thoughts, and who was contrary enough himself to champion Charles
Bradlaugh, the most notorious free thinker of all, when he became MP
for Northampton, but who on entering Parliament refused to take the
traditional sacred oath, wishing instead to make a secular declaration.

Things were changing, but much remained the same, a cloying
reminder of the past. Yet how were those who were dissatisfied going to
change the past? All those Victorian dreamers dreamt of a new Jerusalem,
but one which the next generations were supposed to build. One of
Winwood Reade's adherents, Susan Isaacs, an early promoter of nursery
education, put her particular faith in the free imaginations of children.

For many nineteenth-century outsiders, the question was this: now
I have lost my faith in God, religion and society, how am I to be reborn
into that reality that is more myself and more closely resembles the
reality that others do not see; how is one spiritually resurrected and in
whose name? The answer was clear. First one must detach oneself from

bourgeois mores, become 'bohemian' internally if not also in external appearance; communalism; rational dress, sandals and a diet of nuts were solutions that satisfied some; Marxist-socialism satisfied others; occultism, new religions, free-love and drugs appealed to others. Many looked to the East, to the Arab world or Hinduism to release them from bourgeois desire and delusion, while others looked to history itself to free them. Either way, the outsider's refusal was to be an act of rebellion, both against society and parenthood, against any influence by others.

'What is a rebel?' asked Albert Camus. He is 'a man who says no: but whose refusal does not imply a renunciation'. This 'no' is effectively a type of affirmation of future intent. 'Metaphysical rebellion is the means by which [a person] protests against [their] condition and against the whole of creation.' From the pronouncements of the French Revolution onwards, nineteenth-century rebellion was dedicated to the notion of future time, itself incarnated in the historical process. Nothing was left from the ruins of the past except outdated concepts and outdated relationships. The world could only be put back together if the over-arching certainties of religion and religious observance, tied as they were to outmoded concepts of metaphysical virtue, could be ditched and replaced by the inexorable march of history towards a positive future. History was now to be defined as ethical progress replacing the City of God with that of humanity.

And yet first one had to go through a type of crisis that was both self-induced and external. As the religious mystic 'Octavia' languished in asylum after asylum suffering from delusion and 'melancholia', she concluded that 'I cannot regain myself. I have lost myself. I am without a character which is of any value'. The 'outsider' struggles with problems that are far away from neurosis but close to the social and psychic make-up of rationality itself; unreasonableness is there to reinforce the unnoticed presence of reason itself.

By the end of the nineteenth century, everyone knew that Darwinisn taught that species evolve and that some die out. Herbert Spenser had applied Darwinian ideas to society and others had extrapolated from it to predict the end of the 'upper class' (the 'carriage trade' or 'society' as it was known), but the aristocracy was more powerful than ever, social inequality more marked and more entrenched, psychological questions more burdensome and terrifying. In so many ways, Darwinism solved nothing – neither explaining the existential pain of the intellectual and artist nor the spiritual void of the toiling masses. It would take other conceptual frameworks and other visions to provide answers to these mysteries.

George Bernard Shaw himself was a man profoundly dissatisfied and frustrated with his circumstances, an attitude given expression in his play *John Bull's Other Island*:

Keegan: You feel at home in the world then?
Broadbent: Of course. Don't you?
Keegan (from the very depths of his nature): No.

Although Shaw was far from a peripheral character, his ideas and prejudices irritated and angered those who knew him. Nevertheless, in his head he existed outside of society, his was the feeling of being 'the eternal man outside' and this motivated him. Like many others, Shaw was an 'outsider' figure. The outsider is effectively the sole repository of the movement of the times, for, whilst others are trapped in the prison of pretence and conformity (both of which are illusionary), a prison from which they do not wish to escape, the outsider clearly sees his status 'because he stands for truth'. Only by so doing may he escape the invisible prison of conformity. The outsider's conundrum is how to live whilst others are 'dead', how to make sense out of chaos and meaning out of meaninglessness, live the 'truth' and not be labelled a madman or put in an asylum. The central question of freedom is where to locate the 'reality' of existence in such a way as both to embody that reality and to present it to others clearly.

This would be the problem that would motivate such diverse personalities as Aleister Crowley, T.E. Lawrence or Oscar Wilde, but it would also drive others to insanity explaining the other side of the story of the myth of Victorian certainties.

TWO

RADICAL LUNACY

Princess Victoria was born on 24 May 1819 at Kensington Palace, the daughter of Edward Augustus, Duke of Kent and fourth son of George III. The Duke of Kent had married his wife after 28 years with his mistress, Madame de St Laurent. The importance of the royal child was predicated on the fact that the previous heir to the throne, Princess Charlotte, had died in childbirth, leaving Victoria third in line after her ageing uncle William. The Duke of Kent as an 'extra' royal was always rather at a loss as to how to conduct his life. After a career in the army, he settled down with his mistress in straitened circumstances, which meant that he had to live as frugally as possible on the Continent. At all events, he died in 1820, leaving Victoria in the care of a rather scheming mother and her confidant Sir John Conroy, who both tried to manipulate the young princess. Both were to be thwarted. After the death of William IV on 20 June 1837, Victoria, at the age of 18, ascended the throne. As she did so, her mother and Conroy were dismissed to the background and others of a more reasonable but flattering type came into the limelight. Lord Melbourne was her friend in these first years and she remained an old-fashioned Whig all her life, disliking change in her household or in the country but forced unwillingly to bow to both.

Victoria was crowned in Westminster Abbey on 28 June 1838, with a civil list allowance of several hundred thousand pounds a year to play with rather than the relative poverty of her youth. On 10 February 1840, she married Albert of Saxe-Coburg and Gotha. The Tories fretted over the cost, over the fact that he wasn't British and over the fear that he was a Catholic. 'Monsters', raged the Queen in her journal, 'Revenge, Revenge!'

It may be hardly surprising that an age awash with poisons such as mercury, arsenic, lead and narcotics such as opium should produce strange behaviour, but perhaps strange behaviour was already present and merely exacerbated by deadly chemicals. Moments of heightened national excitement seemed to exaggerate strange activity. Thus, when Queen Victoria came to the throne, all the deranged came out to play. There was Captain John Goode, who accosted the Queen's coach in Birdcage Walk in November and who screamed abuse at her, including: 'You damned----, you usurper, I'll have you off the throne before this day week!' Apparently, the officer believed he was the son of George IV and thus John II.

At his trial, Goode declared that if he were allowed near the Queen, he would tear her to pieces. He also wanted to empty all the royal tombs and scatter the bones, and to hang and disembowel all traitors, particularly the members of the Russian and Danish embassies. When taken away in a coach after being sentenced to be confined in Bedlam, he smashed all the windows and yelled out 'Guards of England, do your duty and rescue your sovereign!', to the astonishment of bystanders. He was transferred to Broadmoor in 1864; he died there, a wreck of a man, in 1883, maintaining his delusion to the last. There was also Charles Stuber, a bankrupt baker who wrote letters to the monarch, threatening a 'dreadful murder' because 'we don't want Kings and Queens in this country!' He was also confined to an asylum.

Most of the early threats to Victoria were of a republican nature borrowed from the previous decade, where men like Arthur Thistlewood and his group of back-to-the-land Spencians had threatened to create a revolution and murder the government. The 1820s had been dangerous days for the monarchy. Were they to be repeated in the new reign?

Queen Victoria's accession, it is said, put paid to the debauched and overwrought reigns of her uncles. Nevertheless, the voices of another place and another age were never quite silent. Patriotism for one's country, for a cause or for the self might outweigh love of one's monarch. Two years after Victoria came to the throne, Chartist agitation and violence broke out in many British cities with an actual insurrection in Newport (1839), armed workers drilled on lonely moors and huge protest rallies filled most city centres, whilst factories and farms were continuously liable to attack from disgruntled labourers. In 1848, as revolution rocked Europe, Victoria was forced to flee for her life to Osborne House on the Isle of Wight because Albert had heard that the Chartists were marching on Windsor, while at Osborne the rumour was that the Chartists were already at the gates.

Edward Oxford was only 19 when he took a shot at the newly wed Queen and her consort as they were being driven in an open carriage through Hyde Park. When questioned, Oxford claimed his pistol had never been loaded but was used merely to frighten the Queen. However, he had also issued a 'proclamation' claiming that an army of revolutionary republicans would rise on his orders. He had drawn up a set of rules for his version of 'Young England', which included arming all members, an oath of allegiance, the use of fictitious names and the need to travel in disguise. Found guilty of high treason, he was acquitted on the grounds of insanity and sent to Bethlem Royal Hospital and then to Broadmoor, from whence he was conditionally discharged 27 years later on 27 October 1867. Warned in no uncertain terms to quit the country or be returned to Broadmoor, and taking the hint, he sailed on 30 December 1867 aboard the ship *Suffolk* bound for Melbourne, Australia and obscurity.

Victoria's reign was haunted by revolutionaries. Yet all was not merely revolutionary turmoil, for Victoria was courted too. In January 1837, Patrick Lynden tried to deliver a love letter to her, but was apprehended and sent to Broadmoor after he attacked the police constables who had him in their care. The Polish Count Dombriski tried to gain the Queen's attention with a love note thrown into her carriage – he left for the United States before being incarcerated. Arthur Tucker tried to get to the Queen to warn her of a conspiracy against her and her mother; found to be harmless, he was discharged into the care of his brother. There was also Thomas Flower, a silversmith, discovered asleep in a chair in the picture gallery in Buckingham Palace, exhausted after searching for Victoria's bedchamber where he wished to leave a love note; he was said to be a 'dangerous lunatic' when roused. Sent to Tothill Fields Prison, he was finally discharged only to turn up again in different circumstances when he violently assaulted a policeman and was again imprisoned.

The strangest case of royal obsessiveness was the first royal stalker, Edward 'the Boy' Jones, who persistently hid in Buckingham Palace and became a minor celebrity and a chronic nuisance. Although poor and strangely ugly, Jones was intelligent and lively, could read and seemed to attract people to his cause. His obsession with the Queen became the talk of the town and magistrates were at first inclined to look positively upon a youth who was clearly not malicious, but merely overly inquisitive. The papers loved his antics, which the law had no recourse to stop. Imprisoned, probably illegally, and transported to Australia, he was spotted many years later as a seller of hot pies and died after a drunken fall off a bridge in 1893. In 1910 the *New York Times* mistakenly thought Jones had ended his days at Broadmoor, a neighbour of the incarcerated Jack the Ripper! Jones was always withdrawn, obsessional and voyeuristic, but not deluded or hallucinatory; schizoid rather than schizophrenic.

Victorians were haunted by madness too. Edgar Allan Poe, a convinced Anglophile, filled his tales with psychotics on hallucinatory drugs (drugs that were freely available at chemists, pubs and in the hedgerows) based on the earlier very English celebration of opium by Thomas de Quincey; John Clare languished in Dr Matthew Allen's asylum in High Beach deep in Epping Forest, believing himself a prize fighter, whilst Alfred Tennyson, who could lose himself in self-induced hypnotic 'fugues', had his own brother (a victim of the family's 'black blood') committed with a Dr Matthews. Writing in 1874 to the American Benjamin Flood, who believed anaesthetics were the way to produce 'revelations', Tennyson commented that:

I have never had any revelations through anaesthetics: but 'a kind of waking trance' (this for lack of a better word) I have frequently had quite up from boyhood. When I have been all alone. This has often come upon me through repeating my own name to myself silently, till all at once as it were out of the intensity of the consciousness of individuality the individuality itself seemed to dissolve and fade away into boundless being – and this not a confused state but the clearest of the clearest, the surest of the surest, utterly beyond words – where Death was an almost laughable impossibility – the loss of personality (if so it were) seeming no extinction but the only true life.

The repetition of a name, Tennyson's own name, led him inexorably from egotism to dissolution as the ego boundaries dissolved and left the 'self' adrift. The strange loss of self was to become a theme in the Victorian imagination and for some an all too fearful reality. To be all alone with nothing but your name as a repeated mantra was both a confirmation of eternal life and a dangerous trap whereby the 'self' descended into the void of non-being. The nature of the loss of ego boundaries would haunt the Victorian consciousness, but would also become the means of escape from Victorian social propriety.

In 1842 Tennyson wrote *Locksley Hall*, an epic poem detailing the alienated consciousness of the narrator after a thwarted love affair, but it was also a poem that documented the factors that were the key to the fragmentation of the age: capitalist madness, hallucination and greed, future wars, imperialism and savagery:

> Cursed be the sickly forms that err from honest Nature's rule!
> Cursed be the gold that gilds the straiten'd forehead of the fool!…
> Am I mad, that I should cherish that which bears but bitter fruit?…
> Where is comfort? in division of the records of the mind?
> Drug thy memories, lest thou learn it, lest thy heart be put to proof,
> In the dead unhappy night, and when the rain is on the roof.
> Like a dog, he hunts in dreams, and thou art staring at the wall,
> Where the dying night-lamp flickers, and the shadows rise and fall…
> Thou shalt hear the 'Never, never,' whisper'd by the phantom years,
> Every door is barr'd with gold, and opens but to golden keys.
> Every gate is throng'd with suitors, all the markets overflow.
> I have but an angry fancy: what is that which I should do?
> I had been content to perish, falling on the foeman's ground,
> When the ranks are roll'd in vapour, and the winds are laid with sound.
> But the jingling of the guinea helps the hurt that Honour feels,
> And the nations do but murmur, snarling at each other's heels.

In the end, the trouble came down to the fault of the age itself: 'thou wondrous Mother-Age!'; the age itself, feminine and tainted, starving its population and on the brink of apocalypse, ruled by a matriarchal (and possibly fickle and treacherous) Queen and thwarted men – the age itself was marked by the irresolvable contradictions of science and progress, of war, imperialism and self-hatred.

What, if anything, asked Tennyson, was the point of the future? In an age without hope, where will it lead? *Locksley Hall* talked of mid-century paralysis and frustrated ambition as the essence of the age itself. All that was left was the void and lost meanings, and the meaningless desire for endless self-numbing action in order to forget the very presence of a disgusted and 'jaundiced' self.

The whole of historical time and all man's energies are reduced to this one betrayal, not merely of one man's love but of an age's promise. What is left is the dregs and self-loathing. Where to run? Perhaps to the East where so many British revolutionaries were to run and perhaps to a 'savage' and exotic mistress whose sexual allure would blot out thought. Only a type of self-induced madness numbs the senses and allows us to carry on:

I triumph'd ere my passion sweeping thro' me left me dry,
Left me with the palsied heart, and left me with the jaundiced eye;
Eye, to which all order festers, all things here are out of joint,…
Weakness to be wroth with weakness! woman's pleasure, woman's pain—
Nature made them blinder motions bounded in a shallower brain:
Woman is the lesser man, and all thy passions, match'd with mine,…
Ah, for some retreat
Deep in yonder shining Orient…
Never comes the trader, never floats an European flag;…
There the passions cramp'd no longer shall have scope and breathing-space;
I will take some savage woman, she shall rear my dusky race.
Fool, again the dream, the fancy! but I know my words are wild,
But I count the gray barbarian lower than the Christian child.
Mated with a squalid savage—what to me were sun or clime?
I the heir of all the ages, in the foremost files of time—
Let the great world spin for ever down the ringing grooves of change…
Better fifty years of Europe than a cycle of Cathay.
Mother-Age (for mine I knew not) help me as when life begun:…
Comes a vapour from the margin, blackening over heath and holt,
Cramming all the blast before it, in its breast a thunderbolt.
Let it fall on Locksley Hall, with rain or hail, or fire or snow;
For the mighty wind arises, roaring seaward, and I go.

In 1848, six years after Tennyson had damned his age in poetry, the Northamptonshire poet John Clare, having spent long years in asylums and in the care of others, the reincarnation, so he thought, of Shakespeare and Byron, torn between the literary world of London and the almost inarticulate world of rural existence, forever searching for a lost lover, but with seven real children and a destitute wife, sat down and wrote his best-known poem *I Am*:

> I am: yet what I am none cares or knows,
> My friends forsake me like a memory lost;
> I am the self-consumer of my woes,
> They rise and vanish in oblivious host,
> Like shades in love and death's oblivion lost;
> And yet I am, and live with shadows tost
> Into the nothingness of scorn and noise,
> Into the living sea of waking dreams,
> Where there is neither sense of life nor joys,
> But the vast shipwreck of my life's esteems;
> And e'en the dearest--that I loved the best—
> Are strange—nay, rather stranger than the rest.
> I long for scenes where man has never trod,
> A place where woman never smiled or wept;
> There to abide with my creator, God,
> And sleep as I in childhood sweetly slept:
> Untroubling and untroubled where I lie,
> The grass below—above the vaulted sky.

Clare contemplated the contradictions of his life that had become intolerable because they were irresolvable and had driven him insane. All that remained was a future marked by the ideal of the past as a return to the womb, represented as a paradise of existential oblivion far from the present moment of utter alienation, the future dragged back into the mythic past of selfhood and aloneness. The completion of the self, for Clare was to be found only in the essential and innate self, left long ago far behind in the womb, but dreamed of as a future state of bliss. The death wish and rebirth sentiments in this poem encapsulate the mid-century angst of artists and thinkers riddled with self-guilt, disappointment in others and the incapacitated self, forever misunderstood or ignored.

For Tennyson and Clare, their poetry started with the self and with the self's struggle with its own identity. There was something wrong with the painter Richard Dadd too. A highly gifted artist and draughtsman of national stature, and a member of 'the Clique', a group of painters who were highly sought after, he nevertheless grew more difficult, more eccentric and downright dangerous. Trouble had first shown itself when he agreed to accompany Sir Thomas Phillips on the Grand Tour. Phillips had been at the centre of the Chartist violence in Newport, Wales, defending the status quo against an armed group of Chartists hell-bent on revolution. He had been knighted for his part in suppressing the disturbances which had greatly frightened the middle classes. The air of England in the 1840s still had the sulphurous smell of revolution left over from the disturbances of the 1820s.

Philips travelled across Europe and the Middle East in search of the picturesque, and Dadd, whose fame had been built on that strange Victorian obsession with pictures of fairies and goblins illustrating Shakespeare's texts, was there to record in paint what was seen. The two travellers sailed up the Nile and Dadd sketched. Later they returned to Cairo and thence to Europe, where, unexpectedly, Dadd began to become outspoken about religious ideas, making claims for ancient Egyptian religion and expressing a belief that he was being watched. He even attempted to kill Pope Gregory XVI, who was, nevertheless, so strong a believer in conspiracy theories himself that he was well protected. For unexplained reasons, Dadd then returned without Phillips, riding to the packet boat post-haste from Paris as if on a mission.

His arrival in London was greeted with disbelief and his growing fear that he might be demonically possessed worried his former companions and his family. Some old friends even began to fear his presence as his persecution mania increased. Dadd 'knew' he was being constantly watched, but by whom and why? Nevertheless, his work remained rational and intelligible. He was still painting in a luminescent style reminiscent of the Pre-Raphaelites and his work showed no signs of the peculiarities of his personal circumstances.

Finally taken by his father to get some treatment and a diagnosis, the doctor concluded that Dadd was a danger and should be hospitalised. Dadd's father delayed incarcerating him as Dadd junior apparently wished to impart something of importance his father him and wished to be free to do so. The two left for a short holiday in Cobham in Kent and went walking together. As the father turned away to relieve himself, Dadd hit him on the head and attempted to batter him and cut his throat, finally knifing his father to death. Dadd later recalled the scene in a conversation with his doctor which his physician recorded:

Describing the scene of patricide, he [Dadd] said he was impelled to the act of killing his father ('if he was his father' he said) by a feeling that some such sacrifice was demanded by the gods & spirits above. He said that they were walking side by side in Cobham Park when Richard suddenly sprang upon his father & stabbed him in the left side. When his father fell, Dadd (posing himself with upstretched arm) apostrophised the starry bodes 'Go,' said he' & tell the great god Osiris that I have done the deed which is to set him free'.

Dadd fled from the scene to France, apparently on his way to assassinate the Emperor of Austria, but instead attacked others on a coach when a 'sign' in the night sky revealed his destiny. He was apprehended on 30 August 1843 and was finally sent back to England in July 1844. He never denied the charges of murder and assault and, although he showed no moral regret or emotion and was coherent, he was, however, evidently disturbed both in his deportment and speech (to invisible interlocutors). It emerged that he believed that he had been incarnated as the son of Osiris whom he saw as the sun god; his father was a demonic interloper who had deceived him. He explained that he was 'the son and envoy of God, sent to exterminate the men most possessed with [sic] the demon'. Later in court:

Nothing could be more changeable than the expression of his fine count- enance and his demeanour. At one moment he was laughing with almost childish glee; the next he would appear deeply agitated, drawing his breath with a hissing noise and grinding his teeth; then mild and affected almost to tears, with his head bent nearly to his knees, and afterwards erect, with a fierce bullying aspect and loud voice.

Apparently, Dadd suffered from Capgras syndrome in which doubles and imposters predominate and in which family members may really be demons in disguise, the real person having vanished: a type of disassociative identity disorder. This may have been caused by mercury poisoning as the childhood home was also where Dadd's father worked using noxious chemicals (his siblings also went 'mad'), or perhaps Dadd suffered from heatstroke in the Middle East, a favourite diagnosis at the time. In effect, he was, in modern terms, schizophrenic, although those around him were happy with the catch-all title of 'monomania homicide', a term invented in 1825 by Etienne-Jean Georget. Yet his ideas were expressed in the terms of his social circumstances, were only those of many current thinkers and were quite 'logical':

> The belief of the unfortunate parricide, Mr Dadd, in Osiris and the religion of ancient Egypt, was far more dignified, and scarcely more absurd, than the religion of the Mormons, the Lampeter brethren, the followers of Johanna Southcott, or Swedenborg. It could not therefore on its own merits or demerits be pronounced to be an insane delusion.

The nature of Dadd's delusions 'entwined themselves around reality' and were therefore 'not gibberish', his illness, at least in part, evolving as 'the sane world … develops'. What separated Dadd was his belief that human nature was under the control of demons and that painting was a waste of time, as only demons would ultimately be the audience. 'Perhaps', thought Dadd, 'the artist is himself the greatest victim of delusion – self-delusion. Pleasing oneself is like trying to be satisfied with a gross mistake. If you try to please a devil, a more implacable customer you cannot meet. And as he is more subtle than most artists – and all men or women have the devil in them – how can they please themselves except by fallacies? And what lies, what fallacies pictures are – in the grand style of art especially'.

Meanwhile, Dadd painted more and more detailed, but more and more elusive pictures. In one sense, the sense of his social awareness, he was not straightforwardly insane. Indeed, interest in the Egyptian gods went back to the eighteenth century and often stood for reason itself, as in Mozart's 'The Magic Flute'. In the 1830s and 1840s there was a mania for all things Egyptian, with Egyptian motifs turning up at the Mansion House and at the fashionable Highgate Cemetery. This interest remained for most of the next 60 years in novels such as Richard Marsh's *The Beetle* (1897) and later in Bram Stoker's *The Jewel of Seven Stars* (1903), and returned in the 1920s with the discovery and 'legend' of Tutankhamun's tomb.

Dadd's madness was peculiarly silent and inward. His oeuvre is both strangely absolutely static and inexorably tangled. His own paranoia (where other people's reality is just beyond reach) was the belief in the imposture of his father, which itself seemed to be part of contemporary fears regarding the anonymity of the crowd and the historically specific experience of nineteenth-century automatism, alienation, out-of-body experiences and helplessness, something captured by E.T.A. Hoffman's tale *Der Sandmann* (1816), Baudelaire's idea of the flaneur and Edgar Allan Poe's tale *The Man of the Crowd* (1840).

In *The Man of the Crowd* an unnamed narrator projects his own alienation onto an anonymous passer-by, a passer-by whose eternal sins and criminality (a persecutory projection of the narrator's own imagination) are ignored by the multitude and whose real personality can only be discerned by the penetrating eye of the voyeuristic watcher:

> It was well said of a certain German book that 'es lasst sich nicht lessen' – it does not permit itself to be read. There are some secrets which do not permit themselves to be told. Men die nightly in their beds, wringing the hands of ghostly confessors, and looking them piteously in the eyes – die with despair of heart and convulsion of throat, on account of the hideousness of mysteries which will not suffer themselves to be revealed. Now and then, alas, the conscience of man takes up a burthen so heavy in horror that it can be thrown down only into the grave. And thus the essence of all crime is undivulged.

Was in fact schizophrenia itself a symptom of the new crowd mentality beginning with the new urbanisation of the late eighteenth century? The new concept of anti-social criminality certainly was, as was the obsession with degeneracy. However the syndrome originated, it was characteristic of the Victorians that they turned to phrenology and primitive psychology and even to Shakespeare to find out the materiality of inexpressible fears.

Dadd's own fascination with the minutiae of demonic life came out in his own interest in Shakespearian psychology. He painted two pictures from this investigation, both of exquisite detail and inexplicable symbolism. His interest in Oberon and Titania was expressed in his picture *Contradiction* (1854–8), whilst his enquiry into the minor Shakespearian fairy Queen Mab is evident in the canvass *The Fairy Feller's Masterstroke* (1855–64), a picture he worked on for almost ten years.

Dadd's own logic may have been wilfully perverse itself, *The Fairy Feller's Masterstroke* providing a taxonomy of 'humours', workers and fairies, just as his friend William Frith produced pictures which were taxonomies of Victorian class: *Ramsgate Sands* (1852–4) and *Derby Day* (1858). Dadd's perversity may have extended to complex visual jokes, such as the one in *The Child's Problem* (1857), in which a strange child attempts to cheat in a game of chess whilst his opponent, a 'woman' dressed in men's clothing, sleeps. The child's resemblance to Napoleon is striking, as is the sleeping female's to Wellington.

At the centre of *The Fairy Feller's Masterstroke* sits a staring 'pedagogue' scrutinising the action and going cross-eyed trying to explain it. Dadd's picture remains a puzzle, the fairies gathered to 'fix some dubious point' only understood by 'fairies ... or to the lonely thoughtful ... recluse', a comment explained, if at all, by Dadd's own long bizarre poem that is supposedly the key to the riddle, but that is also tantalisingly opaque. At the centre of the picture sits the 'arch magician', a patriarch-like figure reminiscent of both the pope and God.

Dadd's purpose may have been simpler than a complicated meditation on fairy folk; his painting a complex visual pun, regarding 'cracking a nut', or simply solving a problem, itself unspoken and unspeakable in words, instead being explained in the complex and highly personal iconography contained in a secret visual language, a language only half-understood by the 'lonely thoughtful ... recluse', but capable in its opaqueness of driving him either into or out of sanity. Here the self is directly in touch with the invisible forces determining one's destiny, for which, perhaps, only insanity will do.

The very density of the picture's imagery combined with the detailed coverage of every inch of canvas is suggestive of complex mathematical formulae or simply the need to account for everything at once in one plane and within one vision. As the Victorian age became more complex, it is not silly to imagine this visually obsessive painter, whose very existence seems to have been determined both by an addiction to the quotidian and to fairyland, trying to account for his experience – and therefore that of his fellows – through the analysis of Shakespeare's 'psychology'. For Dadd, the key to Shakespeare was the key to Dadd, and the minute details of Shakespeare's textual density were the key to Dadd's dense vision as a painter of that which doesn't exist except in his head, but is now realised as the 'truth' of a general experience which cannot be explained but may be experienced.

Dadd came closest to capturing the contradictory world of his thoughts in a small portrait, believed to be of another inmate at the asylum where he lived. *Crazy Jane* (1855) is a portrait of a lunatic transvestite. He is clothed in a borrowed dress such as were traditionally worn by rural incendiaries and machine-breaking Luddites; crows gather and there is a ruined gothic castle in the background. The portrait is a contradiction. It depicts a 'man-woman', typical of the rural incendiaries at the time who cross-dressed in women's clothing as a symbol of the world turned upside down. This was the sane-insane revolutionary symbol of the Welsh Chartism that his mentor Sir Thomas Phillips had prosecuted, now gone crazy and aimlessly wandering. It was a picture that summed up the confusion of the mid-century.

Dadd's specific mania was his own, but it was expressed in the imagery and actions of his time; a combination of extravagant orientalism, spirit fantasies, leftover anti-Catholicism, Egyptiana and the idea of the deceptive doppelganger. These fantasies as they mixed in the personality of Richard Dadd were a recipe for psychosis and alienation, in others only of mild strangeness and curiosity. Fairies provided fantasies for

Sir Arthur Conan Doyle, Arthur Machen and J.M. Barrie, doppelgangers and duplicitous individuals can be found aplenty in the gothic yarns of the 1840s, while orientalism proved the key to William Quilliam, who converted to Islam in the 1880s, began missionary work in Liverpool, took the name Abdullah and gathered 500 followers, or to T.E. Lawrence tramping the sands of Arabia looking for crusader castles. Egypt also provided the impetus to Aleister Crowley; Chartism inspired Marx and Engels, and Charles Dickens confessed to hearing the voices of his characters waiting to get out of his head.

All these ideas provided the material for Dadd's obsessions. From the exotic to the political, not one of these other people was a murderer and not one was incarcerated. Dadd's psychosis was tempered by the times; his murderous rage was also a product of irreconcilable tensions within mid-century conservatism and change. Dadd's mentor Thomas Phillips was a bastion of conservative conformity and hatred of Chartist revolutionaries, and Dadd, who remained an unreconstructed Tory social authoritarian, was also a thoroughly revolutionary individual in his personal artistic expression, the tensions and repressions of one side of his life given vent elsewhere.

The psychological disturbances of Richard Dadd were nothing compared to the downright neuroses of Victorian literature, which becomes more 'unhinged' in inverse proportion to the conformism of the age. Nothing in Dadd is as disturbing as the journalist Richard Marsh's late Victorian orientalist tale of Egyptiania, *The Beetle*, which begins with a description of a homeless man stumbling into an apparently empty room in an empty house in search of a bed for the night. However, the room proves to be a bedroom in which time and reality are endlessly distorted to the point of insanity. On entering, the protagonist feels something on his leg:

It was as though it were some gigantic spider – a spider of the nightmares; a monstrous conception of some dreadful vision. It pressed lightly against my clothing with what might … for all the world, have been spider's legs … They embraced me softly, stickily, as if the creature glued and unglued them, each time it moved.

Marsh's victim is a homeless vagrant, an anonymous drifter amidst the London throng. Since the 1880s, the homeless vagrant had become a 'new' London type, the cause of at least two major city riots against the rich, and was the archetypal image of the disfunctionality of the metropolis.

The next uncanny experience turns the visitor into an 'automaton' without the will to move, for on the bed opposite something weird stirs:

There was not a hair upon his face or head, but, to make up for it, the skin, which was a saffron yellow, was an amazing mass of wrinkles. The Cranium, and, indeed, the whole skull, was so small as to be disagreeably suggestive of something animal. The nose, on the other hand, was abnormally large; so extravagant were its dimensions, and so peculiar its shape, it resembled the beak of some bird of prey. A characteristic of the face – and an uncomfortable one! – was that, practically, it stopped short at the mouth. The mouth, with its blubber lips, came immediately underneath the nose, and chin, to all intents and purposes, there was none. This deformity – for the absence of chin amounted to that – it was which gave to the face the appearance of something not human – that, and the eyes. For so marked a feature of the man were his eyes, that, ere long, it seemed to me that he was nothing but eyes.

The experience of the 'spider' creature is terrifying, but the experience of the living corpse lying in the bed brings on a profound existential crisis:

What had happened to me I could not guess. That I probably wore some of the external evidences of death my instinct told me – I knew I did. Paradoxical though it may sound, I felt as a man might feel who had actually died – as, in moments of speculation, in the days gone by, I had imagined it as quite possible that he would feel. It is very far from certain that feeling necessarily expires with what we call life. I continually asked myself if I could be dead – the inquiry pressed itself on me with awful iteration. Does the body die, and the brain – the I, the ego – still live on? God only knows ... The agony of the thought.

Here was a description of inexplicable terror belonging to a series of 'networks of anxiety' as they have been termed by historian Ben Wilson. Anxiety explains these marginal later Victorian and Edwardian peculiarities of feeling. These networks were also ways of coping with dread and ways of mobilising half-realised and half-expressed desires. Each one of these rebellions, however peculiar they first appeared to the general public, was to become a cultural, political or spiritual force in the future.

THREE
THE SHOCK OF VRIL

I t took over a century for the old regime to crumble. Strains on the social fabric haunted the Victorian mind. The only solution was to reconcile the irreconcilable by papering over the cracks. Such was the Victorian masquerade we call hypocrisy, but which was essential for the framework of social norms to remain stable. The nineteenth century was a period where opposites might be reconciled without any sense of contradiction. On the one hand, the period was notable for its material, technological and scientific sense of progress, whilst on the other, it was a period filled with forebodings of moral decay and physical disaster. The Victorians lived their lives as much in the material here-and-now as in an hallucinatory elsewhere exemplified by their obsession with the spirit realms of drugs, fairies and ectoplasm.

As the nineteenth century wore on, personal or identity 'politics' came to the fore driven by industrialisation, the overwhelming weight of the metropolis, the burden of empire and immigration, technological advances and the significance of an ever-present and fully functioning capitalism which exposed divisions in society that were explained by the idea of the 'survival of the fittest' that had grown up to account for what seemed to be an age that had lost its meaning in the scramble for position. For many, this meant an existential crisis that went to the heart of both the individual, his or her status and presence, and the sociological dimension in which he or she functioned.

This change of mental landscape could not have happened without a radical shift in attitudes, not the least of which was a 'new' ideology of death, an ideology that at its height amounted to a metaphysical politics. The dead were swiftly becoming the companions of the living. Indeed, mid-century trips out of town to the fashionable private cemeteries around London were accompanied by a morbid obsession with death itself, an obsession started by the Queen, whose unearthly shrieks upon the death of Prince Albert had started the cult of mourning and her own state of perpetual purdah.

The form of spiritualism that evolved in the Victorian era represented a decisive break from all previous supernaturalism: a revolutionary leap from an essentially archaic religious belief system concerned with the limits of sin and redemption (and fear of the dead) to one that was, in most respects, materialist, religiously ambivalent or agnostic (and fascinated with the dying and the dead). The development of carefully constructed mourning rituals and the belief that the dead were only 'asleep' and not departed went hand in hand with a new gothic monumentality in funereal sculpture and private cemetery gardens designed for picnics. The dead were not to be quarantined, but embraced in monumental architecture and symbolism which clearly demonstrated that the deceased were not inert, but merely asleep or 'living' on another plane of existence parallel to ours.

The Victorian body had to ascend to heaven whole and corporeal. Nevertheless, there was a growing body of educated opinion that was swayed by Hindu or 'Aryan' cremation practice, something that was strictly anathema in Catholicism and frowned upon by Protestants. In 1874 Sir Henry Thompson wrote an article in defence of cremation entitled 'The Treatment of the Body after Death', which he published in *The Contemporary Review* in January 1874. His reasons for arguing for what was seen as a heathen practice were practical because 'it was becoming a necessary sanitary precaution against the propagation of disease among a population daily growing larger in relation to the area it occupied'. The argument had little weight in terms of its appeal to cleanliness and his further argument about using the ashes as fertiliser was seen as a rather tasteless joke. However, it still garnered huge interest and much support, and a movement began to have cremated remains deposited in columbaria in the new private cemeteries. Thus encouraged in his thoughts, Thompson called a meeting at his house at 35 Wimpole Street on 13 January 1874, which was attended by many of the leaders in the arts, literature and medicine, including Shirley Brooks, Frederick Lehmann, John Everett Millais, John Tenniel, Anthony Trollope and Sir

T. Spencer Wells, and at which a declaration was drawn up and signed by those present. The meeting declared that:

> We, the undersigned, disapprove [of] the present custom of burying the dead, and we desire to substitute some mode which shall rapidly resolve the body into its component elements, by a process which cannot offend the living, and shall render the remains perfectly innocuous. Until some better method is devised we desire to adopt that usually known as cremation.

Following the gathering, the participants formed the Cremation Society of England. According to Thompson, who was its founder, the Society was 'organised expressly for the purpose of obtaining and disseminating information on the subject and for adopting the best method of performing the process, as soon as this could be determined, provided that the act was not contrary to Law'. Membership of the Society was constituted by subscription to the declaration, which had been carefully drawn up so as to ensure the approval of a principle rather than adhesion to any specific practice. Land was purchased and a furnace was built by Professor Gorini, an Italian who tested a cremation machine on the body of a horse on 17 March 1879. The experiment showed that it took approximately two hours to consume a body. For spiritualists, cremation allowed the spirit to escape from the grave. Indeed, some spiritualists believed that the dead were actually trapped in their coffins unless released by burning.

This movement suggested a real change from the eighteenth century, where ghosts were often not merely tangible, but could speak and interact with the living as reanimated corpses or skeletons. Immanuel Kant would have none of it and set about attacking the leading philosopher of the spirit world perspective, Emanuel Swedenborg, in his *Geisterseher* (translated as *Dreams of a Ghost or [Spirit] Seer*) of 1766, but even Kant, who dismissed individual ghost encounters as superstitious and delusional nonsense, believed in the totality of the phenomena, as he was later to make clear in his inaugural university lecture of 1770:

> The same ignorance makes me so bold as to absolutely deny the truth of the various ghost stories, and yet with the common, although queer, reservation

that while I doubt any one of them, still I have a certain faith in the whole
of them taken together.

Horace Walpole was the inventor not only of the neo-gothic as an
architectural form at his home in Strawberry Hill, Twickenham, but also
of the literary gothic, which used ghosts as devices or plot props. In *The
Castle of Otranto* (1764) he conjures up one such stage ghost to deliver a
prophecy that could not be delivered in any other way:

> The marquis was about to return, when the figure rising, stood some
> moments fixed in meditation, without regarding him. The marquis, expec-
> ting the holy person to come forth, and meaning to excuse his uncivil
> interruption, said, Reverend father, I sought the lady Hippolita. – Hippolita!
> Replied a hollow voice: camest thou to this castle to seek Hippolita? – And
> then the figure, turning slowly round, discovered to Frederic the fleshless
> jaws and empty sockets of a skeleton, wrapt in a hermit's cowl. Angels of
> grace, protect me! Cried Frederic recoiling. Deserve their protection, said
> the spectre, Frederic, falling on his knees, adjured the phantom to take
> pity on him. Dost thou not remember me? Said the apparition. Remember
> the wood of Joppa! Art thou that holy hermit? Cried Frederic trembling –
> can I do aught for thy eternal peace? Wast thou delivered from bondage,
> said the spectre, to pursue carnal delights? Hast thou forgotten the buried
> saber, and the behest of heaven engraven on it? I have not, I have not, said
> Frederic – But say, blest spirit, what is thy errand to me? What remains to
> be done? To forget Matilda! Said the apparition – and vanished.

Such ghostly presences owed their origins to Shakespeare's ideas of
the revenant, such as Hamlet's father and Banquo, or the tormented
villain, such as Richard III. They also owe something to those graveyard
spectres which increasingly amused the jaded tastes of the late eighteenth
century. The early gothic 'ghost' is part of the architecture of terror,
rattling its chains in torment as do the ghosts which inhabit Matthew
Lewis' *The Monk* (1796). They appear at moments of high drama or
when conscience is finally pricked. Above all, they are present as solid
creatures with solid aims, brought back by the earthly actions of the
protagonists, conjured from the past by bad conscience. They may be

called up, but only by the spells of those fictional necromancers whose models are the witches of the 'Scottish play'. In essence, ghosts were fictional devices and fictional props not to be taken too seriously.

Yet attitudes were rapidly changing. A mere 100 years after *The Castle of Otranto*, there was no room for rattling chains and cowled skeletons. Instead, ghosts started to become ethereal, either real presences or the hallucinations of the psychologically scarred as they appear in Henry James' *The Turn of the Screw* (1898). In *Green Tea*, by Sheridan Le Fanu, the 'ghost' has become the alienated self, not a skeleton monk. Written in 1872 as part of a sequence of short stories gathered under the title *In a Glass Darkly*, the tale is related to the investigations of Dr Martin Hesselius, an expert in 'metaphysical medicine' and a follower of Immanuel Swedenburg, whose studies lead him to believe:

> That the essential man is a spirit, that the spirit is an organized substance, but as different in point of material from what we ordinarily understand by matter as light or electricity is; that the material body is, in the literal sense, a vesture, and death consequently no interruption of the living man's existence, but simply his extrication from the natural body – a process which commences at the moment of what we term death, and the completion of which, at the furthest a few day's later, is the resurrection 'in power'.

Horrors lay not in mouldering gothic castles, but in the mind itself, symbolised by the ambience of 'the dark house'. The haunted and suicidal Reverend Jennings, the central figure of *Green Tea*, exists within the space of a 'perfectly silent room, of a very silent house, with a peculiar foreboding; and its darkness, and solemn clothing of books … helped this sombre feeling'.

The ghost was now the hallucination that kills or drives you to madness, the demonic presence of past lives and past sins. It could be conjured now not by the potions of witches' brews, but by the far more dangerous expedient of the Black Mass, which gained popularity towards the end of the century. The ghost may have ceased to rattle chains and moan, but it now seemed to issue from realms both more terrifying and more real. This, however, was not the whole story. Alongside the ghouls and spectres of the late gothic imagination were those spectres which could be called across the veil by the act of mediumship. Such ectoplasmic 'ghosts' were not only harmless, but positively benevolent, calming and giving hope to the bereaved.

The decisive break in the history of supernaturalism occurred with the advent of spiritualism in 1848. While revolution disturbed Europe (and Marx mused in gothic metaphors over the 'spectre' of communism in *The Manifesto of the Communist Party*, better known as *The Communist Manifesto*), John Fox, his wife Margaret and his daughters Margaret and Kate moved into their new home in Hydesville, New York State. Within weeks the family had become the victims of strange rapping noises. One night, one of the daughters challenged this phenomenon with the words, 'Here, Mr. Splitfoot, do as I do' (the reference to the devil was soon conveniently forgotten), after which time the sisters became the centre and the controllers of the weird activity.

It might have been expected that the happenings at Hydesville would have quietly passed into one of the more peculiar backwaters of history, especially since the sisters were exposed by three professors from the University of Buffalo on 17 February 1851, who 'proved' the noises were those of cracking knee joints, and both sisters themselves made and then retracted statements about fraudulent practice, but this was not to be the case, for their own brand of non-denominational mysticism and inspiration was steeped in the peculiarly hysterical and histrionic atmosphere of American religious practice, and participated in the millennialism and apocalyptic imagination of New York State. On the day of the first Fox phenomena, it was claimed by Andrew Jackson Davis, 'The Seer of Poughkeepsie', a self-taught healer and mystic, that a voice had spoken to him, proclaiming 'Brother, the great work has begun'. The Fox sisters and their small house became the centre of a cult and they had found their John the Baptist.

By the 1850s there was a positive epidemic of spiritualistic phenomena and mediums flourished on both sides of the Atlantic, mainly led by American spiritualists and charismatics or British spiritualist preachers who chose to settle in the United States, such as Emma Britten, the Bang Sisters of Lily Dale near Buffalo, Thomas Lake Herm and Daniel Dunglas Home. It was the feats of levitation by Home that inspired Henry Sidgwick and Frederick Myers among others to found the Society for Psychical Research in 1882. Myers was particularly interested in telepathy, whilst Edward Gurney and Eleanor Sidgwick produced work with titles such as *Phantasms of the Living* and *Phantasms of the Dead*, works that insisted on the particularity but ordinariness of what was observed.

Change in sentiments regarding otherworldliness began at first as the after-dinner curiosity of the middle classes, but it was also a revelatory experience for many. Nowhere was this change of attitude more apparent than in the occurrences of 14 March 1855 in Hartford, Connecticut. A group of believers which included a journalist from the *Hartford Times* had gathered to hold a séance. At the centre of the events that unfolded was an extraordinary person: Daniel Home. As the party looked on, the supernatural, with all its gothic trappings, seemed to enter the airless room:

> The table-cloth was plainly lifted up, on the side opposite the medium, and in the full light of the lamp. It presented the appearance of something under it, for it moved about under the cloth … Soon after this, the thing, (whatever it was) … reached forward and touched one of the party … the hand – if it was a hand, left its protection of the table-cloth, and commenced touching the party in succession … But nothing could be seen!

To add to the marvels of the night, a heavy guitar was then carried by something invisible to the door where it started to play, after which a 'heavy mahogany chair' was dragged around and the guitar levitated by 'the invisibles'. Then a pencil was thrown on the table, whereupon it was taken up by the unseen hand from the table-cloth and 'began to write'. By now the company was not only convinced that unseen forces had crossed into the material realm through a 'medium', they were also considerably rattled, for 'the hand … came and shook hands with each one present. [The] journalist felt it minutely … it was soft and warm. IT ENDED AT THE WRIST [sic]'.

Some years earlier in August 1852, in the house of a wealthy Connecticut silk weaver, something took place which convinced witnesses that Home was indeed guided by spirits from another dimension. After a display which included the sounds and feelings of a recent shipwreck in which some relatives of one of the sitters had died:

> Mr Home was taken up in the air! [one of the guests] had hold of his hand at the time, and ... others felt his feet – they were lifted a foot from the floor. He palpitated from head to foot apparently with the contending emotions of joy and fear which choked his utterance. Again and again he was taken from the floor, and the third time he was carried to the lofty ceiling of the apartment.

Daniel Dunglas Home, born in Scotland to a clairvoyant mother, but now domiciled in the United States, was the most famous psychic of his day. William Thackeray saw and believed, as did Elizabeth Barrett Browning, Robert Owen, Mrs Trollope, the pope (he was expelled from Rome as a necromancer), the Tsar of Russia and the Empress Eugenie of France. Charles Dickens remained sceptical, but would not give up his attendance at séances; Napoleon III, Leo Tolstoy and Robert Browning hated him, whilst Charles Darwin was eager to put him to the test.

This celebrated friend of the powerful began his career with a vision, just like his mother. One night he saw 'in a cloud of brightness' a childhood friend who had died three days earlier. Indeed, 'the ghostly figure made three circles in the air with his hand and the hand began slowly to disappear, then the arm, and finally the whole body melted away'. The vision left Home paralysed for a while. Unlike his mother, Home would become not just another local village wise man, but one of the first transatlantic celebrities.

From a quite different starting point, Mary Baker Eddy had in 1879 founded the first 'Church of Christian Scientist' whose ambiguously and oxymoronically named system became the other part of the evangelical appeal of spiritualist belief. By the early twentieth century, Lily Dale had become spiritualism's largest summer camp, its focal point the now moved and resurrected cottage of John and Margaret Fox! Alongside this, Christian Science had taken on the trappings of respectable religious belief.

Meanwhile, Mary Baker Eddy joined her own belief in the healing powers of 'truth in Christ' to the strictly materialistic methods she had learned from her mentor Phineas Quimby. After Quimby's death in 1866, she added a theological gloss to his ideas and made them her raison d'être. At one point she even created a 'metaphysical college'. With these, the new occult gained its creed and its geography, and it was into these that believers were able to insert their own personal and idiosyncratic narratives. Although attempting to differentiate her belief system from spiritualism in general and materialism in particular, she still reproduced much that was central to the emergence of modern supernaturalism. Her arguments often differed only in the degree of phrasing from much that preceded them. Christian Science rewrote Christianity from a natural or rational perspective and rethought science from a metaphysical perspective.

Spiritualism soon became all the rage in Britain and much of its activity was based in London. In 1863 James Burns had set up the Progressive Library and Spiritual Institute in Southampton Row, where phrenology could be witnessed on a Tuesday, while on a Friday night one could watch a medium for a shilling; dark séances, costing two shillings, attracted a better class of visitor, perhaps. In the house of Edward Cox, the Serjeant at Arms, serious research was being conducted into these new and strange phenomena. With the formation of the London Dialectical Society in 1869, people like Alfred Wallace, Francis Galton, William Crookes and Thomas Huxley began a series of experiments at Cox's home to test the validity of the miraculous energy which emanated from mediums at séances, which Crookes later announced 'appear conclusively to establish the existence of a new force, in some unknown manner connected with the human organization, which for convenience may be called Psychic Force', the term itself being coined by Cox to sidestep the unscientific belief in ghostly goings on. Cox also formed the Psychological Society of Great Britain, where Galton and others tried to measure the 'weight' of this new energy. The British National Association of Spiritualists began in 1873, whilst the Society for Psychical Research (SPR) began its investigations in 1882, at the home of Hensleigh Wedgewood, a cousin of Charles Darwin. Changing its address, however, to a better area than that around Bloomsbury allowed the SPR to attract a more salubrious audience, including William Gladstone.

Perhaps the strangest and most sensational of the various home-grown incidents surrounding psychic investigations and the reason for the scientific hysteria following its 'discovery' was the apparent ability to generate enough energy to move across time and space, as one medium found to her cost:

> In one … incident in 1871, another prominent medium, Mrs Guppy, was minding her own business writing her shopping list in Highbury Hill only to enter a trance state and apparently vanish. At a Lamb's Conduit Street séance … at the same time 'an object was felt to come upon the table, and when the light was struck, their visitor was found to be Mrs Guppy.' Mrs Guppy had astrally travelled across a mile and a half across London, her famously ample frame thumping rather materially onto the table in midst of writing 'onions'.

None of this might have had an impact (and might indeed have been written off as mere fantasy or delusion) but for the coincidental publication of a popular novel which combined unknown races, new power sources and spiritual awakening of a distinctly orientalist nature. In the same year as Mrs Guppy was teleporting across London, Edward Bulwar-Lytton published a fantasy romance called *The Coming* Race in which an American adventurer, having fallen through a mine shaft, comes across a lost civilisation of super beings, half Native Americans, half angels, but certainly beings who produced in humans feelings of 'awe and terror':

> And now there came out of this building a form – human – was it human? It stood on the broad way and looked around, beheld me and approached. It came within a few yards of me, and at the sight and presence of it an indescribable awe and tremor seized me, rooting my feet to the ground. It reminded me of symbolical images of Genius or Demon that are seen on Etruscan vases or limned on the walls of Eastern sepulchers – images that borrow the outlines of man, and are yet of another race. It was tall, not gigantic, but tall as the tallest man below the height of giants.

> Its chief covering seemed to me to be composed of large wings folded over its breast and reaching to its knees; the rest of its attire was composed of an

under tunic and leggings of some thin fibrous material. It wore on its head a kind of tiara that shone with jewels, and carried in its right hand a slender staff of bright metal like polished steel. But the face! It was that which inspired my awe and my terror. It was the face of man, but yet of a type of man distinct from our known extant races. The nearest approach to it in outline and expression is the face of the sculptured sphinx – so regular in its calm, intellectual, mysterious beauty. Its colour was peculiar, more like that of the red man than any other variety of our species, and yet different from it – a richer and a softer hue, with large black eyes, deep and brilliant, and brows arched as a semicircle. The face was beardless; but a nameless something in the aspect, tranquil though the expression, and beauteous though the features, roused that instinct of danger that the sight of a tiger or serpent arouses. I felt that this manlike image was endowed with forces inimical to man. As it drew near, a cold shudder came over me. I fell on my knees and covered my face with my hands.

These Sphinx-like creatures whose language and origins appear to be 'Aryan or Indo-Germanic' control a powerful 'electric' force called 'Vril':

'I have long held an opinion,' says that illustrious experimentalist, 'almost amounting to a conviction, in common, I believe, with many other lovers of natural knowledge, that the various forms under which the forces of matter are made manifest, have one common origin, or, in other words, are so directly related and mutually dependent that they are convertible, as it were into one another, and possess equivalents of power in their action. These subterranean philosophers assert that by one operation of vril, which Faraday would perhaps call "atmospheric magnetism", they can influence the variations of temperature – in plain words, the weather; that by operations, akin to those ascribed to mesmerism, electro-biology, odic force, etc., but applied scientifically, through vril conductors, they can exercise influence over minds, and bodies animal and vegetable, to an extent not surpassed in the romances of our mystics. To all such agencies they give the common name of vril.'

The novel was pure fantasy, but so powerful an impression did it make that readers would not believe it was just an invention. This coming race of super beings was destined, as Lytton told his friend John Forster, to fulfil the 'Darwinian position that a coming race [was] destined to supplant our races' and people waited with bated breath for the coming of the Vril-ya from its subterranean, Tibetan, Atlantean, Antarctic or vaguely Eastern hiding places.

Arthur Lovell formed the Vril-ya Club dedicted to 'human transmutation' in which sun tans, moon bathing and deep breathing were encouraged to bring on Vril power. In 1891 Dr Herbert Tibbits, the director of the London Massage and Galvanic Hospital, held a 'Coming Race Bazaar' at the Albert Hall. As late as 1903, the Fifth Royal Irish Lancers arranged themselves to spell out VRIL at the Royal Tournament held that year. Percy Fawcett, that redoubtable original of Indiana Jones, dedicated his life to discovering the troglodytic race of Atlantean supermen hidden in the hollow earth below the Brazilian rainforests. The most enduring symbol of Vril potency, however, is the beef drink 'Bovril', invented by the manufacturers of Johnstone's Liquid Beef to sell 'liquid life' in a jar.

Yet the development of Vril and of the 'traditional' spiritualistic ghost tale went hand in hand with a nostalgia for the very landscape of a 'lost' England and Anglo-Saxonism vanishing under the weight of modernity. England (never Britain) now became 'olde' England, a haunted landscape with mock-Tudor revival buildings, tourist guides to the quaint and forgotten, and tea rooms for cyclists.

Much of this complex situation regarding the politics of Victorian and Edwardian popular culture is exemplified by Rudyard Kipling and his own ambiguous relationship with writing for children. On 7 October 1904 Kipling sat down at his desk at Bateman's, his Sussex home since 1902, to write a rather strange invitation to his friend, the journalist and editor Howell Gwynne. In it was a request for Gwynne to get 'from some London toyshop a donkey's head mask, either in paper or cloth sufficiently large to go over a man's head'. He also wanted 'a pair of fairy wings'. Fearing his friend might think him quite mad, Kipling explained:

Don't think I'm mad but the kids are next month doing a little piece of Midsummer Night's Dream, … I've got to be Bottom with the ass's head and Elsie is going to be Titania. Hence, the wings. But if I don't have a proper donkey's head I'll get into trouble from Elsie. John is going to be Puck but I don't think he wants wings.

What lay behind the home theatricals was an idea that had been in Kipling's mind since the end of the 1890s, when he had become fascinated with the Roman occupation of Britain and the deeply buried layers of history that were suggested by the hints in the Sussex countryside. Workmen carrying out repairs at Bateman's had unearthed 'a Jacobean tobacco-pipe, a worn Cromwellian latten spoon and … the bronze cheek of a Roman horsebit'. And close by an old iron works called Welland's Forge was 'supposed to have been worked by the Phoenicians and Romans and, since then, uninterruptedly till the middle of the eighteenth century'. It was in a quarry nearby that:

> it pleased our children to act for us, in the open, what they remembered of A Midsummer-Night's Dream … And in a near pasture of the water-meadows lay out an old and unshifting Fairy Ring … You see how patiently the cards were stacked and dealt into my hands? The Old Things of our Valley glided into every aspect of our outdoor works. Earth, Air, Water and People had been – I saw it at last – in full conspiracy to give me ten times as much as I could compass, even if I wrote a complete history of England, as that might have touched or reached our valley.

What emerged from Kipling's pen, after a type of long incubation, was *Puck of Pook's Hill* (1906), a book of stories illustrating the history of England in which, as he told Edward Bok, the Dutch-American author, in 1905, he wanted:

> To give children not a notion of history but a notion of the time sense which is at the bottom of all knowledge of history and history rightly understanded [sic] means love of one's fellow men and the lands one lives in.

Kipling chose as the central character of the stories Shakespeare's figure of the hobgoblin Puck, acting as psycho-pomp in the children's quest through the fabric of English history. If 'the present was the moving edge of the past', then nothing could be understood without an awareness of a long receding, rapidly fading and almost forgotten history, which was being lost in the rush of the new. Yet *Puck of Pook's Hill* was no straightforward elegy to a lost England. It was neither strident like the books of G.A. Henty and R.M. Ballantyne, nor maudlin like the works of Frederick Farrar, whose school tale *Eric* (1858) was mercilessly spoofed in Kipling's own *Stalky and Co* (1899) (and for which he had to apologise to Farrar!). Rather, through tales of Roman invaders, Norman conquerors, iron masters, local peasants and Jewish doctors, Kipling tried to open up English history as a tapestry rather than a chronology – Englishness as a concoction of differences and similarities that somehow made a community through time.

Puck was to be the conductor of a journey through identity, in which the 'British' (and more particularly its Edwardian synonym, the 'English') were not only confronted with their past but also participated in the past, which was also their past, one in which participation was all. Yet historical community was also 'mythic' where continuity could only be taught by the 'last of the race' of the 'People of the Hills'. By releasing Puck from his captivity, the children achieve their passport to the historical struggle for identity within community:

> You've done something that Kings and Knights and Scholars in old days would have given their crowns and spurs and books to find out. If Merlin himself had helped you, you couldn't have managed better! You've broken the Hills – you've broken the Hills! It hasn't happened in a thousand years.

Kipling found Puck's universe neither by pursing the fashion for spiritualism that had already swallowed up W.B. Yeats and Arthur Conan Doyle, nor by dwelling too long on the dusty pursuit of lost antiquarian books, but in the very heart of modernity. Kipling found his history in the technology of speed and the romance of driving:

> To me it is a land full of stupefying marvels and mysteries, and a day in the car in an English county is a day in some fairy museum where all

the exhibits are alive and real and yet none the less delightfully mixed up with the books. For instance, in six hours, I can go from the land of the Ingoldsby Legends by way of the Norman Conquest and the Barons' War into Richard Jefferies' country, and so through the Regency, one of Arthur Young's less known tours, and Celia's Arbour, into Gilbert White's territory ... in England the dead, twelve coffin deep, clutch hold of my wheels at every turn, till I sometimes wonder that the very road does not bleed. That is the real joy of motoring – the exploration of this amazing England.

It was an irony not entirely lost on Kipling's generation that the 'olde England' that they sought could only be found along roads built for the very cars that threatened their idyll. 'Never before have so many people been searching for England' wrote the journalist and travel writer H.V. Morton in 1927, before setting off on his own motor quest down England's leafy lanes. Yet what was England and where was it to be found?

In the multi-layered, partly ruined landscape of England was a history that was never quite remembered, never quite a totality, an evanescent but not quite tangible reality, to which the isolated facts of actual town and country pointed, but could never explain or be reconciled to present thought. Thus, to remind children of their country's history was already tragic, as it implied a history already forgotten or, even worse, repressed. Puck's history is a multicultural, multi-racial confusion that can be grasped only in the retelling of tales. Such history is represented as primal, beyond and outside of memory, locked in the thousand-year dream of the Hill People.

Kipling's history – and a type of history it certainly is (more real than 'the facts') – is an attempt to reconcile two types of forgetting. First is the forgetting caused by the rush of the present; second is the primal history of self and community built upon layers of the dead, which only exists in communal values, religion, superstitions and habits of mind that are themselves the unacknowledged roots of self-reflection. In *Puck of Pook's Hill*, the certainty of Henty and Ballantyne was already gone, replaced by the attempt to recapture what was already perceived as lost. For Kipling, this loss had already occurred in childhood and could only be recalled as a type of 'trace' memory when meditated upon by the adult writer:

> Since the tales had to be read by children, before people realized that they were meant for grown-ups … I worked the material in three or four overlaid tints and textures, which might reveal themselves according to the shifting light of sex, youth, and experience.

History, like childhood can never be recovered, only grasped in a dream of history, never more than the potential of its remembering. Nowhere does this become so self-evident than in the introduction to *Rewards and Fairies* which Kipling produced in 1910 as a follow-up to *Puck of Pook's Hill*. The heart of England is neither Roman, Saxon, nor Norman, but archaic, occulted, repressed. To reach England is to see beyond into trees, stones and landscape, into lost languages and habits of mind. Englishness is connected to the present by that almost ironic wish of E.M. Forster's to 'only connect'. To connect to history is to go beyond the merely historical into a dream of England induced by the fairies:

> Once upon a time, Dan and Una, brother and sister, living in the English country, had the good fortune to meet with Puck, alias Robin Goodfellow, alias Nick o'Lincoln, alias Lob-lie-by-the-Fire, the last survivor in England of those whom mortals call Fairies. Their proper name, of course, is 'The People of the Hills.' This Puck, by means of the magic of Oak, Ash, and Thorn, gave the children power – To see what they should see and hear what they should hear. Though it should have happened three thousand year[s ago].

Puck however, is the spirit of primal repression 'careful, of course, to take away [the children's memory] of their walks and talks and conversations', but Kipling, as opposed to Puck, is the spirit of tortured memory, bringing to the record what Puck chooses to forget about the communities that lived, toiled and died generations ago and which are preserved in the fragments of 'the stories [Kipling is] trying to tell … about those people'. For over 100 years, British children's writers (including the Scots and the Welsh) have been on a quest for a lost, repressed England. Yet this 'lost' England (a golden age taking many forms) never really existed, its absence continuously 'replaced' by a mystical landscape of the imagination which never quite filled the void.

The Edwardians concocted this territory from their own social, personal, political and technological neuroses and from the rapidly changing intellectual landscape they inherited from the late Victorians. This world of disturbance and uncertainty was bequeathed to two generations brought up in the shadow of trench warfare, aerial bombardment, class division and economic and imperial decline, and was passed on to later generations for whom the creation of a multicultural, multi-perspective United Kingdom still left unanswered the questions asked in the long lost summers before the First World War.

The loss, which could never be retrieved or replaced (because it was never really there), created a type of melancholia, best summed up in the enormous success of A.E. Housman's collection of poems about loss and death called *A Shropshire Lad*, but also found in the wanderings of Arthur Hugh Clough's *Where Lies the Land?*:

Where lies the land to which the ship would go?
Far, far ahead, is all her seamen know.
And where the land she travels from? Away,
Far, far behind, is all that they can say.

It was always an endless, hopeless search for what was believed lost by the rush of the nineteenth century that nevertheless projected a type of imaginative nostalgic 'reality' wherever it went, not the least of which was into the trenches of the First World War, where Wilfred Owen could dream of Camelot or Edward Thomas could conjure up the peace of Adlestrop station with its chorus of blackbirds singing as a heavenly choir from the depths of Oxfordshire and Gloucestershire in the lull between the machine guns.

Surprisingly, this older 'forgotten' world was rediscovered in motor cars and charabancs – England had become a gigantic ghostly palimpsest available to the inquisitive and adventurous tourist of whom Rudyard Kipling was one of the first.

For adventurous visitors who strayed off the beaten track, the charm of the English manor house or castle was encapsulated both in ruin and in ghostly presences which still haunted its ancient battlements, but this time merely for an ornamental and picturesque purpose and often as an adjunct to a canny sales pitch when selling real estate:

> The two towers are crowned by turrets, named the watch and signal turrets. A moat surrounds the castle, and was spanned by a drawbridge, the vertical slits on each side of the central recessed window being fitted with levers for raising and lowering the bridge. Over the archway are the arms of the Fiennes family, a wolf-dog with its paws on a banner and three lions rampant. If we were to pass through this gate we should find the ruins of an immense castle, a veritable town … The ghosts of its great owners seem to haunt the scene of their former splendour, and one noted uneasy spirit inhabited Drummer's hall, and marched along the battlements beating a devil's tattoo on his drum. But perhaps he was only a gardener in league with the smugglers, and used this ghostly means for conveying to them a needful signal. Ghosts often frequent the old houses of England and our artist's sketch of the haunted house, Harvington Hall, Worcestershire, which looks delightfully picturesque in the moonlight, certainly suggests the appearance of a ghostly resident or visitor.

Ghosts no longer fed the thrills of the gothic imagination and they no longer clanked and shrieked. Instead, they were imbued with psychic energy of a preternatural type and as such remained behind as spiritual reminders of a buried history and tradition, something not to be tampered with or questioned, charming and inviting rather than alarming, reminders of psychic and cultural repression:

> We know of such a house in Lancashire, which, like Harvington Hall, is encircled by a moat. It contains a skull in a case let into the wall of the staircase. This skull has been cast into the moat, buried in the ground, and removed in many other ways; but terrible happenings ensue: storms rage and lightnings flash, and groans are heard, until the skull is brought back

to its niche, when peace ensues ... These ancient traditions, ghosts and legends, add greatly to the charm of our old houses.

By the end of the nineteenth century, ghosts no longer rose from the grave to rattle chains and deliver prophecies; instead, they came at will, clothed in ectoplasm and speaking through mediums of the world to come, of higher plains of experience and of the democratic possibilities of 'passing over'.

FOUR

MASSACRE AT TRAFALGAR

The spiritualist Helena Petrovna Blavatsky, better known as Madame Blavatsky, had begun her rise to fame after visiting the Eddy Farm (home to Mary Baker Eddy's daughter and scene of extraordinary mediumistic performances by her grandchildren) in Vermont in 1874. With some psychic ability and much personal presence, she was taken up by one Colonel Olcott and together they formed a 'Miracle Club', followed by the Theosophical Society, which they founded in 1875 with William Quem Judge. Inspired first by the mysterious entity 'Tuit Bey', Blavatsky moved on to India where further inspirational entities led her to complete an occult cosmography described in *Isis Unveiled* (1877) and *The Secret Doctrine* (1888).

Despite the scorn felt by theosophists for Darwin (Madame Blavatsky kept a stuffed baboon dressed as a Darwinian professor in her apartments), theosophical spiritism follows the logic of materialism. Regardless of the debates that flared up in the late nineteenth century, spiritualism was never able to demonstrate the distinction between spirit and matter or to clarify their interconnectedness. Colonel Olcott (who influenced Blavatsky) could never decide if his belief system was scientific or spiritual. Unlike science, spiritualistic knowledge aimed to provide a particular form of ontology based on the conjunction of personality and death. In this model of evolution, death is demoted to a peculiarly minor stage of life.

Theosophy's immense success at the end of the nineteenth century was due in part to its own logic which was at once apparently laudable and reasonable as well as inherently revolutionary in its democratic and pluralistic vision of one human family. It stood for the formation of a universal human brotherhood without distinction in terms of race, creed, sex, caste or colour; the encouragement of studies in comparative religion, philosophy and science; and the investigation of unexplained laws of nature and the powers latent in man. However, these general principles coalesced with the ideas of survival after death, disembodied spirit guidance, contact by select illuminate, out of body travel, psychokinesis, automatic writing, space travel and mystic and occult brotherhood. These further principles were indispensable to Theosophy, despite its attempts to differentiate itself from spiritualism as a general set of vaguely located beliefs.

Theosophy, it was supposed by its followers, would replace the Christian religion (and all other religions) and the rationalism of modern science with a spiritual knowledge that was free from associations with sin and guilt and which did not carry within it the usual moral imperative that religious belief implied. Theosophy changed scientific knowledge into spiritual knowledge. Theosophy and Christian Science were to become the most powerful spiritual forces at play on the moral landscape: they were American, individualist and progressive – a new way of living from the New World. No wonder that they grew in importance with those who were already on a quest for social and religious enlightenment in an age with few signposts. One such was Annie Besant.

The life and work of Annie Besant best represents the tensions and contradictions of the latter half of the nineteenth century and the pressures on radicals, both in terms of their social vision and inner convictions. Born into a Catholic family of Irish descent, Besant married early, but soon rubbed against both an oppressive husband and the oppressive religion he represented. The near-death of both her children severely tested her faith, which, when it broke, led to marital estrangement and divorce, a court case that left her without her children and a reputation for being an 'infidel' and a divorcee. What had been gained was a freethinking temperament which sought a place for women's particular expression and which was scientific in focus and independent in outlook. All her life, Besant struggled against the bigotry of traditionalists and those guardians of public morals who wished to force her back into the role of 'angel of the hearth'. She learned to speak in public as a woman working for *The Freethinker* and other risqué publications and was hounded as a female who it was best not to know. As a scholar, she completed her studies at the University of London and as a radical she embraced anti-imperialism, freedom of thought, republicanism, Malthusian and utilitarian population control (advocating methods of birth control and therefore greater family happiness) and atheism, the latter belief being one she had to defend and explain all her life.

As her radicalism evolved (for her it was no swift revelation), she befriended the notorious radical Charles Bradlaugh, the MP for Northampton whose atheism (and republicanism) made him a bête noir for almost everyone in power and whose attempts to take his seat in the Commons by 'affirming' rather than swearing the oath produced some of most explosive scenes Parliament had seen since the Civil War (more than once they ended in his arrest and once in his violent expulsion from the chamber).

Bradlaugh and Besant saw in each other fellow seekers after justice and rational equity, and they worked together almost until Bradlaugh died in 1891. They were both prosecuted for publishing an 'obscene' pamphlet on birth control, although the pamphlet had been happily sold for years, and both were hounded for libellous, treasonous and immoral journalism. Like Bradlaugh, Besant was a radical of the old school, the term then referring not to socialists or revolutionaries but to those extreme Liberals and Independents who stood, like John Lilburne in the seventeeth century, for the absolute right of liberty of conscience and for its consequences which were often free thought, hatred of landed (or aristocratic) interest, unorthodox religious beliefs, secularism and materialism, individualism and the primacy of the 'citizen as person'.

In the 1860s and 1870s, these radical principles put both Bradlaugh and Besant up against the ire of an increasingly moralistic and patriotic middle class, a revived Christianity and the whole of what was known as the 'carriage trade', those at society's top. The views of both Bradlaugh and Besant were nevertheless taken up by the national radical popular newspapers, the organised working class and the growing number of freethinking Victorians who packed the halls where they spoke. Yet this type of radicalism was fast becoming obsolete and the obsolescence would lead to a split between Bradlaugh and Besant, for Besant was on a journey, whereas Bradlaugh had arrived. Bradlaugh in many ways represented the end of a tradition that embraced Henry Hunt, Richard Carlile, William Cobbett and even the Cato Street conspirators, but it would not survive the economic and social changes that were taking place in the last third of the nineteenth century.

Besant was always looking for strong and idealistic men who espoused a cause and with whom she could work. Therefore, her first encounter with Edward Aveling as she studied science was bound to create a dynamic change and one which would ultimately lead to her separation from Bradlaugh. Aveling opened her eyes to the suffering of the poor and to that particular form of economic explanation that would suggest that the clash of classes was a fundamental but neglected aspect of her version of freedom of expression. The poor became a cause that would assuage her innate religiosity and still allow her to stay a materialist and atheist at heart. Her new religion from now on would be the religion of suffering humanity preached by socialism, and salvation would be the new Jerusalem of human cooperation and community. She took up the socialist cause wholeheartedly and became a follower of the ideas of Henry Hyndman and William Morris, Beatrice and Sydney Webb and Edward Aveling (all of whom she admired) and George Bernard Shaw (who she was originally offended by). Soon she had become a full and active member of the Fabian Society. She was a 'spiritual' and idealist communal socialist, and even though she knew Eleanor Marx, who lived with Aveling, she was never a Marxist revolutionary.

Nevertheless, this interest in the science of the sociological and the creed of socialism eventually led her into conflict with the old individualist radicalism of Bradlaugh, who disagreed profoundly with the principles of socialism and with the Marxist brand of revolution in particular. The break between them came about as a result of the events of 13 November 1887 in Trafalgar Square, known thereafter as Bloody Sunday. The day was intended as a protest against the Irish Land War and the imprisonment of the Irish MP William O'Brien. The day itself was organised by the Social Democratic Federation and the Irish National League, and was to be the culmination of a series of ever-bloodier clashes between the unemployed and the middle classes – the East End versus the West End. Around 10,000 protesters filed into Trafalgar Square led by Besant, George Bernard Shaw, John Burns, William Morris and all the leading socialists. Arrayed against them were police and soldiers, and the ensuing melee, initiated primarily by the police, ended in three deaths. In her autobiographical reminiscences of 1893, Besant recalled the 'massacre':

> The procession I was in started from Clerkenwell Green, and walked with its banner in front … As we were moving slowly and quietly along one of the narrow streets debouching on Trafalgar Square … there was a sudden charge, and without a word the police were upon us with uplifted truncheons; the banner was struck down, and men and women were falling under a hail of blows. There was no attempt at resistance, the people were too much astounded at the unprepared attack. They scattered, leaving some on the ground too much injured … [Trafalgar Square] was garrisoned by police, drawn up in serried ranks … John Burns … [was] savagely cut about the head and arrested … the horse-police charged in squadrons … rolling men and women over like nine pins … At last a rattle of cavalry, and up came the Life Guards … and then the Scots Guards with bayonets fixed … The soldiers were ready to fire, the people unarmed; it would have been a massacre.

The subsequent funerals of three protestors were stage-managed affairs and the following demonstration on 20 November 1887 saw the killing of another demonstrator called Alfred Linnell. Bradlaugh absolutely refused to have anything to do with the demonstrations, which he thought were ill-chosen confrontations. Indeed, he believed that the protests had been stage-managed to produce violence and thus show the police in the worst possible light to prove that they were merely the lackeys of arbitrary and authoritarian government. This proved correct, as the subsequent writings of Besant, the journalist W.T. Stead and William Morris proved. Nevertheless, the demonstration was a defining point in nineteenth-century radical politics whose impact was that of the riot in St Peter's Field, Manchester (popularly known as the Peterloo Massacre) in 1819. It was also the end of a short phase of confrontation politics which gave way, in only a few years, to the gradualism of the trade union movement. Yet it also marked the political boundaries. Whose side were you on? Besant threw herself in with the aims and ideals of the socialists and Bradlaugh became ever more distant and apparently more reactionary.

Yet, as Besant became more socialist, she also became aware that socialism without the leaven of human warmth was itself destructive of the very freedoms she wished to support. It was an impasse. Her atheism was firmly rooted in scientific materialism and the here-and-now of social interaction, but none of this seemed to elevate the spiritual needs of individuals. Even as she struggled with that investigative and campaigning journalism which would expose the exploitation of the Bryant and May matchgirls, she was also wrestling with her beliefs.

What formed the centre of human life – was it the economic system or the soul, however defined? The answer came as Besant read deeper into Theosophy and occultism, to be finally confirmed by her meeting with Madame Blavatsky in 1889. The idea of reincarnation, cycles of existence and a general 'Hindu'-influenced cosmology convinced her that there was a soul and that it had a material existence that went on eternally and in cosmic cycles of reincarnation. This represented a move from neo-Malthusian materialism to the 'School of Occultism' and the 'Science of the Soul'. It satisfied her innate desire for a firm belief system that did not contradict her deeply felt scientific materialism and that also upheld her socialist values. The whole concept was sufficient to revolt Bradlaugh, who wrote of it:

[Theosophists] appear to me to have sought to rehabilitate a kind of Spiritualism in Eastern phraseology. I think many of their allegations utterly erroneous, and their reasonings wholly unsound.

Nevertheless, Besant was convinced of Theosophy's truths and set up with Blavatsky a theosophical and socialist club for working girls in the East End. She was drawn to the plights of the working class and of Indians under British imperialism, and became increasingly drawn into spiritualism.

Bradlaugh died on 30 January 1891 and Blavatsky on 8 May of the same year. This double blow left Besant free to pursue Theosophy without the disapprobation of her former friend and finally to become the inheritor of Blavatsky's legacy. Besant had long ago resigned her place as Vice-President of the National Secular Society and co-editor of *The National Reformer* and was taken up as co-editor of Blavatsky's journal *Lucifer*. Blavatsky named her as her 'right-hand woman', an 'intellectual' who nevertheless heard the 'Master's voice when alone'. She had penetrated into the inner circle of 'the esoteric section of the Society' and was open to 'spirit-control'. When Blavatsky died, Besant became the head of the London branch of the organisation and on the death of Colonel Olcott (Blavatsky's partner) in 1907, she became its World President.

Blavatsky herself was fascinated with Indian thought and incorporated much of it into her teachings. Theosophy's international headquarters was in Adyar near Madras. Many 'Westernised' Indians were drawn to this revival of Indian culture. A young Mohandas Gandhi even attended Blavatsky's funeral. Besant was drawn to the Indian culture and from there to Indian civilisation, which she believed could only flourish if it became independent of empire, and for that a socialist model was necessary. She found an Indian teacher of mysticism called Professor Gyanendra Chakravarti, which led her by stages to the precocious Brahmin 'messiah' J. Krishnamurti. This inevitably led to her visiting India in 1893, where she set about helping to raise funds for the Central Hindu College. She now believed that she was the reincarnation of past Indians whose previous lives had coalesced in hers.

Moreover, Besant was taken seriously in India, where she met Gandhi, Jawaharlal Nehru and Mohammed Ali Jinnah and began, in 1914, to plan with them an independent, non-sectarian India embodying 'the ideal of self-government ... along colonial lines' and run on cooperative principles with 'the obliteration of all racial privileges' and the establishment of 'Home Rule'. For this she was temporarily interned as a subversive in 1917. On her release, she was elected President of the National Congress of India, a post she had to resign from in 1919 after political differences with Gandhi. Nevertheless, she was given the honorific title 'Mother of India'.

In many ways, Besant represents a halfway house between the modern revolutionary tendencies of socialism and the spiritual socialism which created the Labour Party. She was drawn to strong causes and the strong men and women who espoused them. Always a woman who needed heroes and heroines, she attached herself to Bradlaugh, to Shaw and to Blavatsky as a way of confirming her beliefs, which were often extreme and sometimes eccentric, but always intellectually defended and often able to find root in foreign soil, especially her ideas on Theosophy, which in a European context might have consigned her to the very outer margins of sane discussion, but which in another culture found rational support. Shaw thought that she was the only person he had met who had no private life, her causes taking up all her leisure hours. She died an active socialist and occultist on 21 September 1933.

FIVE

SHERLOCK HOLMES AND THE FAIRIES

In its more theorised aspects, spiritualism was engaged in an aggressive debate with Darwinism or the consequences of Darwinism, and Darwin himself took a lively interest in the doings of clairvoyants. This 'revolution' was driven by the belief that contact with the dead and other disembodied spirit entities was a desirable thing. This was in direct opposition to the archaic belief that such contact should be feared and shunned and its practitioners treated as necromancers. The new 'rational' supernatural was believed to go beyond religion and science and explain both. Although this advance was supposedly based on 'natural law' and a type of spiritualised universal mechanics, it was founded on one central dogmatic assertion: survival after death as proven 'beyond doubt'.

The last two decades of the nineteenth century was both a period of intense complacency and intense doubt. It is against such rapid change in experience that Doyle's Sherlock Holmes must be seen. He is, despite his quirky love of old shag tobacco, drugs, avant-garde art and strange violin music, a bulwark against the damnable 'isms' of the age. Holmes may be a detective, but he is a detective who has a unique vocation and whose powers of deduction are based not on intuition but on observation and logical deduction. What cannot be seen cannot be explained. He is, in short, a materialist whose very materialism gives assurance of a greater good beyond the material realm.

Holmes put back what was missing from the puzzle of existence in order to reassure the world of the continuity of the status quo and the rightness of reason's rule. Whether the enemy is a vampire in southern England or a hell hound in the north, the explanation is consistently rational, material and mundane. Everything is reduced to what may be observed and consequently to the assertion that human beings wear their motives in their clothing and their innermost thoughts in the torn scraps of detritus that cling to them: literally, for Holmes, manners maketh the man. One only has to read the opening deductions regarding Dr Mortimer in *The Hound of the Baskervilles* to see the absurdity of the position. In Holmes's world there is only the behaviour of social beings, but social beings whose actions are perverted and who therefore have to be eliminated from society.

Although Doyle was tinkering with Holmes in 1886, the detective finally came to the public's notice in 1887, a year marked by bloody clashes with those godless socialists so threatening to Victorian sobriety. If the Church could no longer assuage middle-class doubts, Holmes could at least protect against existential fears, a talisman against change in a godless universe, a universe where, a year later, the likes of Jack the Ripper stalked like an invisible 'terrorist' (to use George Bernard Shaw's colourful description). The police were flatfoots precisely because the society that they protected was no longer stable, because it was no longer grounded. Holmes is really not a detective; rather, he is the high priest of stability in a destabilised world.

Despite the importance of science and technology in the Western world and the advances of rational thought, a general belief in the paranormal remained both widespread and deeply felt. Curiously, this shift in attitudes towards the dead was the product of the neuroses of a technological modern society. If there is a story to be read in this ethereal realm, it is not that of the eternal return of the non-living, but rather the narration of a progressive and inclusive modernity in which supernaturalism was an integral part of the contemporary experience of the Victorian and Edwardian mind.

There is therefore a conundrum inside Doyle and inside Sherlock Holmes. Why did the creator of the master of deduction turn to a belief in fairies and all things invisible? Why did a rational man (who in his very actions and hobbies defined the age in which he lived) with the most rational of heroes turn to the 'invisible', and why do we still refuse to see that the author's swerve into esoteric belief is at one with the nature of his creation? Why was Doyle condemned for a naivety that Sherlock Holmes was never subject to? Indeed, how did Doyle come to stand for the opposite values of his own creation?

Doyle had, after a long search, at last found the truth that reconciled the spiritual with the material. He had become spiritualism's last great advocate and its most famous believer:

> I seemed suddenly to see that this subject with which I had so long dallied was not merely a study of a force outside the rules of science, but that it was really something tremendous, a breaking down of the walls between two worlds, a direct undeniable message from beyond, a call of hope and of guidance to the human race at the time of its deepest afflictions.

Doyle had, of course, been born into a period of intense spiritual change. By the time of his birth on 22 May 1859, more than half the population of the United States believed in spiritualism and there were 25,000 practising mediums; séances and levitations were all the rage amongst crowned heads and society notables. In his twenties, Doyle was still a 'convinced materialist', but was becoming more fascinated by the subject, attending séances and table tipping between 1885 and 1888. Some prominent scientists were also becoming convinced of the reality of an 'unseen universe of Spirit'.

At the very point that Doyle was thinking about the first Holmes story, he was also wondering about faith. He refused to accept the tenets of organised religion and, although not an atheist, was attracted to spiritual theories which kept an idea of God, but ditched the paraphernalia of worship. From the late 1880s, he was reading mystic literature, but writing rationalist detective fiction. By 9 May 1889, he was a convinced spiritualist actually signing a letter to the *Portsmouth Evening News* 'a Spiritualist'. His friends drew back, yet he advanced, becoming more embroiled with spiritualist-minded people to the exclusion of others.

During 1916, Doyle was suggesting that spiritualism was a 'revolution' in thought more profound than any political revolution, looking towards a new millennium of hope and consolation where the living could commune with the dead, and by 1917, he had joined Sir Oliver Lodge in the London Spiritualist Alliance. By 1920, and against the evidence of his own eyes (or expressly because of it), he had embraced the Cottingley Fairies and wrote several articles to say so, articles that simply brought ridicule upon him.

The editor of *The Strand* begged Doyle to desist from publication if it led to the devaluation of all that Holmes stood for and all that Doyle epitomised as the pipe-smoking 'embodiment of common sense'. For E.T. Raymond, writing in *The Living Age* in 1920, Doyle had now become a 'fictional' character whose views were opposed to those of Holmes; 'instead of common sense', there was the 'wildest mysticism', but when had Holmes ever exemplified common sense? Meanwhile, *Punch* ribbed Doyle with a ditty:

> If you, Sir Conan Doyle, believe in fairies,
> Must I believe in Mister Sherlock Holmes?
> If you believe that round us all the air is
> Just thick with elves and little men and gnomes,
> Then must I believe in Doctor Watson
> And speckled bands and things? Oh, no! My hat!
> Though all the t's are crossed and i's have dots on
> I simply can't. So that's that!

Although fairies, elves and gnomes were the staple of much mid-Victorian art and belief, Tinker Bell did not arrive until 1904, and Doyle's own grandfather made a living out of painting them. Doyle became progressively convinced of the materialisation in this world of the hitherto unseen. A revelation was at hand. Materialism had given way to a new sense of time and space, not because of the dubious activities of mediums but because of the tested methods used by scientists to prove mediumship authentic and show their access between 'two worlds' to be a real phenomenon. As early as 2 July 1887, he had written an article in the magazine *Light* on his new beliefs:

> [Death] makes no abrupt change in the process of development, nor does it make an impassable chasm between those who are on either side. No trait of the form and no peculiarity of the mind are changed by death but all are continued … in recent years there has come to us from divine sources

a new revelation … by far the greatest religious event since the death of Christ … it is a revolution in religious thought, a revolution which gives us as a by-product an utter fearlessness of death.

Doyle always had a rocky relationship with organised religion, believed in divorce on equal terms and was open to non-orthodox spiritual explanations of the universe. For weeks on end, he pondered the mystery of spiritualist belief.

The Edwardian world had inherited the Victorian militarist whirlwind and an apocalyptic war with France, Germany or Russia seemed inevitable. It is in this atmosphere of anxiety that Doyle moved closer to the spirit world. In the latter half of his life, however, he turned increasingly towards an interest in life after death and used the science fiction tales of his new hero, Professor Challenger, to explore the conundrum, especially in Challenger's penultimate novel of 1926, *The Land of Mist*, where the Professor's best friend and his daughter go on a spiritual adventure in order to reveal the truths of spiritualism and prove to the sceptical materialist professor the significance of ectoplasm:

> For the second time in her life Enid had to pinch herself hard to satisfy herself that she was not dreaming. Was this graceful creature, who had now sat down in the centre of the circle, a real materialization of ectoplasm, used for the moment as a machine for expression … or was it an illusion of the senses, or was it a fraud? There were the three possibilities. An illusion was absurd when all had the same impression. Was it a fraud? … And the cabinet was fraud-proof. It had been meticulously examined. Then it was true. But if it were true, what a vista of possibilities opened out. Was it not far the greatest matter which could claim the attention of the world!

In its origins the new spiritualist movement that gave rise to the idea of cremation (with its Hindu undertones) contained a belief that a veil had been rent in consciousness (first hinted at by mesmerism at the start of the century) and that the spirit world was now within touch. In the same way that electricity remained for many years a mysterious force, so too the 'advances' in 'spiritism' suggested possibilities that hinted at a vast invisible liquid ether suffusing everything and harnessable by a few highly tuned minds, a 'conducting medium … which extends from star to star and pervades the whole universe', as Doyle put it in an earlier Professor Challenger tale, *The Poisoned Belt* (1913). Yet it soon became clear that this ether was also the gateway to the dead and that the parlour tricks of the new clairvoyants were the first stages in contacting those who had 'passed over'.

By the Edwardian period, Challenger is no longer the explorer of lost realms, but merely an old-fashioned materialist curmudgeon refusing to acknowledge the new revelation: 'this soul talk is the Animism of savages. It is superstition, a myth … [humans are] four buckets of water and a bagful of salt … when you're dead you're dead'. His friend Malone disagrees on philosophical lines and is slowly convinced that even 'ectoplasm' has a material basis, and by turns comes to the conclusion of life after death as a reality, material science giving way to 'spiritual progress', all nevertheless repressed by the vindictive nature of the police and the ignorance of judges. Spiritualism was not only revelation, it was also revolution.

Doyle also embraced the sense of equality and levelling of those churchmen who had effectively broken away from the orthodox Church. Nevertheless, he rejected the collectivism of the new 'socialist' churches. Instead, for him, spiritualism was essentially about individual salvation. Thus, he was able to reconcile the new revolution in spirituality with the status quo; he always remained a political Liberal in his head, if a radical spiritual socialist in his heart. In his late 'Challenger' novel, *The Land of Mist*, he points out:

> There is no such leveller of classes as spiritualism, and the char woman with psychic force is the superior of the millionaire who lacks it. [The poor] and the aristocrats fraternize instantly. The Duchess [asked] for admission to the grocer's circle … It makes me see red when I remember these folk, Lady This and Countess That, declaring all the comfort they have had [from spiritualism], and the leaving those who gave it to die in the gutter or rot in the work house.

The reconciliation of democracy, social equality, materialism and spiritualism in Doyle's work was not after all an aberration of a deluded man, but instead the fulfilment of much that Holmes stood for (and much that the age stood for too), a rational explanation of inexplicable phenomena in a confused world. In spiritualism, Doyle reconciled his lapsed Catholicism with a new religious conviction of the survival of life after death, which itself ironically confirmed and upheld his belief in the reality of the nature of material evidence, even if that material was now invisible and strange.

This new revelation would kill off Holmes more surely than a fall off a high cliff because Holmes would no longer be needed to reassure us. Of course, Doyle was often naïve, too gullible and easily convinced, too willing to grasp at straws to prove a slim theory, but in all this he shared the delusions of his age rather than stood against them; indeed, he stood for the Victorian he was and remained 'the one fixed point in a changing world', as Holmes remarks to Watson in the midst of the First World War. Doyle was a patriot and imperialist, but he shared more than he realised with the anarchists and socialists whom Holmes constantly defeated, and with a Church that Holmes himself had long since forsaken. What Doyle saw was a new world order and a new beginning, not so much socialist and Christian as personal and spiritual, the final reconciliation of opposites. His delusions were to him certainties, spiritualism the one veil Holmes could not penetrate: the final problem finally solved.

Doyle's mental turmoil seemed not to be a debate between faith and reason, but rather two forms of logic. Indeed, most writers on the occult insisted upon the conspiratorial nature of both conventional science and established religion, which (against the evidence of history) had worked together in order to conceal a set of truths they only dimly understood but which they nevertheless fully comprehended would destroy their power should such truths be revealed to a wider public. 'Illuminated knowledge' would, clairvoyants believed, soon replace both science and religion: séances and clairvoyancy were the portals to a new revelation.

If science emphasised effect (not self-based), then 'magical' encounters emphasised affect (where subjectivity is a necessary corollary of determination: the self as conduit). Magical encounters were suffused with an overabundance of affect, where a 'fact' in the world was determined by the presence of subjectivity and then returned as an effect (bells ringing, levitation, spirit hands). Spectators at such events were not mere onlookers but were witnesses to a new revelation of history in which time itself was abolished and with it the linear idea of events.

Such hallucinationatory states and the experience of them 'in the world' aspired, for believers, to the conditions of history. Yet such experiences were excluded not only by the derision of intelligent non-believers but also by the inability of the experienced phenomena to conform to historical chronology and materialist determination (nor even to the theological determination of the miraculous – of which it falls short). Excluded from history although experienced as an event, the supernatural was relegated by its own processes and procedures to pseudo-history and the marginal, confronting history but incapable of being incorporated within it. Supernatural experience occurred within history but lacked significance: the effort of becoming an event was too great for the weight of its signification, leaving it only a mere anecdotal status.

It is this dislocation that makes the hallucination an event but prevents it from becoming history. Instead, all is determined by a certain scenario, a theatre of staging, witnessing and participation at once cerebral and visceral. This scenario, according to its script, setting and direction, creates a framework whose dynamic tends towards zero: a trajectory out of time altogether into the ritualistic and mythic.

The new arts were not immune from the influence of the spirit world. Photography, that most scientific of artistic forms, was soon to be put to use in trying to capture the ethereal world of spirits conjured by the occultists. In photography it was felt that the fleeting and invisible would become visible and permanent. In capturing the spectral on what was already a spectral apparatus (later Arthur Conan Doyle would hope to talk to spirits through the telephone), photographers would redeem their medium from one that was only good for recording the mundane. It happened as an accident, when William H. Mumbler caught the fleeting trace of a (real) women on his photographic plate, but others thought that this was the way into the spirit world. The loss of life in inexplicable catastrophes such as the Commune of Paris, the American Civil War and the First World War prompted collusion with mediums as well as experimentation with the medium.

Spirit photography took off in America, wafted to France and thence to Britain. It was most popular during the 1860s and 1870s, and it curiously accompanies that other foray into the unknown, the pornographic photo. Both aimed to achieve large commercial profit, and whilst some photographers were genuinely interested in ectoplasm and spiritualism, most were happy to produce spoof photos of shrouded spectres and ectoplasmic extrusions. The use of white sheets to produce 'ghosts' as well as the use of 'ghost stamps' (a technical device to distort a normal picture by adding a light source not present) kept an avid public more than happy. The exhibitionist spirit medium 'Eva P' sat nude for photographs with ectoplasm coming from her vagina and sliding over her breasts, creating, in so doing, a spectacular and legitimated pornographic theatre of which photography became the accomplice. And yet belief in spirit photography remained high as it was the only verifiable way of exhibiting the scientific proof of the phenomena. Doyle again caught the mood:

'By the way, you should try for a psychic picture.' …
'I always thought that that at least was fraud.'
'On the contrary, I should say that it was the best established of all phenomena, the one which leaves the most permanent proof.'

The powerful combination of non-conformist religion and Theosophy or similar doctrines created a new area of popular culture – essentially modern, American and plebeian, which found a quick and easy acceptance in Britain. It is this Anglo-Americanism which dominated the modern popular revival of belief in the occult and which grew independently of the more aristocratic and arcane European versions, which owed many of their ideas to this side of the Channel. Indeed, the Anglo-American version of spiritualism often merged and subsumed independent European Romantic magical and spiritual traditions which appeared to develop independently but, when investigated more closely, were tied to developments that may be considered broadly Anglo-American or which were associated with the European émigré culture in Anglophone countries. Doyle, a grand patriot, always thought this higher plane of experience was essentially 'Anglo-Celtic'. More than anything, it was democratic.

A pattern of plebian revelation had already established itself in the wanderings of American 'holy men' and seers and their fundamentalist followers. Spiritualism was a product of the mid-nineteenth century with its emphasis on individualism, populist mass culture, democratic inclusion, market choice, religiosity and revolutionary dreaming. It found a ready home in Victorian Britain, first as the answer to middle-class social and religious qualms and then later as a compensation for working-class poverty and exploitation. One commentator, Ronald Pearsall, has noted that spiritualism 'was the first popular movement to be imported from the United States' into Britain, a movement not only 'tailor made for the nineteenth century' but inherently tied to an entrepreneurial and acquisitive age:

[The Victorians] wanted marvels and wonders … and because Victorian England [and America] was a capitalist country subsisting on the laws of supply and demand, they got them.

As Pearsall further points out, right from the beginning:

The entrepreneurs were cashing in on the occult mood. In Florence 'guaranteed' turning tables were being sold with the tag 'It Moves!' In London, crystal balls were all the rage, and the 'original' was bought by Lady Blessington from an 'Egyptian magician', though she admitted that she never got the hang of it. An optician in London was turning them out by the dozen.

The séance became the defining scene of spiritualist activity. The spiritualist salon was filled with mediumistic levitation, kinetic movement of objects, raps and taps, cracks and whistles, snatches of birdsong and spirit voices, spirit drawing and writing, ectoplasmic extrusions and floating trumpets, the appearance of spirit bodies or dematerialised hands or limbs, and the sudden appearance of rings, coins, flowers or even sugar plums. Nevertheless, a new ghostly phenomenon was about to appear.

As real bodies dematerialised in séances and on photographic plates, the nineteenth-century American holding company took on legal flesh and bones. This was the materialisation of Frankenstein's monster in reality – not made of the remnants of the graveyard, but nevertheless real and immortal, the creation of the legal profession and of finance.

In the United States, the corporation would have a fertile new life. Corporations were the creatures of government and could be made immortal and could be given whatever powers the lawmakers wished for them. Sir Edward Coke, seventeenth-century champion of common law rights against a tyrant king, warned that corporations 'cannot commit treason, nor be outlawed nor excommunicated, for they have no souls'. In the twentieth century, Daniel Boorstin noted that:

> Corporations [in the United States] ... would spread over the land, and finally permeate every citizen's daily life ... The corporation had many advantages over the enterprising individual ... A creature of the law, it was immortal ... Lawyers presided over the mysteries of corporation law. Property became a new realm of the occult.

Secret business trusts in the United States, when outlawed, metamorphosed in the hands of managing lawyers (of whom the chief magician was Rockefeller's Samuel C.T. Dodd) into the 'holding company', of which Standard Oil was the first in 1899. A paper delivered at the annual meeting of the American Bar Association in 1900 proclaimed that 'there is ... complete freedom of contract; competition is now universal, and as merciless as nature and natural selection'. Far removed (at least on paper) from human (i.e. fallible) interference, the 'immortal' but 'soulless' corporation retained the same rights as actual humans, but avoided the responsibilities. The corporation was entirely the creation of law: an animus without anima moving with its ghostly presence through

American history defended by the 6th and 14th Amendments and protected by 'due process', enjoying the rights of a 'natural person' but without substance or consciousness and yet endowed with an immutable and immortal purposive 'will'. The corporation had rights in exact proportion to its non-materiality. Here was a new spectral economic and legal body against which popular and populist refusals had little effect.

Borrowing a gothic metaphor, Karl Marx described the haunting 'spectre' of communism in *The Communist Manifesto* which was the ghostly double and terrifying nemesis of that other spectre: money. Money was both the alchemical principle of transubstantiation and the principle of eternal production. 'It is as though, for example, the discovery of a stone granted me possession of all the sciences, irrespective of my individuality.' Money was the *élan vital*, the new linking force within society and capable of infinite and eternal transformation. Ironically, it was money which combined the material and spiritual universes through its infinite power of reproduction. 'All commodities are perishable money', said Marx and 'money is imperishable commodity.'

SIX
KNOCKING ON HEAVEN'S DOOR

Against the inhuman forces of the universe little could be done, but society itself was already showing signs of evident decadence before the nineteenth century had even begun and the decline in morals and social purpose might be addressed. There seemed three choices for survival: there was either the nihilistic individualism of bohemians who would overcome the travails of life and the degeneration and ugliness of society by an aesthetics of doomed beauty, there were the socialists who would heal society with world revolution and there were those who kept firm to a belief in the return of the Messiah. The sacrifice of the alienated but superior artist would lead to fascism, just as that of the alienated revolutionary socialist would lead to communism and religious mania would lead to delusion and failure.

The greatest contradiction and tensions of the period were within the political, social, sexual and philosophical lives of spiritual men and women who progressively gave up the struggle to act as they felt other men or women of their class would expect them to and as they might be expected to by others. Alongside madness and mesmerism, there was religious mania which slowly through the century became the province of those men and women who were cut off from other means of expression. However, this process began in the late eighteenth century.

The 'prophet' Richard Brothers was born in Newfoundland in 1757 and was educated at Woolwich before becoming a naval lieutenant in 1783. Discharged on half-pay (the usual course of events when naval officers were not wanted), he refused to take the money if it required him swearing an oath to the crown. Penniless, he was therefore sent to the workhouse, where he declared himself the 'Napoleon of the Almighty' and began to prophesy, becoming so troublesome that he was actually indicted for treason, but was found to be so entirely mad (perhaps he was schizophrenic) that he was confined as a criminal lunatic. Yet even in this state he gained a number of followers, including John Finlayson, with whom he finally came to live and in whose house in Marylebone he died in 1824.

Yet Brothers was not the only one to see the light of revelation. Of all those who believed the millennium was coming, the most significant was Joanna Southcott. She was born the fourth child of William and Hannah Southcott of Ottery St Mary, Devon in 1750. She grew up to become a proud, hard-working girl who had a gift for prophecy, which brought her to the attention of a wider public and inevitably led to accusations of lunacy and fraud. Joanna had begun prophesying in 1792. The date was significant as the French Revolution at that point was reaching its climax at the guillotine. The world was turning upside down. The radical and scientist Joseph Priestley, for instance, published the sermon *The Present State of Europe Compared with Ancient Prophecies* in 1794, in which he saw the French Revolution as the fulfilment of the apocalyptic message of the Book of Revelation.

Southcott had already begun her own campaign of prophecy and soon identified Napoleon as the antichrist; she distributed papers to those around the country willing to listen on which she had written 'seals' to protect the wearer. On 22 October 1803, the *Leeds Mercury* noted that: 'The object of her visit is to distribute Celestial Seals to the faithful: and as these seals ... will protect the possessor from all danger even at the cannon's mouth, we recommend the Volunteers to lay in a stock preparatory to the arrival of Bonaparte and his sharp-shooters.' In a credulous and worried age, with rapid change and constant war, Southcott appealed to all levels of the population. Indeed, most interestingly, her appeal seemed to have been to the more educated middle classes, who found solace in her teachings. Many of her dreams, for instance, related ordinary domestic activities (such as the squabble between a cat and a dog) to the wider picture of the war with France.

Finally unable to persuade the Church that her revelations were real, she 'became' pregnant at the age of 64, declaring the baby the 'Prince of Peace' and calling him Shiloh. Despite her age, many believed her actually to be pregnant and her followers laid aside numerous gifts for the baby. So famous was she at this point that there was even a cartoon by Thomas Rowlandson (8 September 1814) dedicated to the event and she was soon the talk of medical society, many doctors being unsure if it actually was a pregnancy or a cancerous tumour. Inevitably she died on 27 December 1814, with no sign of Shiloh. The 'woman clothed with the sun', as Southcott called herself, died with devoted followers who still eagerly awaited the birth of the Saviour.

One of these followers was her faithful companion Jane Townley, the daughter of the High Sheriff of Lancashire who became Southcott's supporter and eventually believed that Shiloh was the Prince Regent himself. There was also the Reverend Thomas Foley, an Anglican Churchman and guardian of Southcott's mysterious closed box which was to be opened when 24 bishops were willing to sit in judgment at a time of great crisis. Foley remained faithful to the end and even in the twentieth century, the box was advertised in the Sunday newspapers as awaiting its opening. Others followed Foley's lead. William Sharp, an engraver and friend of Thomas Paine and John Horne Tooke, was a member of the Society for Constitutional Information and a revolutionary who, nevertheless, believed in the revelations of Richard Brothers. There was also the maverick George Turner, who was so sufficiently problematic as to be committed to a Quaker asylum. After his release, he too predicted the coming of Shiloh, but died in 1821 still awaiting his appearance. It was an age of superstitious belief and credulousness. A Leeds woman by the name of Mary Bateman, a disciple of Brothers, even claimed that her hen was laying eggs with the message 'Christ is Coming'. Such beliefs were taken seriously by many.

In this atmosphere, the strangest of all revolutionaries stepped into the rural landscape of Kent almost from nowhere. This man was born plain John Nicols Thom, the son of a farmer and maltster of St Columb in Cornwall who worked for a time in a wine merchant's warehouse in Truro. When the firm closed, he started trading on his own as a wine merchant and hop dealer, but unfortunately his business burnt down in an 'accidental' fire for which he claimed rather too much insurance. It was not long before he recovered from his loss and achieved considerable success dealing in malt, which he seems to have disposed of in Liverpool.

For a couple of years he vanishes from the records, only to return as Sir William Percy Honeywood Courtenay, Knight of Malta, no longer in Liverpool but now in Canterbury. His eccentric title was apparently borrowed from the real Sir William, who was at that time abroad. Previously he had gone about as Sir Moses Rothschild. During 1832 he stood as a parliamentary candidate for Canterbury and was able to gain many respectable admirers, despite the eccentricity of his manners and the sheer peculiarity of his dress, which consisted of a braided red velvet suit topped with epaulettes, a short cloak and a floppy medieval-style cap crowned with a tassel. For armament he carried a curved Turkish-style sword which he called 'Excalibur'.

Although he did not win a parliamentary seat, Courtenay began inveighing against the Poor Laws and gained a following from the local farm labourers. Indeed, he wrote a number of publications and took issue with a number of social and political wrongs. In his publication *Liberty* (motto: 'the British lion will be free'), he addressed himself to the 'lower orders of society' in order that they should have the 'opportunity to read on a Sunday' and in the issue of Saturday, 27 April 1833, he attacked both the Church and the moneyed classes. 'Landlords' he insisted, lived off the backs of the 'working classes', 'the poor stands [sic] as it were upon a gibbet' and 'for a country to prosper, the working classes, can never have too good wages'. The consequences for a parliament, 'not being the voice of the people', was that 'England must go to a revolution', but at the same time no country in 'Christendom' could stand 'upon a republican form of government'.

It is now that Courtenay becomes delusional. His next action was rather bizarre as he gave perjured evidence in a smuggling case (for which he had no reason to appear) and was found guilty at Maidstone Assizes during 1833. By this time his actions were becoming more outlandish and his friends, having by now discovered his whereabouts, persuaded the judge that he was not of his right mind and had him incarcerated in a local lunatic asylum. Falling into dispute with his guardian, however, he left the asylum to take up residence near the small village of Dunkirk near Faversham in Kent. Sir William now metamorphosised again. It was his greatest impersonation, for by this time the locals had started to believe that he was the reincarnation of Christ, and certainly many of the women of the village were fearful that if their husbands did not do as he said, 'fire would come from heaven and burn them'.

The villages of Kent were rural and isolated, prone to rumour and superstition. Nevertheless, it would be wrong to imagine that Courtenay's little band of disciples were all ignorant farm labourers. There were many labourers, but there were also distressed farmers (with smallholdings of between seven and 20 acres), brewers, a gardener, a shoemaker, a bailiff and a mole catcher. More than half could read and a number were noted for their strict attendance at church. A high proportion was also over 40 and so were not likely to be hotheads yet were likely to be cynical about their lot. In short, these were not the rambunctious material of the industrial villages, although almost ten years of rural disturbance had made them disaffected and rebellious. These were older men perhaps inclined to think that they had little or nothing to lose by their efforts. As for the area, it was relatively isolated, sitting some way from the nearest town of Faversham at an angle to the old Roman road to Canterbury. The area was also heavily wooded and a good hiding place for smugglers or thieves, especially as there were few inhabitants. Dominating the area, then as now, is Mount Ephraim, a large country estate.

Courtenay led his followers out on 29 May 1838 riding a horse, armed with a brace of pistols and a sabre, and looking like a mixture of pirate king and Banditti leader. His followers carried his 'standard', a lion rampant, and held aloft a loaf of bread attached to a pole. They toured the local villages for two days calling for volunteers and promising the return of better days. By the second day, they had a little force of some 36–49 men according to the estimates of Norton Knatchbull, a local gentleman and self-appointed snoop who shadowed them as they gathered. Enough was enough and the local magistrate, the Reverend John Poore, issued warrants for the apprehension of Courtenay who was being followed at this point by a large force of local gentry and special constables.

By now the rebels were at Dunkirk and Courtenay was ensconced in a farmhouse. When the special constables arrived, Courtenay pointed a gun at them and pulled the trigger. One of the constables was killed. Afterwards Courtney hacked the body and threw it in a ditch. No longer could his antics be ignored and a detachment of the 45th Infantry, newly returned at Canterbury barracks from India, was called up. The infantry marched to Bossenden Wood where the rebels were camped. The two sides sized each other up, the one armed with muskets and the other armed with sticks. There was little time for thought as Courtenay threw himself at Lieutenant Henry Bennett, aged 29 and a veteran of the Burma campaign. Both fired and both dropped dead, Bennett being the last soldier to die on active service on English soil and the very first to die in Victoria's reign. Then pandemonium ensued: a volley, bayoneting, 20 dead. After the 'battle', the owner of Mount Ephraim collected souvenirs: a lion banner carried by Courtney; an ivory whistle; a comb; two swords; a money pouch and some bullets; and a broken watch.

The question remains as to what exactly happened at Bossenden. It was called a riot by contemporaries, but no rioting took place and it was not an uprising in any straightforward sense. Was it a sort of mad holiday or a religious parade to bring on the millennium? Recruitment by Courtney had began on 29 May or Oak Apple Day, commemorating the restoration of Charles II, but also the traditional day for making a holiday in the ritual of the rural year. Courtenay's language and manner were suffused with apocalyptic imagery. Before the murder of the special constable, Courtenay had told his followers that this was 'the first day of the Millennium – and this day I will put the crown upon my own head'. After the murder he exclaimed that he was only 'executing the justice of heaven in consequence of the power God has given me'. He had already delivered a sermon on nearby Boughton Hill about the inequities of the rich which he had taken from the general epistle from St James, and he was already known for his compassion for the poor and his hatred of the rich, which was couched in biblical terminology. As Barry Reay notes:

Witnesses attested to his claim that he was not like earthly men: 'I fell down from the clouds and nobody knew where I came from.' He said that all he had to do was to place his left hand on the muscle of his right arm and 10,000 would be slain. He pretended to shoot out the stars with inflammable liquid steeped in oil with iron filings, so that when he fired his pistols the shots emitted sparkles of light. He convinced some of his followers that they were invulnerable to bullets. When Courtenay lay dead, his lover, Sarah Culver, attempted to revive him with water – he had told her that if he appeared dead he would only be sleeping ... William Wills [one of his followers] believed that Courtenay could hear everything that was said even though he was a mile away.

His followers believed him to be the Messiah and 'Christ come down from the Cross', and Courtenay offered to show them the nail holes in his hands. At Bossenden, the apocalyptic tone became more strident, with two followers, Alexander Foad and a man called Blanchard, worshipping Courtenay on bended knees as Christ re-risen. After Courtenay's death, he was laid out in the Red Lion at Dunkirk, his wounds showing prominently, but this did not prevent one local woman, Lydia Hadlow, expecting his resurrection. Many locals kept his portrait on their walls or treasured souvenirs of his life. A delusional fantasist and a serial liar Courtenay may have been, but he was also a man created in his own image who gave hope, however briefly, to those with very little and who to all intents and purposes were still living in the seventeenth-century world of the Fifth Monarchists. It was the last peasant's revolt.

There was more to come from Kent in the next 100 years where Fifth Monarchism had not yet died out. Fifth Monarchy men had been active during the latter half of the seventeenth century following the upheavals caused by the Civil War. They preached revolution and republicanism until the imminent return of the Messiah and the end of the world. Their beliefs were taken from the Book of Revelation, where it was said that 144,000 would be saved on the Day of Judgment. Added to this belief some time later was a strong sense that England was where the 144,000 were to be found and that they were, in fact, to be made up from the ten lost tribes of Israel (rather than all 12) waiting to be ingathered. Thus, England waited and hoped.

Richard Brothers had hoped to lead the chosen back to Palestine to await the latter days, believing himself to be the nephew of God; Joanna

Southcott was to give birth to the Messiah called Shiloh. British Israelite belief hinged on the twin ideas of the salvation of the 144,000 and the birth of the Messiah; both of these occurrences were to happen in nineteenth-century England.

British-Israelites waited in vain for a sign. A shoemaker called John Ward woke up one day in 1827 and proclaimed himself Shiloh, adopting the name Zion Ward as he preached. He gathered some followers but died in 1837. Others also made claims, but George Turner and William Shaw proved only to be pseudo-Shilohs, which was not the case with John Wroe, a charismatic who grew his hair to biblical proportions and who successfully attracted followers in Ashton-under-Lyne in the 1820s. Wroe soon had communities in Kent in Chatham, Maidstone, Gillingham and Gravesend, but was forced to make a quick exit to Australia after a scandal regarding sexual improprieties with young women in his flock. He died there in 1863.

There were now Wroeite communities of 'Christian-Israelites' in both the north and south of England, in the United States and in Australia, and all were still hungry for revelation. Into this strange world came James Rowland White of the 16th Regiment of Foot. Here was a mystery indeed, for no one ever established White's real name or his age, family or origins. The Israelites had split in Chatham into two factions and to one of these factions White came one day looking for 'salvation'. Over more visits White appeared to his teachers more and more like the awaited Messiah. He was already making enigmatic comments and on Christmas Eve 1875 he called the little congregation together to proclaim that he was indeed the 'Messenger of the Lord' and read from his *The Flying Roll*, itself a Fifth Monarchist means of expression, now oddly tempered with a patriotic, royalist and anti-imperialist tone:

'Blow the Trumpet in this land of England first, and say "England! The day of thy judgement is come: thou shalt be the first to be judged and the first to be redeemed. England! Thou art the land of Joseph, the granary of the Lord's corn, wine, honey and milk. All Israel shall be driven into this land; there shall 144,000 bones of the Virgin be gathered, when the Trumpet of War shall sound over the earth, but no foreign sword shall enter

thy borders!'" ... We sound the trumpet, and call upon all ... the seed of
Israel ... to flee for their lives to the city of Jerusalem above ... O happy
England ... the last country where there will be a king ... then all nations
will flock to England, and all Israel will be gathered there; and the vessels
which they have prepared to carry men into many nations, will bring Israel
home.

Scandalised by his ideas, the little group split again, by which time White
was calling himself James Jershom Jezreel or 'JJJ' in acknowledgement
of Joanna Southcott and John Wroe. He also claimed to be the 'sixth
Trumpeter' of the Book of Joel, the others being the five dead English
prophets who had preceded him. In Chatham he gathered a flock who
were known as the 'New and Latter House of Israel', the men growing
their hair long. Their church would be the last before the final apocalypse.

However, White had not yet left the army and was duly posted to
India with his regiment in 1876, where his companions found him
decidedly odd. After five years he returned from his duties, left the army,
set up as the Messiah and married a local girl called Clarissa Rogers. He
was probably in his forties, she just into her twenties, but no shrinking
violet, having travelled to the United States to pass on the word of the
'Stranger' (Jezreel's term for himself as someone in an 'alien' land) and
made a number of conversions whilst writing to Jezreel in Calicut. In
1882 the newly married couple were invited to tour America to preach
the Word as old-time revivalists, but arrangements soured with their
hosts and they returned home. Life was hectic as Jezreel tried to win
followers amongst Wroeite sects in Lincoln, Ashton and even Australia,
where he travelled in 1883.

By 1883, there were sufficient followers to plan a future. A large
meeting hall was opened in Gillingham in 1883, where prayer meetings
would be accompanied by harp music and a small orchestra. This
proved a winner where entertainment was scarce and congregations
flourished. To finance his plans, Jezreel taxed his followers of their
savings, but few objected as he provided work and a good living in the
many small businesses he set up. He was, as it turned out, able to serve
both Mammon and God very successfully all his life. His various shops

offered no credit and were strictly cash only. Life was sweet, and Jezreel and Clarissa moved into a spacious house called 'Woodlands' and set up 'Israel's International College' in the grounds. Here he held open air rallies with music, food and 'no collection'! He now had at least 2,000 followers, which made his plans even more ambitious.

Finally, in 1884, Jezreel decided to create the new Jerusalem for the 144,000 he had dreamed of in *The Flying Roll*. It would be on Chatham Hill, looking for all the world like an Assyrian fortress or the walls of the Holy City, six storeys high with towers adorned with the mystic symbols of the Book of Revelation: trumpets, the Flying Roll, crossed swords and the feathers of the Prince of Wales signifying the Trinity. The building was to house an assembly room, offices and work spaces designed in ultra-modern steel and concrete with electric lights and central heating. Structurally, it was the very first 'modernist' building in Britain, pre-dating the Cenotaph by 36 years. P.G. Rogers, Jezreel's biographer, points out that the building 'looked to all the world like a strange wizard's tower rising on its hill, an impression reinforced by its mystical dimensions: a perfect cube with sides 144 feet long'.

Then an unexpected disaster occurred. On 1 March 1885, Jezreel died. He was buried without lamentation in an ordinary grave with a Church of England service. Rumours abounded in the press as to his sexual improprieties, odd rituals and peculiar lifestyle, but all seemed to have been unfounded. His successor was his redoubtable wife, now 'reincarnated' as 'Queen Esther', a formidable lady who continued the building work on 'Israel's Sanctuary', but was litigious and frivolous by turns and lost followers and money as a result. Nevertheless she started a newspaper and continued to live a relatively privileged lifestyle.

By the 1880s, times were unsettled and atheistic foreign anarchists with cloaks and beards seemed to lurk behind every doorway. Such times brought new recruits, as Queen Esther recalled:

I had occasion one day – some four years ago now – to call the attention of a policeman, who was on duty outside my shop in Oxford Street, to a suspicious-looking parcel which had been left on my counter, and was supposed to be a package containing tea. Upon a careful examination I found sawdust trickling out of it, and knowing the many explosions of dynamite which had taken place in London and elsewhere, I felt considerably relieved when we ascertained that the contents of the parcel were quite harmless. This circumstance led however to an interesting conversation as to the unsettled state of affairs, and in fact the state of the world in general. We spoke about the signs of the time, and presently discussed the subject of the restoration of the lost tribes. This led to his introducing to my notice a copy of a book entitled Extracts from the Flying Roll.

Indeed, by 1887, the New and Latter House of Israel had communities in London, Chatham, Gillingham, Maidstone, Brighton, Lincoln, Holyhead, Ashton-under-Lyme, Kilmarnock, Glasgow, the Channel Islands, New Zealand, America and Australia. The tower rose and the faithful waited, the band played and the 'gentiles' (as non-believers were called) gawped; the press, both local and national, couldn't get enough. Then disaster came a second time. Queen Esther died suddenly in 1888, giving 'birth' to Shiloh. She actually died of peritonitis aged only 28. The sect declined and split in the wake of the death of its two colourful and charismatic leaders. Income rapidly fell and the sect's businesses closed; the tower remained unfinished and abandoned. One Edward Rogers led the sect for a time as its 'overseer' whilst William Forsyth led the 'Outcasts of Israel'.

Finally, an American called Michael Keyfor Mills appeared. He had been born in Detroit in 1857 and had lived in Canada before reading Jezreel's *Flying Roll*. Converted himself, his methods of converting others (sex landed him in a Detroit jail for five years) were dubious. Upon his release, he continued to preach in his 'God-House' in Detroit until 1906, when he travelled to 'Israel' in Gillingham as 'Prince Michael', accompanied by 'Princess Michael' and his secretary, a Mr 'Mackay', whose real name was David Livingstone (his mother had admired the explorer and missionary).

What struck people was that Mackay had a strange resemblance to Christ. He had joined Michael when he had been miraculously cured of 'headaches'. Later as a fine media manipulator, Mackay signed off as 'David the Living Stone, slayer of Goliath' and may have been responsible for the detection of more auspicious signs and wonders in a notice recording the sinking of the *Titanic*:

By the sinking of the above vessel a special warning has been given and symbol shown of the coming fall of Babylon. In addition to the prophecies referred to above (in another notice) this fall was also foretold by the late James Jershom Jezreel in the Flying Roll Series … which speaks of the horse and his rider (Christendom) being overthrown in the sea. In the sinking of the Titanic the prophecy has received its fulfilment in figure, the horse being symbolized by Mr. Stead, the 'steed' of Christendom, and the rider by Mr. Astor … The boat was considered unsinkable, but she was swallowed up by the waters, and Babylon will just as certainly fall, for the one is the figure of the other.

Slowly but surely, Prince Michael convinced everyone, including the local council, that he was the spiritual inheritor of Jezreel. He was liked as a person and as a local celebrity, and the Jezreelites brought jobs, money and fame to Gillingham. All seemed well, but Michael's love of fast cars was his undoing. After a spin in yet another new vehicle, both Michael and his consort the Princess became ill. In January 1922 both died suddenly. Things drifted, fell apart and died. The sect broke up, the buildings crumbled. The tower was to be sold off as 'a brewery or an asylum', but stood on its hill into the Second World War, during which it was believed that it housed a top-secret 'death ray'.

On the whole, Jezreel's followers were not fanatics, although they all felt that they were 'peculiar' people in the non-conformist sense. They were, for the most part, former Southcottians or Wroeites looking for assurance in a confused and confusing world. They seemed mostly to come from the working classes or lower middle classes, looking for assurance from a charismatic leader and his wife whose exotic background and lifestyle gave hope to lives that had lost their way. Jezreel imposed few rules and even if men had to grow their hair inordinately long, they were not forbidden from smoking or required to take the pledge, there were no sexual restrictions and no weird cult practices or uniforms either. The sacrifice of one's earnings seemed to be recompensed by the promise of eternal bliss and by the social relationships built up within the community and with the trades that brought followers into contact with the 'gentiles' living around them. For the most part, the sect lived an amiable life with its non-believing neighbours, who formed an affection for the brethren which was reinforced by their admiration for the canny financial acumen of their leader, who owned property, ran businesses and dealt in stocks and shares – in every way a respectable Victorian entrepreneur who just thought he was the Messiah.

The Jezreelites slowly faded into insignificance, their money and membership seeping away with the ever-delayed arrival of the messiah Shiloh. At Jezreel's death in 1885 there had been about 1,400 members of the sect, a small but respectable number, with more allies in Australia and the United States, but on the death of Queen Esther, the community had dwindled to around 250 spread around Maidstone, Gillingham and London, with others spread as far as New Zealand and Scotland. Nevertheless, frustrations and money troubles had reduced the core followers to around 50 by 1894 and by the Second World War, they were merely a half-forgotten memory. Jezreel's Tower was bought and sold by various developers and was finally demolished on 1 March 1961, while Woodlands, lingering on as Gillingham Museum until 1956, was demolished in 1958, and the graves of Jezreel, Queen Esther and Prince Michael were left to moulder in the local cemetery, forgotten and unloved.

Messiahs may come from the least likely surroundings. Such was the case of Mabel Bartrop, who, by degrees, led a revolution of sorts in female emancipation. She was born the second child of Augustus and Katherine Andrews on 11 January 1866 in Peckham, south London. Her father was a banker's clerk and the son of the Congregationalist preacher who had taught the young John Ruskin. Her cousin by marriage was the Catholic poet Coventry Patmore, who had done so much to mythologise the role of women as the 'angel of the hearth'. Mabel married a vicar and became, to all intents and purposes, the dutiful wife of Mr Andrews of Bedford. Unfortunately, Mr Andrews died quickly and Mabel began to suffer breakdowns. She was already dissatisfied with the Church of England and its disregard for women in its services, but she had no outlet for her frustrations. Then, one day in September 1914, she went to her local library and discovered a small book by Joanna Southcott. It seemed a revelation. Mabel was no youngster. She was 40, had a family and was a widow, but had felt no purpose as a woman. Southcott and neurotic breakdowns changed all that.

The rest of Mabel's life was a struggle to overcome illness and reconcile her suffering with God's purpose. It was an intellectual as well as an emotional journey, determined by the desire to know God by faith and her own role by conviction. Luckily, others came to believe in her holy mission. Suffering a complete mental collapse after her husband's death in 1906, Mabel placed herself voluntarily in the local Three Counties Asylum, believing it to be a place where 'gentle women' might rest and recuperate – a type of secular nunnery. Diagnosed with 'domestic worry' and 'melancholia', she was treated like any actually insane person and had to live amongst the deranged. Throughout the war she was in and out of hospitals, remaining a year and a half in Northampton General Lunatic Asylum between April 1915 and October 1916. Curiously, it was the hospital where John Clare, in his final reincarnation as himself, had written *I Am*, publishing it in the *Bedford Times* on New Year's Day 1848. Twice Mabel was actually sectioned by her husband's sister, as she seemed to be suffering from 'delusions', 'possession by the devil for unpardonable sins', 'depression' and violent behaviour. At 49, these symptoms may have been caused by the 'change', but Mabel was long on the way to seeing her mission. In the end, she mythologised this suffering as the female equivalent of Christ's crucifixion.

Whilst in hospital Mabel made friends with Minnie Oppenheim, the mentally unstable but psychic sister of E. Phillips Oppenheim, the most popular writer of the day. Minnie channelled a message from Mabel's husband reassuring her of her great mission, one that seemed peculiarly connected to her obsession with Joanna Southcott.

In one sense Mabel was 'mad' and in need of care, while in another she was not, a female victim of a system that could not recognise new forms of women's emancipation and women's activity. For a while she was trapped between two worlds. The need was to translate the world of delusion into the reality of rational experience. Her stay in hospital was later rethought in theological terms as a time of inner struggle and enlightenment. Southcott was the key and Minnie channelled messages from her to Mabel.

Replying to her best friend, Kate Firth, Mabel showed glimmerings of awareness about her new role. She concluded that: 'You … are very stupid about asylums. They are chock full of extremely gifted people and I say if God chooses to bring Joana out of a Lunatic Asylum [sic] you can't stop it.' Nevertheless, others were the solution. Whilst in hospital during the First World War, Mabel took up automatic writing and started to feel inner compulsions about her new role as a messiah called 'Octavia'. She was, in effect, reinventing herself. The doctors were more cynical. They concluded that '[Octavia] imagines she has a special mission to perform. She apparently imagines she has had a special Revelation from God telling her how the War was caused and the way to stop it'. You did not have to be in an asylum to have such delusions. She was in good company, as W.B. Yeats, Samuel Liddell, MacGregor Mathers, Aleister Crowley and many other respectable members of the occult society known as the Hermetic Order of the Golden Dawn all thought they too knew how to end the war by equally magical means.

Why should Mabel think such aberrant thoughts? Because others were seekers too. The women's suffrage movement had created a rupture in women's thinking. Newly empowered, if not yet enfranchised, women who were not attracted to the suffragettes but who nevertheless wanted something more for their lives began to look for new ways of expressing their coming liberation. One way was in religion, still a powerful force but one needing a new revelation. Her first follower was Rachel Fox, a cousin by marriage and herself a practitioner of automatic writing, while another was Helen Shepstone, the spiritualist wife of a colonial administrator who channelled messages about the Second Coming and who was in correspondence with Fox. Another seeker was Ellen Oliver, who was to play a key role in what happened next.

All four women were looking for the answer to the appearance of 'Shiloh', Southcott's baby that turned out to be the tumour that killed her. Neither Fox, Shepstone nor Oliver believed this version of things. All believed the baby had been 'born' in Heaven and was awaiting its incarnation on earth. The time was ripe, as Mabel had left her life in the asylums for good and returned to Bedford in 1916. On her return, Mabel had a revelation that 'Bedford is the place of God's glory', the site of the new Jerusalem, the place where the Israelites would be gathered in. Then, on 14 February 1919, Oliver came to the astounding conclusion that Mabel Bartrop herself was the baby Shiloh, a conclusion she had revealed to her after reading James Jezreel's *The Flying Roll*. 'No wonder', she exclaimed, 'M.B. has a look of Joanna for she is Joanna's Spiritual Child [sic] – Shiloh!'

It was the piece of the puzzle that squared the circle; the age of the spiritual realm of the female messiah had arrived and women's emotions were to be the guide to this new world (Mabel had no use for the intellects of men, which just caused trouble, nor indeed the political aspirations of women, which she rejected as looking in the wrong direction and trying to be 'masculine'). Mabel herself had begun to reach the same conclusion from hearing the voice of God:

> Behold I am with thee always, I am knit unto thee, My Child. Dost thou know who thou art, even My Child sown into the womb of thy Mother Joanna, and caught away unto the heavenly places until I found a body likely to suffer, into which, after sufferings great and terrible, My Child Shiloh should enter and dwell there. Didst thou not come into the work one hundred years after thy Mother's death?

She was reborn as 'Octavia', son/daughter of Joanna Southcott, the incarnation of the cosmic female principle. Reason, Octavia argued, was the spawn of the devil:

> As to REASON [sic], you cannot bring REASON into the woman's movement. The charm of a woman is her 'sweet unreasonableness!' But 'God knows the comparative values of reason as against intuition'.

And this was why, she believed, 'He has chosen woman to finish the whole thing for the very reason that she does not reason'. She then went on, paradoxically to demonstrate her own logical ability: 'Reason only comes from the verb ratio, I think. Well, thinking is a very dangerous thing, and in spiritual realms it easily becomes the sin of self-communing. Mens or mind, men's mind, implies a man, and man thinks. Now for aught we know the trouble lies here.'

What was needed instead was not religious fanatics or wild-eyed proselytising revolutionaries but:

> The simple facts are, that God requires a few sensible, matter-of-fact women to take on the housekeeping on earth, and to begin to give their orders by word of mouth and on His behalf, until the defeat of Satan and the Divine Jurisdiction begins.

Octavia's followers turned out to be a mixed bunch, but amongst them were a number of suffragists looking for a more 'female' world amidst the disturbances caused by the war and the revolutionary strikes that had followed in 1919. Ellen Oliver had spent time in Holloway Gaol for her involvement with the suffragettes as well as the suffragists; Alice Jones, Ellen's friend, belonged to the Church League for Women's Suffrage; Charlotte Despard, President of the Women's Freedom League, was a believer in the imminent second coming and the appearance of the 'Divine Mother-Spirit'; Dora Marsden, founder of the journal *The Freewoman* in 1911, was a spiritualist and suffered from mental breakdowns that put her almost permanently in psychiatric hospitals; Francis Swiney, writer of *The Awakening of Women* in 1915, took it into her head that Judaism was the worship of the 'mother-essence'; Eva Gore-Booth, the mystical poet and theosophist, wished to 'erase sexual differences'; Emmeline Pethick-Lawrence, one-time treasurer to the suffragettes who nevertheless preached at the all-women Church of the New Ideal in Manchester between 1916 and the 1920s.

For all these women, women's suffrage was as much about the self and spirituality as about politics and equality with men. In 1920, just as Sylvia Pankhurst and others founded their version of a British communist party, the Panacea Society was formed in Bedford 'for the purpose of gathering Israel'. They were two sides of the female radical coin.

* * *

Religious mania was not confined to Britain but reached out into the Empire too. The Doukhobors were a religious sect whose origins dated back to the eighteenth century, when a hermit began gathering followers on the banks of the Volga. By 1779, these followers were under suspicion and were exiled to Siberia, but it did not stop the movement, which had 20,000 followers by the end of the nineteenth century. They thought of themselves as the only true Christians, regarded priestly intervention as unnecessary and believed in pacifism, vegetarianism, non-resistance and disdain for intoxicants and tobacco. In 1895, Peter Verigin, the leader of those Doukhobors in exile, having read Leo Tolstoy, whose views he had come to accept, ordered his followers to resist conscription. The result was persecution and the international condemnation of Russia. Tolstoy tried to raise money for their cause, but the British government went one better. It offered the sect a haven in both Purleigh, Essex and in Canada, where most emigrated, settling in British Columbia, Alberta and Saskatchewan. Once in Canada, many rejected the very people who had invited them as being ungodly. The Doukhobor group, known as the Sons of Freedom, were the most radical, taking to eating only raw foods and the bomb-throwing tactics of anarchists. They refused to assimilate and marched across Manitoba in 1907 completely naked in protest against materialism.

SEVEN

TINKER BELL ON MARS

It is no surprise that belief in the world of spirits and messiahs, belief conditioned essentially by social disenchantment, should cause socially disenfranchised groups to attempt to unite that belief with political and economic arguments derived from utopian socialists. For a time in the nineteenth century there was certainly debate and bridge-building between both spiritualists and socialists, and utopian socialists were also in the spiritualist movement. This was especially so in Britain, where many of the founders of the Labour Party were themselves spiritualists. Spiritualism's egalitarian nature also allowed women to take centre stage in proceedings and created ground for debate on temperance and suffrage. Frustrated revolutionary émigrés escaping from the failed insurrections of the period from 1830 to 1848, arriving from France, Poland, Hungary, Bohemia and Germany also took to spiritualism (or spiritism as it was then called) as a compensation for their impotence in their own national affairs; a symptom of psychic displacement, frustration, fanaticism and despair. The spiritualist movement was not only egalitarian, it was also democratic in the basic sense, not communist but communalist, open to the influence of the Church and scientific reasoning.

Socialism and spiritualism form two means whereby the masses made their revolt. Both ideologies provided for refusal and rebellion and both lead to a restored harmony 'on the other side' – the other side of capitalist history. If the socialist revolution itself led to emancipation from the thrall of history, then for the spiritualist, that emancipation or release came through death. Both propelled their believers into the freedom of a future as yet unrealised. The twin knowledge of death and of history, their secret occulted meanings revealed, allowed those who understood to rise above the mundane and achieve full consciousness.

Such consciousness was the result of understanding the hidden processes of life and its universal or cosmic determinants.

The steady decline in established religious belief amongst intellectuals on the one hand and the working masses on the other during the Victorian period did not halt various forms of religiosity, most notably the congruence of some sort of spiritual belief and the belief in the inevitable rise of socialism: non-conformism was for years the backbone of Liberalism, but Liberalism went into decline (at first very slowly) as non-conformism itself declined and the secular 'religion' of socialism took hold. The majority of the working class (Catholics perhaps excepted) did not attend any form of worship, let alone that of the very people who oppressed them; intellectuals increasingly became outspoken critics of religious superstition. The reaction of Church leaders and congregations was an important factor in modelling a socialism or labourism into a working and coherent party with which to challenge Liberalism and finally defeat it.

The richer classes too were mobilised through Samuel Barnett, the vicar of St Jude's in Whitechapel who founded Toynbee Hall, and Canon Scott Holland, who founded Oxford House, both in 1883. It became fashionable for rich men and women to go 'slumming' in the East End as missionaries to the dark continent of poverty where they made surveys and worked in soup kitchens. It wasn't long before the energy that had once galvanised the dissenting tradition now mobilised the socialist conscience. Joseph Chamberlain, the guru of civic pride and duty, held a grudge against religion for diverting energy away from politics and was pleased 'that part of an Englishman's nature which has found gratification in religion is now drifting into political life'.

Christian 'socialism' had existed in the middle part of the century when religion was in a period of revival amidst a failing economy and dire social conditions. Augustus Pugin, who had hoped to revive Christian fellowship in Catholicism, and John Ruskin, who had hoped to revive the medieval Christian guild, had both gone insane trying. The Christian socialism of the 1880s had grown out of those non-conformist branches that had sprouted from the Methodism of previous decades, but by the end of the nineteenth century, the older disciplines of non-conformist religion had broken down.

The Catholic Church was also worried about atheistic socialists conv-incing the Irish workforce to abandon Catholicism. Cardinal Manning, who was prominent during the settlement of the Docks Strike of 1889, saw the need for gradualist and therefore 'traditionalist' reform tinged with a covert Christian message. Yet this new reforming notion actually came from a strong reaction against organised religion and its middle-class proponents who were in poor areas handing out charity and advice. Indeed, Beatrice Webb recalled of the period that it looked 'as if whole sections of the British proletariat ... would be swept ... into a secularist movement'.

In order to combat secularism amongst workers and at the same time to reimpose Christian virtues on the middle classes, a new type of philanthropism had appeared. This was dedicated not to the old charitable ways of indiscriminate dole, but to an entirely new Christian regime of handing out advice on how to live; Christian charity was thus joined to laissez-faire capital, the moral responsibility and self-help of the individual being at the centre of the programme.

This process had started when the formidable Octavia Hill and her colleagues formed the Charity Organisation Society (COS) in 1869. The Society's immediate aim was to coordinate the various charities working amongst the poor, but its ideological goal was actually to stop monetary charity altogether and replace it with 'help' of every sort of persuasion, including coercion. It was a brilliant plan which absolved the rich from higher taxes and charitable giving whilst passing the burden of blame for poverty onto those who lived in the slums and it was carried on with the passionate fury of self-righteousness. Hill and her group had the monopoly on charitable activity in the middle of the century, being perfectly at ease with market-driven capitalism as long as the poor dragged themselves up by their boot heels and the rich condescended to notice their plight.

This attitude changed when Samuel and Henrietta Barnett broke away from the dogma of self-help that was epitomised by the COS. Samuel was recalled by Beatrice Webb as 'a diminutive body clothed in shabby and badly assorted garments, with a big knobbly and prematurely bald head, small black eyes set close together, sallow complexion and a thin and patchy pretence of a beard'. The first rector of St Jude's Church, he and Henrietta argued that such charity had no effect as long as corrupt landlordism and capitalism were rampant. They were not socialists, but saw in the sociology of socialists a reason for poverty which made sense. From 1892 onwards, Samuel laid out his message. It was a message peppered with Christian values and references to Christ, but his ideas could well have been Buddhist sentiments; stripped of all religiosity, it was a secularist communal message about justice:

> I do not want many alterations to the law ... but I should like the best things made free. We want many more baths and wash-houses, especially swimming baths ... Book and pictures should be freely shown, so that every man may have a public library or a picture gallery as his drawing-room, where he can enjoy what is good with his boys and girls. We want more open spaces, so that every man, woman and child might sit in the open air and see the sky and the sunset ... We want free provision of the best forms of pleasure ... Across my vision passes a figure of perfect Man.

Henrietta too was without that bitterness that ruined many a radical's life; she felt simply that those who exploited others should get a good 'spanking'.

The first group of specifically Christian Socialists had consisted of Frederick Maurice, John Ludlow, Charles Kingsley and Thomas Hughes. This group had flourished between 1848 and 1854, dedicating themselves to the prevention of socialist revolution by the ameliorating power of Christianity. Most of them believed that a new communal and socialistic Christianity would be the outcome of any revolution following the working-class Chartist agitation of the late 1830s to the mid-1850s. The important alliance that they wished to make with the very poorest led to the founding of the Working Men's College in 1854. They also pioneered women's education at Queen's College in Harley Street, London. The vision was to create a communal life based upon the cooperative movement and the socialism of Robert Owen, as well as the community village based on the ideas of the *phalanstère* of Charles Fourier, but all under a Christian umbrella of a reformed and enlightened Anglicanism. Their influence continued long after the demise of the group in the ideas of John Ruskin, William Morris and the Fabian Society.

The second specific conjunction of socialism and the Church was in 1877, when Stewart Headlam, curate of St Matthew's in Bethnal Green, in the heartland of socialist concerns regarding poverty and deprivation, set up the Guild of St Matthew in order to combat the secular propaganda of people like Bradlaugh, then regularly speaking in the area for the National Secular Society. Headlam, however, didn't object to Bradlaugh or his followers and regularly spoke at their venues and worked alongside them. Indeed, Headlam vexed the Anglican establishment more than he ever worried a freethinker. He was born in 1847, was independently wealthy and was educated at Eton and Cambridge. He was ordained as a deacon in 1870, but dressed like a non-conformist and conducted services like a Catholic.

As curate at St John's, Drury Lane, Headlam pledged himself to bettering the moral situation of those in the music-halls who were looked down upon by the established Church as little more than prostitutes and mountebanks, and he was actually supported in this by John Ruskin, who enjoyed dancing, something still considered wicked by many. The National Secular Society met round the corner and Headlam made friends with both Bradlaugh and Besant. When he left for Bethnal Green, he actually joined the local radical club.

The object of the Guild of St Matthew, which was formed when Headlam went to Bethnal Green, was to convince secularists of their mistakes and 'justify God to the people' (rather than the other way round). At one meeting, an atheist tried to shout Headlam down, only to be rebuked by the atheist republican Dan Chatterton, who rounded on the heckler: 'You let him alone. I've been turned out of every public-house debating society in London for saying things which this here parson let me say at his meetings without a murmur. He is fair, this man, and don't you forget it.' The heckler was duly silenced.

Headlam's enthusiasm for fairness and justice got him into frequent controversies and when he appeared as a witness for the defence at Besant and Bradlaugh's trial, it seemed to confirm his waywardness.

He was temporarilly stopped in his tracks after lecturing on the music-halls, banned from preaching and virtually sacked. For a time he was taken in to work and preach by various sympathetic churchmen and he found time to stand side by side with Michael Davitt at one rally. He wrote tracts for the Fabians, held regular church parades and encouraged others to get involved. One sermon by Thomas Hancock was entitled 'The Banner of Christ in the Hands of the Socialists'. Indeed, socialism and Christianity were increasingly being seen by many as the same thing. In 1884 the Guild had established a network of clerics who subscribed to its programme, a third of whom belonged to the Anglican Church. The 'manifesto' was explicit in seeing Christian brotherhood through the prism of economic, political and social theory. It read as follows:

> That whereas the present contrast between the condition of the great body of workers who produce much and consume little and of those classes who produce little and consume much is contrary to the Christian doctrines of Brotherhood and Justice, this meeting urges on all Churchmen the duty of supporting such measures as will tend –
>
> (a) To restore to the people the value which they give to the land;
> (b) To bring about a better distribution of the wealth created by labour;
> (c) To give the whole body of the people a voice in their own government; and
> (d) To abolish false standards of worth and dignity.

Slowly Headlam made progress until he was embraced by the new Bishop of London, Mandell Creighton, but he was still willing to push things to the limit, starting an Anti-Puritan League (APL) with G.K. Chesterton and his brother Cecil. More importantly, he lent £7,000 through the APL to Oscar Wilde at his trial and then urged Wilde to break bail and flee to France! He was political, religious and religiously political all his life; in 1888 he was nominated for a place on the London School Board (Hackney Division), which he won. From then on he remained in local politics, becoming a member of the newly formed London

County Council in 1907. When he died on 18 November 1924, it was the freethinkers who were most liberal with their praise:

> Deeply devoted to religious principles, he held to them with characteristic tenacity, but all the time with the widest and most respectful tolerance of others. Freethinkers were glad to meet such a clergyman, and his relations with them were always of the most cordial nature. His opponents were among his greatest admirers. His love of liberty was all-embracing: liberty of thought, of publication of political and economic freedom. In all the years of his public life no call to action on behalf of freedom of thought or speech ever found him wanting. He taught the Church Catechism to those who were sent to him at Church, but was a life-long advocate of Secular Education in the State schools.

The Labour Church Movement was created by John Trevor, a Unitarian preacher who had been brought up in a religious atmosphere in Wisbech, Cambridgeshire that consisted mostly of the terrors of Hellfire. He finally abandoned the Bible in his early twenties, but returned with a newly blended faith of socialism and Christ. He slowly came to the belief that a new type of religion was needed for the humble of the nineteenth century. He attended the Unitarian Conference of 1885 and heard the union leader Ben Tillett talk of the lack of response by churches to what the working class needed in their lives. The workers, he told the Conference, were not irreligious, just spiritually ill led. To help propagate his new vision, partly inspired by the Fabian economic group to which he belonged, partly by the work and organisation of the Salvation Army, and partially by the idea of a 'New Theology of Modernism' which had come from University Hall where he worked for a time, he decided to hold his first Christian experiment in Manchester in October 1891. A huge audience turned up to see Tillett, P.H. Wicksteed (Trevor's mentor), Tom Mann (who was almost persuaded to became a preacher by Cardinal Manning before actually becoming a communist) and Stanton Coit of the South Place Ethical Society preach the good word. It was said that when Christ was mentioned by name, there was cheering from the audience.

Just as Arthur Conan Doyle tried to reconcile the supposed opposites of rationalism and spiritualism in a new unity, so Trevor and Headlam were trying to reconcile the Christian message with that of the materialist socialists. Trevor's ideas spread around the country and he founded a paper called *The Labour Prophet* in 1892 and organised the Labour Church Union in 1893. Nevertheless, the new churches were mostly confined to the North and never numbered much more than 50, so it was a rather limited crusade at best. A conference was duly held where the following resolution was passed:

1. That the Labour Movement is a Religious Movement.
2. That the Religion of the Labour Movement is not a class Religion, but unites Members of all classes working for the abolition of commercial slavery.
3. That the Religion of the Labour Movement is not Sectarian or Dogmatic, but Free Religion leaving each man free to develop his relations with the Power that brought him into being.
4. That the Emancipation of Labour can only be realized as far as men learn both the Economic and Moral Laws of God and heartily endeavour to obey them.
5. That the development of Personal Character and the improvement of Social Conditions are both essential to man's emancipation from moral and social bondage.

Following the conference, 'Cinderella' clubs were opened to educate and feed poor children as well as to give the poor such treats as outings. These clubs continued into the twentieth century and were often run in conjunction with the Social Democratic Federation or the Independent Labour Party. Eleanor Marx found Christian Socialism risible but harmless. 'There may be only a dozen of them', she said, 'but they are truly convinced and honest people', even though 'one must be English to understand the ludicrous mixture of Christianity and Socialism. They are mainly Anglican churchmen, but their religion is as singular as their socialism'. Yet the socialist movement was itself also religiously rapturous through and through. At a meeting in August 1885, Eleanor

Marx was praised by Henry Hyndman, the creator of the 'Marxist' Social
Democratic Federation, in almost messianic revivalist terms:

> Eleanor Marx made one of the finest speeches I ever heard. The woman
> seemed inspired … as she spoke of the eternal life gained by those who
> fought and fell in the great cause of the uplifting of humanity: an eternal
> life in the material and intellectual improvement of countless generations
> of mankind. It was a bitter cold, snow-swept night in the street outside, but
> in the Hall the warmth of comradeship exceeded that of any Commune
> celebration I have ever attended. We were one that night.

The eventual decline of the Labour churches was accompanied by the
rise of pals clubs, which were part of the Clarion Fellowship. These clubs
encouraged outdoor activity, debate and fellowship. The first of the new
organisations was the Clarion Cycling Club, formed at a meeting of
the Birmingham Labour Church in 1894. In 1907 the fifth Annual
Congress of the Russian Social Democratic Party was held in a London
Brotherhood Church to the fanfare of the press and the ever-watchful
eye of the police. Nevertheless, such churches remained residually
Christian, with prayers, hymns and a lesson as part of the order of
service. James Keir Hardie preached the lesson in Wales with a 'Come
to Jesus' tone in his voice. Nevertheless, it was clear that the attendance
of those Russian delegates in a church boded ill for orthodoxy. Such
was the contradiction that there was even a William Morris Labour
Church in Leek in Staffordshire, Morris himself being a well-known
atheist! It was a contradiction, perhaps, but also a prophecy that this
new religiosity allowed 'the flight of emotion away from the service of
God to the service of Man', as Beatrice Webb had observed.

The apparent enthusiasm for Christian Socialism eventually died
down as a movement, although it was to have a profound effect on
the idea of a political youth organisation in both the Communist and
Labour Parties and the British Union of Fascists, as well as aligning it
with the Scouts and early ecological movements like Kibbo Kift. Yet it
did not die either as an imperative within labourism or within modern
Christianity. It was still evident in the eccentric behaviour of Conrad
le Dispenser Roden Noel, the 'red' vicar of Thaxted who was a leading

British Christian Socialist. Although he was a practising member of the Church of England, Noel was also a member of the Independent Labour Party and a founder of the communist British Socialist Party in 1911; his own foundation, the Catholic Crusade, may even have influenced the origins of Trotskyism in Britain. For Noel, the fundamental message of Christ was one of social harmony in which there should be fundamental respect for the individual within a 'reconstruction' of society ('world reconstruction'); to him, the world of Christ was one 'living organism pervaded by God … the many are one body', as he put it in an essay of 1935. It was not much of an intellectual step to see Christ as 'a socialist collectiviser'.

Noel's belief that there was no contradiction between Christianity and social justice led him to fly both the red flag and the flag of Sinn Fein alongside the flag of St George during 1921, an act which got the students of Cambridge so furious they went on a jolly to rag the vicar and pull down the flags. They did not succeed, although an ecclesiastical court ordered the removal of the offending items.

Questions too were asked in Parliament. On 2 June 1921, *Hansard* reported that the Conservative MP for North Manchester had asked Mr Shortt, the Home Secretary:

> Whether he had had any report upon the proceedings and actions of the Reverend Conrad Noel, vicar of Thaxted, in Essex; and whether he proposes to take steps in regard to the open preaching of sedition in Thaxted church? Mr. Shortt replied to both questions in the negative.

Socialism, theosophy and psychology may have entered the consciousness of many in the late nineteenth century, but atavism was not so easily disregarded and nihilism not so easily avoided.

The American Edith Wharton, thinking back to a period of childhood illness in the 1870s, could vividly remember the delirium brought on by 'typhoid fever' combined with reading 'robber stories' and tales of 'ghosts' which 'brought on a serious relapse' from being haunted by 'formless horrors … like some dark undefinable menace, forever dogging my steps, lurking and threatening'. So bad were these waking nightmares that up to her late twenties she was unable to sleep in a room she knew contained a ghost story. So fearful was she and so superstitious of the results that the ghost books in the library had to be burnt before she could effectively sleep at night. Demons could be in the room or in your head, as Henry James conceded when he wrote *The Turn of the Screw*, where the governess is 'mad' but the ghosts exist. Ghostly thinking was formalised partially in Darwinian terms by Sigmund Freud from the 1890s, who considered such conditions of terror the outcome of repressed and inherited thoughts, something he did not come to formulate until his essay *The Uncanny* of 1916.

Yet was the fear of the supernatural merely an hallucination emanating from our own bodies or repressed thoughts? For many thinkers, such explanations would not wash, or at least would simply add a gloss to fears that were real because they existed in the world, not in the head. The orientalist and horror writer Lefcadio Hearn, for instance, had his own explanation of cosmic dread which he enumerated in in 1900. Unlike Freud, Hearn located our darkest nightmares in the fear of contact not with what is familiar but with that which is forbidden, the ontological and atavistic fear threatening the integrity of both body and soul. It was a question Hearn approached in his tale *Nightmare Touch*. 'What', asks Hearn, 'is the fear of ghosts among those who believe in ghosts?' It was that the 'dead' dressed in the clothes of ghostliness might touch the living, causing logic and rationality to dissolve in cosmic chaos:

The common fear of ghosts is the fear of being touched by ghosts, — or, in other words, that the imagined Supernatural is dreaded mainly because of its imagined power to touch ... And who can ever have had the sensation of being touched by ghosts? The answer is simple: — Everybody who has been seized by phantoms in a dream.

Elements of primeval fears — fears older than humanity — doubtless enter into the child-terror of darkness. But the more definite fear of ghosts may very possibly be composed with inherited results of dream-pain, — ancestral experience of nightmare. And the intuitive terror of supernatural touch can thus be evolutionarily explained.

Hearn's fear is of the disintegration of the self from the touch of the phantasmal 'dead', secreted within the 'race' memory of the absolute other or schizoid double; the self as a reversed mirror of its own existence – Jekyll and Hyde. The nightmare touch was the fear of annihilation and the realisation of cosmic meaninglessness that overwhelmed the senses in dreams:

> It may be doubted whether the phantasms of any particular nightmare have a history older than the brain in which they move. But the shock of the touch would seem to indicate some point of dream-contact with the total race-experience of shadowy seizure. It may be that profundities of Self … are strangely stirred in slumber, and that out of their blackness immediately responds a shuddering of memory, measureless even by millions of years.

The lengthening of cosmic shadows carried hints of the doom that awaited 'England' when Herbert Spencer's speculation of 1864 about the survival of the fittest became late-Victorian dogma. This represented not merely the touch of the dead, but the appearance of the unknown and unknowable; the repressed clothed in the garments of the unthinkable bringing cosmic annihilation in a godless universe.

By the latter half of the Victorian age, there were increasing notes of apocalypse as writers took the theme of foreign invasion by the French, Germans or Russians to its logical conclusion. Yet it was not the nightmare of Russian soldiers with snow on their boots marching down Whitehall that thrilled Victorian readers – there were Martians hovering over the Home Counties and there was the god Pan lurking in the undergrowth. H.G. Wells' science fiction work *The War of the Worlds* (1898) told instead of space-borne attack, the Home Counties a burning wasteland following the invasion of the Martians. Aggression across cosmic distances of 140,000,000 miles of outer space could never have been planned against, leaving the heart of the British Empire in blasted ruin from deadly Martian heat rays. It is not men and guns but bacteria that finally come to rescue humanity from the nightmare:

> In another moment I had scrambled up the earthen rampart and stood upon its crest, and the interior of the redoubt was below me. A mighty

space it was, with gigantic machines here and there within it, huge mounds of material and strange shelter-places. And scattered about it, some in their overturned war-machines, some in the now rigid handling-machines, and a dozen of them stark and silent and laid in a row, were the Martians – dead! – slain by the putrefactive and disease bacteria against which their systems were unprepared; slain as the red weed was being slain; slain, after all man's devices had failed, by the humblest things that God, in his wisdom, has put upon this earth.

It is the Martians who are the vision of the future and there is always the possibility that they might return from the outer reaches of a cosmos without God or meaning:

Dim and wonderful is the vision I have conjured up in my mind of life spreading slowly from this little seed-bed of the solar system throughout the inanimate vastness of sidereal space. But that is a remote dream. It may be, on the other hand, that the destruction of the Martians is only a reprieve. To them, and not to us, perhaps, is the future ordained.

The very small and very great fight in this cosmic battleground and neither has the remotest interest in humanity. The cosmos is silent and threatening, and very material in its power. In such a scenario, men, not Vril-ya, will be forced into the darkness of the underground. Trapped alone with a maniac, the hero of *The War of the Worlds* is forced to listen to a survivalist rant which inverts Bulwer Lytton's own prophecy of a 'Coming Race':

I mean to live underground. I've been thinking about the drains. Of course, those who don't know drains think horrible things; but under this London are miles and miles – hundreds of miles – and a few days' rain and London empty will leave them sweet and clean. The main drains are big enough and airy enough for anyone. Then there's cellars, vaults, stores, from which bolting passages may be made to the drains. And the railway tunnels and subways. Eh? You begin to see? And we form a band – able-bodied, clean-minded men. We're not going to pick up any rubbish that drifts in. Weaklings go out again.

Where was one to turn, caught between the nightmare of Darwinism, the end of mankind, the inevitable indifference of geological time and the spiritual vacuum that seemed to be sucking back the dead? Something else was needed to bring hope.

Another writer would hold part of the answer. In 1891 Kenneth Grahame had already spent 12 years as a loyal member of the Bank of England, and in another seven he would be its Secretary, but his pin-striped dreams lay elsewhere in the artistic bohemia of *The Yellow Book* and the river banks of the Thames. On 25 April 1891 he published a short story in *The National Observer*. It was called *The Rural Pan*, about the gods of the river bank forced to hide from modernity, but ever-present to those who were willing to look beyond mere materialism and the world of city bankers. In 1908 the episode was incorporated into *Wind in the Willows*. In search of Otter's lost son (so many orphans and lost children inhabit the work of children's writing), Rat and Mole find themselves on a small island, bathed in an Avalonian light, at the centre of which is the all-forgiving, all-compassionate Great God Pan: 'the Piper at the Gates of Dawn'.

Pan represented to many late Victorians and Edwardians a dream of social escape and personal release, expressed sometimes as a return to magical thinking and sometimes as a rush towards sexual excess and free love. Pan also stood for unalloyed youth and rural bacchanal sometimes embraced by the 'golden youth' of the pre-war period, as exemplified by Rupert Brooke and his poetry. Yet it had its darker side, a side that was essentially chaotic, degenerate and occult, as suggested in Arthur Machen's novella *The Great God Pan* (a 1890 short story in *The Whirlwind*; revised for re-publication in 1894). Machen was part of the 'Celtic Twilight', one of that rather elite and fashionable occult group called the Golden Dawn. For Machen, who was brought up in Wales, unlike Kipling from England, it was not history that put mystical glamour into the landscape, but the old gods of the Celts who, returning as demonic fairy folk, put terror into the valleys. Machen's landscape was pregnant with the Celtic mystery of the little folk that surrounded his own home, Llanddewi Rectory, where, it seemed to him, the symbol of the house seemed to speak 'a great word in [a] secret language' conveying unfathomable 'mysteries'. No wonder Caerleon-on-Usk, his home town and 'a very ancient place', should be redolent of repressed and alien history, for it was 'once the home of the legions, the centre of an exiled Roman culture in the heart of Celtdom'.

It is in this weird landscape that Dr Raymond, the strange and cold villain of *The Great God Pan*, decides to conduct an occult experiment which will lift the veil that hides the 'real' world from our eyes. To do so, he has convinced a girl called Mary, saved, of course, from 'the gutter', to undergo surgery in his 'laboratory'. This, however, is no ordinary surgery, for it is intended to create a 'trifling rearrangement of certain cells', a rearrangement that would be missed by 'ninety-nine per cent of brain specialists', but which will open a portal in the 'physiology of the brain' to allow the patient to rend the veil of existence and '[see] the God Pan' face to face; in other words, to encounter the primal chaos of existence.

The experiment succeeds and a child is born, the spawn of Pan himself. The child, apparently the result of Mary's rape by the god, is incarnated as the 'scarlet woman', Helen Vaughan. Her mother is reduced to an imbecile in the process, but Helen goes through various predatory and mysterious incarnations until finally ending her life in a Darwinian nightmare of degeneration, dissolution and sexual ambiguity, a polymorphously perverse descent into the primal sludge of creation. A colleague, Dr Robert Matheson, records the grisly end of her existence:

Here ... was all the work by which man had been made repeated before my eyes. I saw the form waver from sex to sex, dividing itself from itself, and then again reunited. Then I saw the body descend to the beasts whence it ascended, and that which was on the heights go down to the depths, even to the abyss of all being.

Nothing is left after the debacle except to retreat into silence where 'such forces cannot be named, cannot be spoken' and where 'they may only be imagined ... under a veil and a symbol'. The Victorian imagination ultimately retreated from the consequences of such explorations into the ancient landscape, unable however quite to shut the door on the lurking fairy folk of myth and legend, not friendly and protecting, but actually murderous and demonic, because they alone are the forgotten dispossessed of our own landscape.

Nevertheless, Pan was embraced by less esoteric writers too. Of all the fictional characters of the Edwardian period, only one has truly transcended its literary origins. Peter Pan is an oddity as he was never a straightforward figure in a children's book and his first appearance on the stage was to an adult audience going to see what they thought was an adult play.

J.M. Barrie was born to a hand-loom weaver family in Kirriemuir near Dundee on 9 May 1860. His father's exertions saw not only his family get very good educations but also a move up the class system, with books and free time available to the children. Barrie could even afford a periodical called *Sunshine* which cost a 'halfpenny or a penny a month', but he also read *Pilgrim's Progress* and works by Edgar Allan Poe, James Fenimore Cooper and R.M. Ballantyne before progressing to Dickens, Thackerey and Carlyle. Of the influence of Ballantyne's *Coral Island* on his own writing, he thought:

> It egged me on, not merely to be wrecked every Saturday for many months in a long-suffering garden, but to my first of work of fiction, a record of our adventures ... we had a sufficiently mysterious cave ... and here we grimly ate coconuts stoned from the trees which not even [characters in R.M. Ballantyne] would have recognised.

A post as the lead writer for the *Nottingham Journal* was soon followed by a career in London where Barrie wrote sketches and short stories which eventually became a book, *Better Dead*, published in 1887. However, his forte was to be the stage, for which he began writing skits and curtain-raisers. Indeed, his most successful play to date, *The Little Minister*, was actually watched with approval by Lewis Carroll. *Quality Street* and *The Admirable Crichton* appeared in 1902 and Barrie's name was made.

Nevertheless, it was with the appearance of Peter Pan, Tinker Bell, Wendy, Hook and the 'Lost Boys' that Barrie found his peculiar métier. Pan emerged from the stories told to the children of Arthur and Sylvia

Llewelyn Davies in Kensington Gardens. After four years of storytelling, Barrie published *The Little White Bird* in 1902, which became, four years later, *Peter Pan in Kensington Gardens*. 'Never Never Land' had not yet appeared, but as the mythology grew, the bird sanctuary in Kensington Gardens was soon identifiable as the place where Hook, the 'redskins' and the lost boys had their adventures. Wendy, an entirely new fictional girl's name, was created through Barrie's friendship with the daughter of W.E. Henley (who died at the age of five).

The pantheon of characters was nevertheless completed and Barrie began writing a play (as with *The Little White Bird,* purely for adults) which was finished early in 1904 and staged at the Duke of York's Theatre on 27 December the same year. The play also took off in the United States, but was not actually published until 1928. So famous was Peter Pan that in 1912 a statue was erected in Kensington Gardens, not to Barrie but to his creation: a little boy in a child's smock playing pan pipes surrounded by benevolent fairies. Indeed, the story of Peter Pan, partly because of its genesis and partly because of its retelling, seems nearer to folk myth than to fiction. Nevertheless, Peter Pan hovers uneasily between repressed desires and revulsions. He is the boy who would not grow up, and his companion, the irritable and frustrated Tinker Bell, and the company of the Lost Boys inhabit a world both attractive and fearful. 'Never Never Land' is the true world of Housman's 'lost content', uneasily just beyond reach, sweeping backwards into a half-dreamed memory of lost childhood thoughts.

Yet what here is lost in the quest for the 'situated' self, a self that is placed within a landscape and a history? Personal as well as communal history is the quest for a 'lost' identity and remains nothing more. It is, of course, only this already defeated search, as Freud first saw and spent the years up to his death codifying, that makes identity in the first place. In *Mourning and Melancholia* (1917), Freud was to write that 'reality testing has shown that the loved object no longer exists'. In so doing, he missed the fact that the loved object is not missing because it once existed and was inexplicably lost, but that it *never* existed in the first place. One may 'mourn' for what never existed but should have.

EIGHT

CHATTERTON'S SCORCHER

Extremes of revolutionary republicanism increased as Victoria's reign went on. The movement of radical ideas which had began 30 years before she came to the throne moved as the century progressed, from the reform club ideals of the late eighteenth century to the Jacobinical republican dreams of the French revolutionary period, on to the Spencian plotters and thence to Chartism by the middle of the century and the foreign revolutionary passions of the period 1848 to 1890. Emigré revolutionaries had arrived by packet boat and had ensconced themselves in clubs filled with tobacco smoke and vitriol in Clerkenwell or drank in the seedy backstreets off the Tottenham Court Road, simply adding to the mix of unorthodox political doctrines. Friedrich Engels, living a double life as gentleman and revolutionary, was about to publish *The Condition of the Working Classes* in 1848 and, on the Continent, Marx was brooding over the inevitability of the collapse of the old order in the coming revolution; *The Communist Manifesto* was first published in German in 1848 and was sufficiently terrifying to get its main author (the other was Engels) exiled to Britain. The Socialist International would follow the collapse of the Paris Commune and would meet in pubs on the Gray's Inn Road, watched by the new Special Branch, Britain's secret police force, with its eye on Irishmen, anarchists, communists and revolutionary madmen.

Whose voice should we listen to in the babble of voices? From whence does an authentic voice emanate and from whom? Certain voices ring clear above the noise, but in the noise, other voices may be discerned, which, even now over 100 years later, are difficult to hear and interpret, marginal voices of madness and revolution that exist in the no-man's land of forgotten anecdote, silenced by the mainstream of historical babble.

One of the voices raging forlornly against the old regime of Victorian values was that of Dan Chatterton, 'Old Chat', in his coal black coat, standing statue-like in some draughty corner, raging like some old-time prophet, dirty and mad, filled with a burning zeal, but denigrated, ignored, laughed at; fighting the century with coruscating words as it fought him with poverty; killing the century he hated, bit by painful bit in his writings and pamphlets, raging against the dying vision.

Chatterton was a maverick, a street-corner orator who took his life's work so seriously that he deposited his pamphlets and his newspaper, *Chatterton's Commune, the Atheistic Communistic Scorcher*, fully catalogued, in the British Museum. Like so many others, he came from a pool of forgotten revolutionaries who formed the 'underbelly' of radical politics. However, he refused to be forgotten. Undisciplined though he was, and unsuitable as he quickly became, for the new socialist politics that emerged in the 1880s, he nevertheless forged an individualistic and anarchic path through the decade, an 'ultra' who attacked every position of established thought. Indeed, he was wild and reckless, but it was a recklessness born out of poverty, frustration and helplessness, giving rise to an irritability at public pronouncements by socialists and the advocacy of violent revolution by one least likely to effect it.

Chatterton was born in August 1820 to a comfortable artisan family in Clerkenwell. His father made a living in furniture lacquering within an area of London known for its independent-minded tradesmen. Indeed, Clerkenwell which was the centre of the radical tradition, had witnessed revolutionary events in the early years of the century and was to prove a fertile breeding ground for many radical groups right up until the twentieth century. Such enlightened tradespeople as his family, reasonably well educated and literate, were, to use Chatterton's words, 'proverbialy [sic] thinkers'. Chatterton's father was an atheist and took his son to meetings from an early age, but an accident of some sort began to undermine his father's 'reason' and he took to acting as a coal merchant or possible coal heaver later in life, something of a disastrous decline in fortune.

Chatterton, meanwhile, went to school in Aylesbury and Barnet, but the family's declining position meant that he would be apprenticed to a bootmaker and thereafter would drift from job to job without settling down. He became a shoemaker, a bookseller, a news vendor, cut up corpses for anatomy lessons, served coffee as a waiter and posted bills. Poverty stricken, he enlisted in the army for the bounty offered and fought in the Crimean War until he was discharged after two years. Having left the army, his thoughts turned to love and he married Emma Cook, an illiterate labourer's daughter who died in St Pancras Workhouse in 1865. Extreme poverty haunted Chatterton, who had several spells in his life where the workhouse was the only option. He married again in 1867, this time to Emily Scott, who at 21 was half his age. She vanished from the records, as do the children of both marriages, most of whom died young with the exception of a boy called Alfred, whose severe physical and mental disabilities must have proved to be an extra burden.

His personal circumstances aside, Chatterton was a born contrarian and one deeply involved in popular politics. He took part in a Chartist rally on Clerkenwell Green in 1848 and another on 23 July 1866, was present at the Reform League riot in Hyde Park and, although a small, frail man, was happy on both occasions to join in the fighting with the police. Slowly penetrating radical circles, he rose to some prominence in the Land and Labour League during the 1870s, but despite this he seems to have become detached from mainstream radicalism soon after, taking no part in the First International, which was the name given to the inaugural meeting of the International Working Men's Association which had met in St Martin's Hall, London in 1864. He was certainly too poor to travel to Geneva in 1866 for the next congress or 'International'. Instead, it was the Paris Commune and the resistance of the Communards that fired his imagination, an imagination now more hectic and fevered where the idea of the 'commune' stood for universal salvation and peace, a rewriting of ideas about the ideal commonwealth of his seventeenth-century predecessors, Gerard Winstanley and John Lilburne.

Chatterton took part in radical debates at the Hole in the Wall pub and, after the police closed the meetings of 'red republicans', helped reconstitute the Patriotic Club in Clerkenwell, where he would lament the poverty and 'misery about him … and [see] aloft the red right arm redress the eternal scales'. By this time, he was known as a 'communist' and in his fifties he began to produce those pamphlets calling for social justice that would become *Chatterton's Commune*, which would run between September 1885 and April 1895, the year he died. In Issue 31, he issued an open letter in his homespun newspaper-cum-pamphlet to Prime Minister Gladstone. The *Atheistic, Communistic, Scorcher* pulled no punches, its acerbity undiluted and its final message unequivocal. It demanded the immediate 'abolition of the Queen … the lords and commons' and called for 'revolt' and 'chaos', and the setting up of 'a commune'. Chatterton's honesty seemed as mad as the dyslexic message itself:

I, Dan. Chatterton. Atheist, & Communist, – 'in Revolt against the Plunder. Blunder. – & Bloody Murder, of King-craft, Priestcraft. Aristocrasy, Landoscrasy, – Moneyocrasy, that – cursed the workers life for years. Demand – that the Fraud, (called) Parliament, At once, – Rescind any Act of Succession, – to Victoria-Guelph. Queen of England. – 'Her (so called) Heirs, to the Throne of England. 'That all Money Payment, be Stopped Instanter, Giving; Her the order to Clear Out at once, – 'That the House of Lords, be declared an Illegal assemblage of Scoundrels, Is Abolished.

Then Disband Army, Navy, & Police Force. – Withdrawing our Accursed Rule, from India, China, Zulu, our many Colonies. – Bringing home Ships Armaments and Men. Leaving them with – Wales, Scotland, Ireland, – Free to the Supreme Voice – of each Peoples. Free from a Blasted Despotism, of Brutal, Bloody, English Rule. –

Finaly, Abolish the House - of Commons. Yielding Posession to the People, who will be Supreme, We. Will be there 'Me Thinks, The Bugle Sound. Calling the People, – To their own Senate, 'To take Instant action to formulate the Structure of A Glorious Commune – No Poverty, – Disease, or – Death. As to Day. 'This Is Our First Duty.

William. Ewart. Gladstone.

'Will You, Do This? – We Think Not. – What Then,? A Bitter Bloody Guerila War, Fight, & Retreat, If Needfull, Fight, & Retreat, every Inch of Ground, Untill We destroy You, – In Details of a Bloody Extermination. –

Sisters, Brothers, – Not Too Much Work, One, Hour, – a Day for every Woman, & Man, 'How will You Get It.? – By Intelligent Industry, Stamping Out Brutal Idleness, – 'Vive La Commune. [Spelling as in original]

When Chatterton died, his colleagues found him hard to sum up, slightly distant and forbidding, the resurrected ghost of revolutions past still stalking the nineteenth century to remind it of unfinished business. 'Who does not remember', reminisced David Nicoll, no mean radical himself:

> A pale haggard old man who used to climb the platform at meetings of the unemployed, or in the closely packed Socialist lecture halls and pour forth wild denunciations of the robbery and injustice that flourishes in our rotten society, mingled with fearful prophecies of the terrible revolution that was coming. He looked as he stood in the glare of the gaslight, with his ghostly face and flashing eyes, clad in an old grey overcoat and black slouched hat, a red woollen scarf knotted around his neck, like some grim spectre evolved from the misery and crime of the London slums, and middle-class men who had entered the meeting from curiosity shuddered as they murmured to themselves 'Marat'.

From his enemies he received 'unqualified disgust', from his colleagues bemusement and from historians such as E.P. Thompson derision, and yet Chatterton's writings and self-publications represent a singular, pure strain of Victorian invective going back through Thomas Paine to John Lilburne and from Lilburne through the Spencian Philanthropists, who marched from Spa Fields in 1816 under the red flag, to the Chartists of the middle of the century to the communist and anarchists at its ending; the type setting and clipped language even reminiscent sometimes of William Blake.

Chatterton's voice is a strained voice, a voice grown hoarse from shouting to people who wilfully will not hear, the voice of an evangelist with no God and of a political vision so radical in its implications that it has nowhere to go, because even sympathisers are scared by its implications. It is nevertheless an authentic voice, steeped in British and continental political demands, typical themselves of the results of Victorian non-conformity. Nowhere is the revolt of the marginalised against the centre more realised than in such voices in the wilderness; in the distraction of the asylum inmate working at his easel and the mania of the political agitator, the Victorian age found its hidden symbolism and occult meaning – the pulse of changing ideas that formed the basis of those revolutions which shaped the future of the self and the state.

Yet, Chatterton proved consistent, if extreme, focused on the sweeping away of social inequality, the supremacy of the liberty of the individual, republicanism, the end of priesthood and the importance of sexual pleasure and birth control; why shouldn't 'shams and swindles' finally be removed to herald in a new world, a world he knew would not appear in his lifetime, for who would listen to a prophet ignored even by those who espoused his views but who found his presence embarrassing?

Chatterton was a home-grown revolutionary, but there were other more measured voices from abroad. Britain may be an island, and the empire may have been vast, but both were vulnerable to the influence of strange ideas from Europe. Such strange ideas slowly coalesced to create a new politics of confrontation that would shake the foundations of late Victorian and Edwardian Britain and find unlikely adherents in the ranks of dissatisfied intellectuals and the new working class. Not least, Britain's enemies, France, Prussia and Russia would produce thinkers and activists who would shape the extreme edges of Britain's political landscape.

Blood, bullets and barricades: across Europe, the revolutions of 1848 heralded the possibility of democratic, national republics. 'A springtime for nations' was declared and the revolutionaries looked with hope to a new world order. They were soon bitterly disappointed as the forces of the old regimes, from Austria, Russia and Prussia, brutally suppressed the uprisings and drove their enemies across the Channel to Britain to seek safety. By 1853, there were 4,380 political refugees of whom 2,500 were Polish, 1,000 were French and 260 were German. Yet the statistics may hide another 5,000 undeclared refugees whose invisibility meant that they never emerged from the shadows.

Of these 10,000 political émigrés, some, like the Poles, the Italians and the Czechs, loved Britain and its customs, while others, like the French, grumbled and continued estranged and alienated in their new home. Still others, like the Germans and the Russians, when they came remained ambivalent. Men such as Alexandre Ledru-Rollin, who had been in the provisional government of France, bitter in his exile, took to attacking his host country, which he considered was run between a conspiracy of corrupt landowners and crooked financiers. One year after his arrival in England, he published *De la decadence de l'Anglererre* (published as *The Decline of England* [1850]), which hardly endeared him to his English hosts, and although he did spend time with some of the more militant and revolutionary Chartists such as Julian Harney and even met William Thackeray, he remained *persona non grata* even in radical households.

Whatever their personal attitude, they were welcomed all the same, not because successive British governments wished to destabilise their enemies abroad, but because, as *The Times* put it on 28 February 1853:

> Every civilised people on the face of the earth must be fully aware that this country is the asylum of nations, and that it will defend the asylum to the last ounce of its treasure, and the last drop of its blood.

Lord Palmerston, then Foreign Secretary, considered that these continental incendiaries would simply languish in a country whose freedoms guaranteed it against revolution. In 1852, he explained his position in a homely analogy that stood for all things British and all things stable:

> A single spark will explode a powder magazine, and a blazing torch will burn out harmless on a turnpike road. If a country be in a state of suppressed internal discontent, a very slight indication may augment that discontent, and produce an explosion; but if the country be well governed, and the people be contented, then letters and proclamations from unhappy refugees will be as harmless as the torch upon the turnpike road.

No refugee was ever deported or even harassed before the twentieth century; no secret foreign policeman answering to his embassy was ever refused entry either. When the exiled royal family of France arrived, they too were welcomed, although they were not endorsed by the British monarchy, Britain never wishing to give a pretext to France for war. Indeed, in 1854, the refugee Johanna Kinkell could note in a letter home that 'the police hinder no one in the development of his talents'. It was a revelation.

It was, however, true that, fearing a wave of undesirables from Continental Europe, the government passed an Aliens Act in 1848 in imitation of other acts during scares in 1793, but it was not enforced and was rescinded in 1850, and was not renewed until a further panic in 1905. Of course, there were panics as long as the foreigners remained. The great Chartist meeting on Kennington Common was considered a French revolutionary plot and Frenchmen disguised as trees were said to be lurking outside the Great Exhibition in Hyde Park just waiting to jump out and start a class war. The plotters were abetted by Catholic priests to boot. Foreign radicals were represented as all having long whiskers and the French were to be distinguished by their moustaches; Karl Marx, it was rumoured, was going to assassinate Queen Victoria.

The French would have preferred a little intervention as they moaned about conditions in their temporarily adopted country. Britain was, on the whole, indifferent; a refugee had to work like any Briton in the dog-eat-dog atmosphere of the middle of the century. One anonymous refugee commented bitterly that he had seen, he thought, an article in *The Times* which had confirmed his worst views of English duplicity. He read that 'the prince-president is quite wrong to spend so much to send the Republicans to Africa ... let him just cast them on our shores, and with the help of our fogs, the wretchedness in which we let them die and languish will soon get rid of them'. Foreign revolutionaries expected welfare and received none; they expected to continue the revolution but could not when faced with no livelihood; teaching, writing and hoping were no substitutes for action. Left to fend for themselves, many either gave up the revolutionary cause to avoid starving (and became teachers or craftsmen) or just gave up and turned themselves in. British tolerance was also short-lived and fickle, as the Poles found out in 1850 when compared to the more influential and colourful Hungarians. John Stuart Mill, writing to a Polish revolutionary in 1850, thought that:

> There is scarcely any sympathy remaining for the Poles. The Tories ... hate them as the promoters of anarchy all over the world; the colder Liberals think they belong to times gone by, to ancient history; the warmer ... feel their interest still more engaged by the Hungarians.

Some refugees, like the Italians Guiseppe Mazzini and Guiseppe Garibaldi, the Hungarian Lojos Kossuth or the Polish heroes of their failed uprisings in 1831 and 1846 (as well as later in 1864), were nevertheless greeted with enthusiasm, being the honourable representatives of national movements which could be understood by the British, their leaders embraced by the fashionable elite of society. They were wined and dined by Cabinet ministers such as Lord Palmerston (who thought most of the indigenous British population 'scum' anyway) and prime ministers such as Lord Russell, for whom there was a mutual affection and to whom their ideas did not pose a threat.

Lord Dudley Coutts Stuart organised support for the Polish émigré aristocracy through the London Literary Association of the Friends of Poland. Yet others were supported by more humble British groups, usually of a more radical or socialist bent. As such, the Polish Democratic Society, less likely to be welcomed by the great and good, could expect assistance from Chartists such as William Linton or Joseph Cowen Junior, who looked after radical Poles, or the 'red republican' Harney, who helped Germans including Marx.

The Hungarian revolutionary Lajos Kossuth, who arrived in 1849, who admired the British constitution and whose command of English was exemplary, was lionised wherever he went, being the recipient of a copy of a set of Shakespeare's plays set in a casket that had been bought by penny subscription and presented to a rather embarrassed hero at the Lord's Tavern pub in London on 6 May 1853. Still others, like the Bohemian-Czech revolutionaries, were ignored by politicians or lectured to as to the futility of independence. Even their own side was often dismissive. Alexander Herzen and Mikhail Bakunin, both of whom were in London and attended a nationalist-socialist revolutionary club meeting in Southampton Street in London, lectured the poor Czechs on the Darwinian law of Slavic culture by which they and all who resisted would be 'swallow[ed]' up in the coming Slavic republic of the Russias.

Disparate groups might unite in common cause for the general liberation of Europe, so that Mazzini's Central European Democratic Committee might include Poles such as the republican Alfred Darasz and the German republican Arnold Ruge, men from the French provisional republican government in exile, Chartists and liberal democrats. The democratic 'Europe of [the] People' would herald the 'springtime for nations' that would never quite arrive but which would be the model for the First International.

Revolutionaries at home might also be brought into the wider circle of European unity by their support for Irish independence, which most supported as a *sine qua non* of international brotherhood and demonstrated at every possible event. The visit of Napoleon III to London in April 1855 was one such occasion. The French émigré paper *L'Homme* had already published a derogatory article by Victor Hugo, then exiled in the Channel Islands, in 1854 and it followed this with another attack on 22 November where it accused Napoleon of being a 'perjurer [and] a murderer'. The piece was undersigned by 60 workers and Chartists, including Ernest Jones. The arrest of Chartists selling Victor Hugo's books, the destruction of his publisher's premises and the much-lauded reciprocal visit of Queen Victoria to France sealed the solidarity of international opposition groups.

So what if, to all intents and purposes, their every move would be checkmated, their every desire delayed indefinitely? Reassured by their convictions, expressed in radical papers like *L'Homme,* international radicals organised themselves across national boundaries.

The final mission concerned the propaganda of the newspaper's subtitle, 'la democratie universelle'. *Republique universelle* began publication in France with the Peace Congress of 1849 in Paris, where French republicans and socialists, but mainly Anglo-Saxon liberal Christian thinkers, gathered together. For people like Victor Hugo, it offered a way of defining a moderate republic, a model for a further 'Etats-Unis d'Europe'.

Dreaming over his books in the British Library Reading Room, Marx might well have hoped for the spontaneous combustion of capitalism and the rise of a workers' state, but the truth was that he would be dead long before the Russian Revolution of 1917, and the capitalist system he so abhorred would outlast the consequences of the theory and principles he created. Despite the march of revolutionary orators and agitators, would-be assassins and terrorists, the ideals of a British socialist republic were essentially the pipedreams of a few 'street' politicians and backstreet clubs held in the back rooms of the capital's less salubrious public houses.

The London Patriotic Society was typical of such clubs. Formed from republican, democrat and Fenian supporters, the club represented 'the head-quarters of ... ultra nonconformity [and] treason'. It met in pubs such as the Hole in the Wall, where republicans could book private rooms, but after the somewhat lavish praise of the Parisian Communards, the police had forced publicans to ban all such meetings. The 'provinces of liberty', as they termed themselves, then called a meeting at the Robin Hood public house in Leather Lane to form a society and rent premises.

The rooms the Society finally found were at 37a Clerkenwell Green (now the Marx Library) in an area notorious with the authorities for its reputation for protest, Sunday speakers, rallies and general political troubles. Spa Fields (the scene of a semi-revolution in 1816) was round the corner, as was the Clerkenwell House of Detention, built on the ruins of a prison destroyed by the Gordon rioters in the eighteenth century. The London Patriotic Society's Club and Institute soon changed into the London Patriotic Club, with members meeting to discuss science, social justice, foreign revolutions and votes for women.

The London Patriotic Club was one of a number of groups that attempted to form alliances between the more extreme elements demanding votes for women, anti-imperial legislation and Irish Home Rule. The Russian revolutionary Peter Kropotkin was, for instance, a guest during his stay in 1881 to 1882 and the club members were supporters of Narodnaya Volya, the Russian revolutionary group that had assassinated Tsar Alexander II. By the second half of the 1880s, clubs such as the London Patriotic were breaking up under the pressure of debates over how social change might best be effected.

Revolutionary and republican socialisms were reimported into British politics by European émigrés and those with European connections, such as Frantz Kitz, who was born in the revolutionary year of 1848 to an English mother and German father. Settling in Soho in the early 1870s, Kitz joined a group called the Democratic and Trades Alliance, in which poor but skilled manual workers could discuss the issues that interested them. Kitz spoke on communism. By 1875, he had helped create the

Manhood Suffrage League, an alliance of both radicals and republicans that publicised the heroic actions of the Parisian Communards. He was committed to revolutionary rather than electoral action and by his use of the phrase, he clearly meant a revolutionary democratic socialism. The distinction was between a total revolutionary social democracy and a partial radical political democracy. Kitz joined and met William Morris when the Democratic Federation was created, but Morris thought him too anarchistic and destructive, although he did recognise the strong anti-state and anti-capitalist organisation that Kitz and others had created in Mile End and Stratford in the East End of London.

Other German and Russian émigrés swelled the numbers of such groups, especially after the German anti-socialist laws. Many joined the English Revolutionary Society, itself part of the Social Democratic Club which met at pubs in Soho. Here members would plot their return home and dream in exile. Alternatively, they might plot more violent action, known as 'propaganda by the deed', essentially campaigns of bombing or assassination. At the same time, the club issued *Freiheit*, a revolutionary paper that was illegal in Germany and was smuggled by sailors.

Pursued to Britain, one of these revolutionaries, Johann Most, found himself on the receiving end of an 18-month prison sentence for incitement to murder heads of state. It was only in 1882 that *Freiheit* was closed down for printing an article approving of the recent murder in Phoenix Park, Dublin of Lord Frederick Cavendish, the Irish Chief Secretary. Such an inflammatory article was the last straw for the more moderate radicals, who decamped, leaving the more revolutionary group to form the Anarchist Club in St Stephen's Mews, Rathbone Place, in 1883.

There were, however, British working men who instinctively moved towards sympathy with the position of the foreigners. One was Joseph Lane, who founded the socialist Homerton Social Democratic Club in Hackney. He also attended the Social Revolutionary and Anarchist Congress in July 1881 at a pub in Euston. Most of the 45 delegates there were from Europe, but five British socialists attended – at least one, 'C. Hall', was a police spy.

The most surprising convert to socialism was Henry Mayers Hyndman, a stockbroker whose political leanings began as those of an independent Tory. After meeting Joseph Lane, he came round to the idea of forming an independent labour party, and held a meeting to that effect at the Westminster Palace Hotel in June 1881. He went on to create the Democratic Federation, an alliance of revolutionaries and reformers. He was a genuine convert to socialism, if an autocratic one. Another convert was William Morris, who turned to 'practical socialism' as a way of restoring the medieval craft society he so loved. However, his socialism was only tangentially linked to the theoretical intricacies of Marxism.

Most radical socialists had joined the Democratic Federation and later transferred to the Social Democratic Federation (SDF) as it became to put forward a Marxist programme for change. Hyndman's federation was the centre of socialist activity in the 1880s (his influence not ending until his death in 1921), a loose grouping of like-minded but volatile people who banded together more for convenience than out of ideological solidarity. Hyndman was a strange and (to many) an unpleasant enigma, a demagogue revolutionary and a jingoistic patriot who hated foreigners (he was anti-semitic) and loathed 'that damned Jew' Marx.

Hyndman was independently wealthy and had had a private education before going up to Cambridge. In 1880 he stood, unsuccessfully, as an 'independent' (i.e. Tory) candidate for Marylebone, but by the following year he had been converted, almost by a miracle, to a form of revolutionary Marxist socialism embraced by neither Marx nor Engels, both of whom had only growing contempt for him as a person and his strange ideas. Engels called him a 'pretty unscrupulous careerist' and Marx dismissed him as 'self-satisfied', but years later Lenin reassessed his career in a more positive light in an article he published in *Zvezda* during 1911. Indeed, Hyndman led the only successful socialist party that there was right up until the First World War.

With his own money, Hyndman built up an effective socialist group and published a newspaper which was the centre of 'extreme' radical debate outside the Liberal Party's more sedate discussions. He championed causes too; for instance, he fought against the subordination of Indian wealth to British interests. In this respect, his ideas, though eccentric, were genuine, but his deportment at meetings in top hat and frock coat, his disparagement of the unions and the working class, and his ambivalent but bombastic manners towards Eleanor Marx (Marx's eldest daughter, whom he considered too 'Jewish'), Engels (too close to Marx) and Morris (not loyal enough) alienated his followers to such an extent that a break was inevitable. The break came about because of his refusal to countenance internationalism, now the very watchword of socialism and in the socialist tradition of the First International that he toyed with but never fully embraced or trusted. In this he paralleled the attitude of other radical groups such as the Fabian Society.

This was all too much for Morris and Eleanor Marx, who, on 16 December 1884, split the SDF on a resolution regarding the supremacy of 'fraternal co-operation' as against the 'arbitrary rule' of Hyndman. A new group called the Socialist League (SL) was formed on 29 December 1884, but in truth the bitter rivalries seemed not to diminish and crossover allegiances were formed when it proved convenient. The SL moved to premises in Farringdon Street in 1885 from whence it produced its manifesto and newspaper. The decisive difference with the SDF was that the SL was internationalist and wanted to educate the masses to prepare for the fall of capitalism, whereas Hyndman seemed contemptuous of the masses and of their labour organisations, the new trade unions. But in all honesty, the SL manifesto read little differently from that of the SDF's own propaganda:

> Our view is that such a body in the present state of things has no function but to educate the people in the principles of Socialism, and to organise such as it can get hold of to take their due places, when the crisis shall come which will force action on us. We believe that to hold out as baits hopes of amelioration of the condition of the workers, to be wrung out of the necessities of the rival factions of our privileged rulers is delusive and mischievous. For carrying out our aims of education and organization no over-shadowing and indispensable leader is required, but only a band of instructed men, each of whom can learn to fulfil, as occasion requires it, the simple functions of the leader of a party of principle.

The truth was that had Hyndman not been so unpleasant a colleague, there would have been no split and Hyndman, Morris, Marx, Aveling and Besant would have cooperated into the 1880s. Nevertheless, all of them continued to be invited to the non-affiliated radical clubs and the Junior Socialist Education Society. They were all present at a Commune anniversary meeting on 19 March 1888, as was Prince Kropotkin.

It was to be an amalgamation of Kropotkin's teaching and the bloody-mindedness of members that finally split the Socialist League. At the fourth annual conference held on 20 May 1888, the Bloomsbury branch put forward two motions: one for the amalgamation of all socialist clubs into a united body and the other that a number of parliamentary seats should be contested at the next election. Both resolutions were decisively defeated, partially because Morris and his faction wished to have nothing to do with Parliament and partially because the anarchist faction under Kropotkin was now in the majority. The movement was split both ways. Morris and the Avelings were trounced and forced to resign from the executive, forming another group called the Bloomsbury Socialist Society. Morris withdrew from this rump in 1890 to form the Hammersmith Socialist League with about 100 members, but it too folded.

Although not part of the SDF, the old London Patriotic Club still cooperated over a number of issues and the Twentieth Century Press, a radical publisher working for the SDF run by Harry Quelch, who edited the SDF publication *Justice*, transferred to the club's premises in Clerkenwell Green in the 1890s. For the most part, the visitors to the London Patriotic Club had no desire to follow the old violent revolutionary path, but contented themselves with the belief that socialism would inevitably triumph. The growth of the trade unions and the rising tide of colonial subjects who refused to do what they were told, not to mention Irish nationalist elements and a growing politicisation of the whole working class (including women), lent credibility to the belief that capitalism would collapse with only the slightest push. How this might eventually be achieved split the aged Chartists from the Marxist-Communists and the creators of the embryonic Labour Party from the anarcho-socialists and the Bolsheviks. Socialism might be the future of humankind, but would it appear by revolutionary or constitutional means?

These socialist groups never numbered more than a few dozen to a few hundred members, but while the SDF had only 400 London recruits

(and perhaps 300 in the rest of Britain), in defence of civil liberties
or parliamentary reform it could call upon thousands of sympathetic
supporters, as happened during the protests against police raids on the
Anarchist International Club and the breaking-up of open-air meetings
in Stratford.

Most socialists belonged to more than one group so that, despite their
differences, memberships duplicated each other and disguised the tiny
number of active members, something that Engels noted with a certain
amount of scepticism. This was especially so as the leading members of
each group seemed to have their own agenda against which, despite the
solidarity of the movement, everybody else was to be judged: Eleanor Marx
hated Annie Besant and Charles Bradlaugh; Engels disliked Hyndman
and H.H. Champion, the editor of *Justice*; Marx, Herzen and Bakunin
fundamentally disagreed on principles; H.G. Wells struggled to convince
the Fabian Society that his ideas held any water; Ben Tillett thought
Beatrice Webb 'rather an aristocratically prejudiced visitor ... somewhat
condescending'; Johann Most, waiting for the arrival of Eleanor Marx
in New York, suggested she should be 'shot' before she arrived and so
keep the anarchist standard in America free from socialism; and all were
agreed that Eleanor's common-law husband, Edward Aveling (who had
already 'mislaid' one wife), was a philanderer, a scrounger and a pretty
johnny-come-lately socialist, as Besant sarcastically pointed out in 1884
after falling out with the man she considered her mentor in socialism:

> Though his [Aveling's] political knowledge, like that of most scientific and
> literary men was very small ... he never touched Socialism in any way or
> knew anything about it until in 1882 he took to reading at the British
> Museum, and unfortunately fell in to the company of some of the Bohemian
> Socialists, male and female, who flourish there.

'Supposing', Mrs Besant went on, 'that his was a "sudden conversion",
Karl Marx acting as a Socialist Moody and Sankey [a guide book of the
time], it could only have taken place two years ago.'

Aveling managed to have spats with everyone including Hyndman,
whose organisation he suggested he still represented, even though he

had resigned, and continuously with Besant, arguments that were part doctrinaire and part private vendetta (mostly on her part). Everyone argued. It was de riguer to support Irish nationalism, but Michael Davitt refused to shake his English supporters' hands because they were atheists. This dissension continued to deepen as the years went by and this amongst only a few hundred followers, perhaps no more than 700 active members of all factions all told, which did not mean (as already mentioned) that they could not call upon several thousand when a special occasion arose.

Adherents fell out one moment and cooperated the next, so that the socialist movement as a whole was ever fluid and unpredictable, or in other words no real threat to the old-style radicals of mainstream liberalism. The fact was that they were often (but not always) a sorry if heroic lot trying to build a 'new order of things', as Morris lamented in 1886. Later that same year, socialists and anarchists were even more divided. Engels couldn't help but despair in 'English [sic] Socialism'. 'Here all is a muddle', he wrote to Laura Marx at about the same time:

Bax and Morris are getting deeper and deeper into the hands of a few anarchist phraseurs, and write nonsense with increasing intensity. The turning of *Commonweal* into a 'weekly' – absurd in every respect – has given Edward [Aveling] a chance of getting out of his responsibility for this now incalculable organ … It would be ridiculous to expect the working class to take the slightest notice of these various vagaries of what is by courtesy called English Socialism, and it is very fortunate that it is so: These gentlemen have quite enough to do to set their own brains in order.

NINE

THE DEATH MACHINE OF HARTMAN THE ANARCHIST

As early as the 1880s, squabbling, personal feuds and ideological differences had begun to paralyse action. William Morris (who flirted with anarchism throughout his career) complained that the 'anarchist element … seem determined to drive us to extremity', whilst Frantz Kitz complained of the affliction of the sort of 'anaemic respectability' that attached itself to Fabian activities. Yet some Britons were, it seems, willing to give revolution a nudge. When British anarchists did turn to 'propaganda by the deed' in imitation of their Continental brethren, the attempts were woefully inadequate to the occasion. One group was caught supposedly planning a bombing campaign in Walsall.

The Walsall anarchists were a strange group of working-class British and European idealists. In the summer of 1891, four itinerant foreign workers came to the unlikely setting of Walsall looking for work. They met up with William Ditchfield and Joseph Deakin. All were members of the local branch of the SDF, and between them they formed the Walsall Socialist Club, for which Deakin acted as secretary. Someone in London working inside the dissident Autonomie Club alerted the newly formed Special Branch to the suspected transportation of explosives by the group, who were allegedly making bombs. The police started to watch the comings and goings at the local railway station, where eventually a foreigner called Jean Battolla appeared who was dressed in sufficient anarchist garb to warrant following. He led them, as expected, straight to the socialist club.

Arrests followed, little was proved, people went unnecessarily to prison (Deakin actually changed his second statement admitting to making bombs – they were never found – to be exported through an agent to Russia against the tsar), but it was actually left to the police to prove their case for conspiracy by manufacturing a bomb from the alleged plans of the anarchists. The bomb (actually a grenade) did not work when tested!

This was a classic piece of police provocation undertaken to 'draw out' dangerous elements and using a long-term double agent, Auguste Coulon. Coulon had come into the Socialist League during the 1890s, but was always too rich and too eager to be trusted. 'One would think he lived on bombs', commented one colleague, the soon to be entrapped David Nicoll, whose life of abject poverty was dedicated to fighting for civil liberties. Once imprisoned, Nicoll actually became deranged. British anarchists and their émigré colleagues lived in an atmosphere of suspicion and double agents were a daily hazard in such cloak-and-dagger proceedings, proceedings often closer to Gilbert and Sullivan than to grand opera.

If anybody was thinking of examples of 'individual action' immediately before the Walsall case broke, they would probably be mostly concerned with the rather farcical action of John Evelyn Barlas (a poet whose collection of poems, *Phantasmagoria*, was published under the pen-name of Evelyn Douglas). On 31 December 1891, a policeman first heard and then saw him discharging several shots from a revolver at the Houses of Parliament at about 9 am. The policeman ran towards him. 'Seeing witness [i.e. policeman] he [i.e. Barlas] handed him the revolver says, "I am an Anarchist and I intended shooting you but then I thought it is a pity to shoot an honest man. What I have done is to show my contempt for the House of Commons".'

At 4.45 pm on 15 February 1894, an explosion was heard in Greenwich Park near the Observatory. It was a strange and surreal event for those who witnessed the event. A park warden was first on the scene of what was first thought to be the discharge of a gun. He found a man who was horrifically injured, having lost his right hand and having a hole in his stomach. It turned out that the injured man was the victim of his own enterprise. A bomb he was carrying had accidentally exploded. The injured man was a Frenchman called Martial Bourdin who was probably taking a bomb from a bomb factory in south London to be used in France for revenge against the authorities. That is what the police thought and Bourdin's death allowed them to close the case.

Although there had been Fenian outrages since the 1860s, this was the first foreign terrorist 'attack' in Britain and, as such, its circumstances and reasons were much debated. Anarchists turned up to hail the hero at his funeral and there was a riot; the authorities pondered and dismissed the issue, and the general public got its first media exposure to anarchist 'dens' and 'laboratories' which would obsess the yellow press and popular novelists well into the 1920s. In the anti-anarchist Rome conference of 1898 that followed the wave of attacks in Europe, the British government would not sign up to anything except an open-door policy for political dissidents, a policy quite opposed to its attitudes towards Irish bombers in the same period.

The revolutionary propagandist H.B. Samuels was a tailor by trade, and his introduction to radical politics led him to become a man 'obsessed with violence' and who saw in the American anarchist movement, in the Spanish massacre at the Liceo Theatre in Barcelona and in the French, Belgian and Russian 'dynamitards' (especially the terrorist Ravachol) perfect models for his own revolutionary fervour. Samuels, who finally became editor of the radical journal *Commonweal* in 1893, acted as the apologist for bombings at the (French) Café Very and Café Terminus (1894). Along with the impoverished anarchist and conspiracy theorist David Nicholl, he also applauded the self-sacrifice of Bourdin, but both failed to match their words with deeds.

By the time of the death of Edward VII, continental politics were becoming frayed, but for the most part, Britain turned a blind eye. Legislation to keep aliens out of Britain would not be passed until 1906 as an emergency and rather panicky measure, but there was little heart for keeping people out, especially when they were suffering oppression elsewhere. Britons still prided themselves on their fair-mindedness and the strong belief in a police force awake to every danger. In this they were to be sadly disappointed. For the most part, Special Branch still looked west to Ireland and America, and had little or no expertise in watching Eastern Europeans. At the 1907 Congress of Social Democrats, however, there was such a fuss in the press that the police had to do something.

By the 1880s, the corruption of the police of the 1870s had been dealt with, but bribery and corruption were small beer in the face of bombs and insurrection. The 'Met' had no expertise in these areas. Once the bomb attacks began in the 1880s, the authorities had to respond. The Home Secretary not only promoted an Explosive Substances Bill, which became the Explosive Substances Act, but also approved the use of Royal Irish Constabulary (RIC) officers in London. This was a force which had long fought terrorists and had foiled James Stephens' Fenian rebellion of 1858. The bombing campaign of 1883–4 following the assassination of Lord Frederick Cavendish, Chief Secretary for Ireland, and his Under-Secretary in Phoenix Park in May 1882 left the government in need of a clear operational policy. A 'special' Irish Branch was duly set up whose secret police force was soon being called by the embarrassing name of 'the Political Branch'.

Counter-subversion in the late nineteenth century had evolved from a civilian (if effective) spy network into the professional work of a police cadre. In the mid-1880s there were five such bodes: uniformed police on guard duty at public buildings; port of entry officers, including plainclothes detectives; special duty 'Irish Branch' men stationed at central office; two intelligence sections; and the RIC. With changes to this organisation came James Monro, known semi-officially as 'the Secret Agent', and with him came a growing bureaucratisation of these forces, with a central group of senior detectives recruited in the war against the Fenians. These detectives would now be paid secretly from imperial coffers rather than being on the Metropolitan payroll. The complexities of the system can be demonstrated by the fact that Scotland Yard's Special Branch was separate from the Irish Branch, known as 'Section D' and recruited from special duty CID personnel until 1911. To confuse matters further, the original Special Branch consisted simply of the four senior officers recruited by Monro in 1887. This was quite different from the 'Special Irish Branch' of CID officers, which was counted as a separate unit. Moreover, it suffered from a distinct lack of identity, being variously called the Special

Confidential Section, Special (Secret) Branch and Home Office Crime Department: Special Branch.

Despite the fact that the police were becoming more sophisticated and that they knew anarchists and Irish nationalists were both operating in international networks, they were still loath to cooperate with the police of other European countries. Austria, Germany and Russia were simply not trusted; France, Spain and Italy were of no account; anarchist bombers at least were simply not attacking British targets. The International Conference of Rome for the Social Defence against Anarchists, held between November and December 1898, aimed to create a pan-European response to the wave of terrorism that had led to over 60 political assassinations, including heads of state (many royalty included) and untold civilian casualties. The Conference attracted 54 delegates from 21 countries, but the central issue of renaming anarchist incidents as merely criminal instead of political acts went against British feelings about both liberty and politics, and the critical British vote was not won.

Therefore, the International Conference of Rome left Britain as before and this meant that Britain it alone would welcome Europeans fleeing oppression. Nevertheless, senior policemen such as Howard Vincent acknowledged that private cooperation between police forces should be encouraged, if not officially acknowledged. In 1904 a secret Protocol for the International War on Anarchism was drawn up in St Petersburg between Austria, Russia, Germany and Denmark amongst others, Britain not being privy to the signing or caring (at least in public) what its European neighbours did to this effect. It was not until 1923 that international cooperation was finally agreed upon with the founding of the International Criminal Police Commission, now known as Interpol. It is interesting to note that Interpol was based in Vienna and that after the Anschluss, a Nazi was appointed as its head of operations! It then had to be refounded after the Second World War in Paris.

The rise of all forms of revolutionary politics from state communism to libertarian communalism or the extremes of violent anarchism were muted in the public's mind as so much wild talk, or relegated to the fringes of a lunatic but essentially harmless foreign volatility which could not touch the British sense of fair play. The social order might be tinkered with, but that was all – the world was fixed and stable, the important radicals were Liberals, the enemy were Tories.

The singular explosion in Greenwich Park, which was symbolically out of all proportion to its actual importance, represented a new sense of unease. It was not only the defining point of insane radicalism but also the window into a world of secret machinations which seemed to suggest a conspiracy not merely of social significance but also of existential proportions. It remained a defining moment until long into the twentieth century. One man had died in lonely if bizarre circumstances, but it was precisely these circumstances that made the Greenwich bomb incident a psychic event in the collective memory.

In many ways, the Greenwich bomb incident was *the* event which defined the periods both before and after its occurrence. It was as if within the mundane surface of late Victorian life there existed a parallel world full of randomness and self-destructive violence, a type of continental virus from which the British felt themselves immune up until this point. Now, here, in Greenwich a bomb had exploded in an act so futile it would need revisiting, pondering and explaining for years to come, both in print as well as in film. The explosion also had the effect of deflecting literary output in a number of ways.

The idea of a random force that was inherently evil starts to suggest itself as a theme in popular fiction after 1894. From now on, a subversive and secret counterweight to law and order that had not existed before the Greenwich explosion would prove irresistibly attractive to readers. The fascination with the anti-matter of evil was most famously mooted by Arthur Conan Doyle in *The Final Problem*, which introduced Dr Moriarty to readers in a story which actually first appeared in *The Strand Magazine* in December 1893.

The introduction of the 'Napoleon of Crime' (based on the American criminal Adam Worth) was to 'kill off' the perfect Holmes through the appearance of his nemesis. Holmes himself, long separated from Watson who had married, is reunited for one last time with his partner, but Holmes is 'paler and thinner', his 'nerves … at the highest tension'. Against him is ranged the genius of evil whose 'hereditary tendencies' are of 'the most diabolical kind'. Indeed, Moriarty is the antithesis and the double of Holmes, for if Holmes is the presiding genius of law and order, Moriarty is in essence the coming corporate and beaurocratic genius who was more than 'an individual' and more like a 'mighty organisation' dedicated to urban chaos, whom Holmes must stop in order to save London. 'The air is sweeter in London for my presence', says Holmes, but Moriarty will poison that air with that criminality which was a euphemism for moral corruption:

> His career has been an extraordinary one. He is a man of good birth and excellent education, endowed by nature with a phenomenal mathematical faculty. At the age of twenty-one he wrote a treatise upon the binomial theorem, which has had a European vogue. On the strength of it he had the mathematical chair at one of our smaller universities, and had, to all appearances, a most brilliant career before him. But the man had hereditary tendencies of the most diabolical kind. A criminal strain ran in his blood, which, instead of being modified, was increased and rendered infinitely more dangerous by his extraordinary mental powers … He is the organizer of half that is evil and of nearly all that is undetected in this great city. He is a genius, a philosopher, an abstract thinker. He has a brain of the first order. He sits motionless, like a spider in the centre of its web, but that web has a thousand radiations, and he knows well every quiver of each of them. He does little himself. He only plans. But his agents are numerous and splendidly organized.

Moriarty heads a great fictional crime syndicate; he is the first of those invisible criminal masterminds who rule the world from behind the scenes and who have fascinated generations of writers ever since. Great crime, Doyle avers, is closer to great philosophical intellect than mere criminality, closer indeed to an aesthetic and academic exercise:

> He is extremely tall and thin, his forehead domes out in a white curve, and his two eyes are deeply sunken in his head. He is clean-shaven, pale, and ascetic-looking, retaining something of the professor in his features. His shoulders are rounded from much study, and his face protrudes forward and is forever slowly oscillating from side to side in a curiously reptilian fashion.

The final confrontation at the Reichenbach Falls is both a cleansing and an annulment. Watson reflects gloomily that 'there deep down in that dreadful cauldron of swirling water and seething foam, will lie for all time the most dangerous criminal and the foremost champion of law'. Of course, the corpse of Sherlock Holmes would not remain dormant for long, but nor indeed would that of Moriarty, who becomes a symbol for the coming age, reappearing in abstracted and occult form in films like Fritz Lang's *Dr Mabuse* series of 1922, 1933 and 1960, and in the 1950 spy novels of Ian Fleming, especially *Dr No.*

Moriarty is the double of Holmes, the schizoid other half which Holmes might just become. The double haunts Victorian Britain, exemplified by the appearance of Robert Louis Stevenson's *The Strange Case of Dr Jekyll and Mr Hyde* in 1886, with its play on the closeness of moral being and the ideas of the new psychology which had not one unified self but a gaggle of selves which competed for attention.

This doubling was best exhibited by the playful appearance of E.W. Hornung's sportsman-thief, the raffish and charming A.J. Raffles in *Cassell's Magazine* in 1898. Hornung was Doyle's brother-in-law, and Raffles and his sidekick Bunny are a type of family joke at the expense of Holmes. Unlike Moriarty, however, Raffles has a perverse conscience, which sees him sacrifice himself in the Boer War as an act of 'atonement'. Nevertheless, it was George Orwell who detected something new in Raffles. Orwell was struck by his 'boyishness' and observance of 'powerful taboos', but also by his remarkable frankness. 'Raffles', as Orwell pointed out, 'has no real moral code, no religion, certainly no social consciousness. All he has is a set of reflexes: the nervous system, as it were, of a gentleman.' All that is left of the Victorian male by the end of the century is a set of cynical reflexes and nervous tensions which reflect a crisis of self and confidence in the solidity of what is around him. All that is left is the last defence, that of a gentleman who may be a thief but who is not a cad.

There was perhaps a fascination with, if not approval of, moral decay in some literary quarters, but there was certainly an abiding interest in the clandestine world of anarchism in general and what it said about modern life and those people so alienated that only wholesale destruction could save the world. For a few, anarchism represented the possibilities of emancipation and freedom from hardship, for some, it showed the way into the new socialist republican future, but for the many, it was nothing but an invitation to a future both chaotic and murderous; that such men were out there in the streets of Britain's major cities prophesying such ideas was incomprehensible and terrifying.

Anarchism gripped the imagination and inspired a number of novels in the late 1890s, including Edward Douglas Fawcett's remarkable *Hartman the Anarchist*, written while the author was in his mid-twenties in 1892. Fawcett was one of that apparent multitude of bizarre and eccentric people thrown up in the late Victorian period. His parents were from Indian army backgrounds, his mother, Myra Macdougall, being the daughter of a colonel in the Bengal Army. The couple returned to Britain for the birth and settled in Hove near Brighton in 1866, where Edward was born. His father seems at some point to have left the army, settling in Torquay, apparently a successful stock broker. The family continued to move around the coast, they were comfortable and more children were born.

Nevertheless, Edward's father died young and Edward found himself adrift until he became an author penning early science-fiction stories which contained prophecies of technological advances and ultimate destruction. He was like a number of late Victorians, interested in the future possibilities of advances in lifestyle which were exemplified in pursuits followed by advanced thinkers. Such advances embraced interests as diverse as chess, anarchism, socialism, motoring, mountain climbing, aeronautics, Theosophy and esoteric Eastern philosophy. His brother Percy was equally flamboyant. An archaeologist, army officer, eugenicist, Nietzschean and South American explorer, Percy died in mysterious circumstances whilst looking for the lost city of 'Z' in Brazil during 1925, a possible model for the fictional Indiana Jones.

Hartman the Anarchist is a study of the anarchist mind pushed to extremes in the fictional year '1920'. Its hero, Stanley, is an evolutionary socialist who, whilst radical in attitude, still wishes to keep the structure of government in order to prevent chaos. As a political candidate in Stepney, East London, his platform neither embraces the extremism of one of his revolutionary opponents nor the conservatism of the other. In a period of serious social change, Stanley is trapped between a rock and a hard place. The 'hydra-headed problem of civilisation' was the only political question in an age of upheaval:

> Things had been looking very black in the closing years of the last century, but the pessimists of that epoch were the optimists of ours. London even in the old days was a bloated, unwieldy city, an abode of smoke and dreariness startled from time to time by the angry murmurs of labour. In 1920 the Colossus of cities held nigh six million souls, and the social problems of the past were intensified … beyond it stretched a restless and dreaded democracy. Commerce had received a sharp check after the late Continental wars, and the depression was severely felt. That bad times were was the settled conviction of the middle classes, and to this belief was due the Coalition Government that held sway during the year in which my story opens. In many quarters a severe reaction had set in against Liberalism, and a stronger executive and repressive laws were urgently clamoured for. At the opposite extreme flew the red flag, and a social revolution was eagerly mooted.

> I myself, though a socialist, was averse to barricades. 'Not revolution, but evolution' was the watchword of my section … What was socialism? The nationalization of land and capital, of the means of production and distribution, in the interests of a vast industrial army.

Stanley has a friend called John Burnett, 'a journalist and agitator' whose leanings are towards 'anarchical communism' and who hates society and the futility of socialist conventions called to remedy its ills, 'your congresses and your socialism – evolutionary, revolutionary, or what not – are played out'. Burnett, in turn, is mixed up with more sinister activists. One is the 'shadow', the pseudonym of a man called Michael Schwartz and his pupil, the infamous arch-anarchist Rudolph Hartman, whom Stanley is acquainted with through knowing Hartman's mother and who hates the present civilisation and what it stands for:

> That is true, but civilization – your industrial civilization – what is it? Not a system to be identified with the cause of human welfare, and hence worth preserving in some form or other at all costs, but a mere vicious outgrowth prejudicial to that welfare as we conceive it. The test of the worth of a civilization is its power to minister to human happiness. Judged by this standard your civilization has proved a failure. Mankind rushed to her

embraces in hope, fought its way thither through long and weary centuries, and has for a reward the sneers of a mistress as exacting as she is icy: 'The third day comes a frost, a killing frost.'

Both Schwartz and Hartman were meant to have perished after a failed attack on Westminster Bridge, where there was an:

attempt of this enthusiast to blow up the German Crown Prince and suite when driving over Westminster Bridge on the occasion of their 1910 visit. Revenge for the severe measures taken against Berlin anarchists was the motive, but by some mischance the mine exploded just after the carriages had passed, wreaking, however, terrible havoc in the process. My sneer about the applewoman must not be taken too seriously, for though it is quite true that one such unfortunate perished, yet fifty to sixty victims fell with her in the crash of a rent arch.

Burdett, ready to 'bite' civilisation once and for all, invites Stanley to a secret rendezvous at which a shoot-out leaves two police dead and Stanley unconscious. On awakening, our hero realises that he is no longer at the scene, but actually in the bowels of a gigantic airship or 'aeronef' called the Attilla. The captain of the ship, which is made of an inpenetrable type of new substance, is, of course, Hartman. It is Hartman's megalomania in visible form – the form of the future, aerial warfare, created to exact Hartman's revenge with the ultimate dynamitard machine. Hartman himself is the epitome of the steampunk science-fiction philosophical revolutionary, a man physically magnificent and intellectually endowed with the giant forehead of the man of genius in the way of all late nineteenth-century master criminals:

Seated before a writing-desk, studded with knobs of electric bells and heaped with maps and instruments, sat a bushy-bearded man with a straight piercing gaze and a forehead physiognomists would have envied. There was the same independent look, the same cruel hardness that had stamped the mien of the youth, but the old impetuous air had given way to a cold inflexible sedateness, far more appropriate to the dread master of the Attila. As I advanced into the room, he rose, a grand specimen of manhood, standing full six feet three inches in his shoes. He shook hands more warmly than I had expected, and motioned me tacitly to a seat.

The mission of the Attila with its 'Napoleon' at the helm is to exterminate rotten civilisation and restore a type of Rousseauesque-style natural humanity through the destruction of cities and the institutions of capital and government. 'The regeneration of man' will take place through the air warfare of the 'fiends of destruction', the crew of red capped international anarchist desperados and their 12,000 agents. A new experimental politics will be initiated after the old world is incinerated:

> But the prospect, I admit, is splendid. Were you to succeed, I say at once that the return would well repay the outlay. I am socialist, you know, but I have felt how selfishness and the risks of reaction hampered all our most promising plans. The egotism of democrats is voracious. It is the curse of our movement. But this scheme of supervised anarchy, well, in some way it is magnificent – still it is only a theory.

The bombs and incendiaries finally drop on London and first to go is the Houses of Parliament 'in a tempest of dynamite, its 'pinnacles … collapsing and walls … riven asunder as the shells burst within'. The aeronef flies disinterestedly by, while a 'blood-red flag' unfurled declares 'THUS RETURNS HARTMAN THE ANARCHIST [sic]'. The Tower of London and the Bank of England, the Stock Exchange and the Royal Exchange are next engulfed in flames. Anarchy rules the streets and the last few pages are a catalogue of horrors only stopped by Hartman's rather sentimental change of heart and regiments of volunteers and regular soldiers (many of whom have gone over to the enemy), who restore order by mass summary executions.

Anarchism inspired a series of 'what if' novels, such as Robert Louis Stevenson's *The Dynamiter* in 1882, Tom Greer's fantasy of Irish revenge, *The Modern Daedalus*, of 1885, G.K. Chesterton's *The Man Who Was Thursday* in 1908 and Frank Harris' *The Bomb* of 1909. The actual Greenwich explosion inspired two specific works: Joseph Conrad's novel *The Secret Agent* of 1907 and Arthur Morrison's short story satire 'The Red Cow Group', which he published in the collection *Mean Streets* in 1894 following the success of his East End sketches in *The National Observer* and the *Pall Mall Gazette* (produced from 1892 onwards).

Morrison had humble beginnings and knew the East End intimately. He had been born in Poplar in 1863, the son of an engine driver, his mother having met his father when she travelled from Kent to London. In 1871 his father died and his mother had to cope with three children, but conditions got better when she took over the running of a haberdasher's shop. Morrison eventually became an office boy, but rose to be Secretary of the Beaumont Trust in charge of the People's Palace in Mile End Road, then the centre of a thriving arts, debating and social scene. Finally he took to journalism, writing a series for *The People* in 1888 and going on to find success as an early realist writer.

'The Red Cow Group' was one of a series of 'snapshots' of East End life at the turn of the century. It concerns a motley group of poor workers who drink and grumble at the Red Cow public house: men who 'had long been plunged in a beery apathy' and who could not care less for the 'social system', but who are confronted by a convinced anarchist called Sotcher. Before the coming of Sotcher, the group was apolitical, apathetic and alcoholic:

> Their talk was rarely of politics, and never of 'social problems': present and immediate facts filled their whole field of contemplation. Their accounts were kept, and their references to pecuniary matters were always stated, in terms of liquid measure. Thus, fourpence was never spoken of in the common way: it was a quart, and a quart was the monetary standard of the community. Even as twopence was a pint, and eightpence was half-a-gallon.

Sotcher had been discovered by one of the group while out drinking in Shadwell:

> he had met Sotcher in a loft at the top of a house in Berners Street, Shadwell. It was a loft where the elect of Anarchism congregated nightly, and where everybody lectured all the others. Sotcher was a very young Anarchist, restless by reason of not being sufficiently listened to, and glad to find outsiders to instruct and to impress with a full sense of his sombre, mystic dare devilry.

The drinking club is made up of poor but respectable artisans; the anarchist himself is not down and out, but affects the decrepitude expected of a revolutionary, a caricature based on both David Nicholl and Dan Chatterton:

> Grease was [Sotcher's] chief exterior characteristic, and his thick hair, turning up over his collar, seemed to have lain long unharried of brush or comb. His face was a sebaceous trickle of long features, and on his hands there was a murky deposit that looked like scales. He wore in all weathers a long black coat with a rectangular rent in the skirt, and at his throat he clipped in a brown neckerchief that on a time had been of the right Anarchist red.

Sotcher, wishing to ingratiate himself with the 'professional' revolutionaries of Tottenham Court Road and Soho for his success in infiltrating the working class in the East End, soon begins to lecture his fellows on the iniquities of the present system:

> 'Wy are we pore?' [sic] asked Sotcher, leaning forward and jerking his extended palm from one to another, as though attempting a hasty collection. 'I ask you straight, wy are we pore? Why is it, my frien's, that awften and awften you find you ain't got a penny in yer pocket, not for to fit a crust o'bread or 'alf a point o' reasonable refreshment? 'Ow is it that 'appens? Agin I ask, 'ow? … I'll tell you, me frien's. It's cos o' the rotten state o' s'ciety. Wy d'you allow the lazy, idle, dirty, do-nothing upper classes, as they call 'em-selves, to reapy all the benefits o'your toil wile you slave an'slave to keep 'em in lukshry an' starve yerselves? Wy don't you go an' take your shares o' the wealth lyin' round you?'
>
> There was another pause. Gunno Polson looked at his friends one after another, spat emphatically, and said 'Coppers' … Make a clean sweep of 'em. Blow 'em up. Then you'll 'ave yer rights. The time's comin.'

The group's only solution appears to be to make a bomb and the anarchist gives them detailed instructions as to how to accomplish this task:

> They should buy nitric acid, he said, of the strongest sort, and twice as much sulphuric acid. The shops where they sold photographic materials were best and cheapest for these things, and no questions were asked. They should

mix the acids, and then add gently, drop by drop, the best glycerine, taking care to keep everything cool. After which the whole lot must be poured into water, to stand for an hour. Then a thick, yellowish, oily stuff would be found to have sunk to the bottom, which must be passed through several pails of water to be cleansed: and there it was, a terrible explosive. You handled it with care, and poured it on brickdust or dry sand, or anything of that sort that would soak it up, and then it could be used with safety to the operator.

But who should they dynamite? Any crowd is suggested, like people at the theatre or a bank, but they finally pick a gasometer. The day arrives and the bomb is prepared, but the group turn the tables and tell Sotcher (who, of course, proves to be a coward) to detonate it. Sotcher finds himself the butt of his own chicanery, robbed and tied up by his companions as an example not to mix with East Enders who aren't anyone's political patsy. It is now that memories of the Greenwich bomb flood back as images of the futility of anarchist politics to solve the problems of the poor. Morrison's fictional conspirators prove 'vulgar' Marxists; knowing the importance of a bob or two, they also know the significance of economic circumstances and prefer a pint to political idealism:

A convulsive movement under the men's hands decided them to throw more beer on Sotcher's face, for he seemed to be fainting. Then his pockets were invaded by Gunno Polson, who turned out each in succession. 'You won't 'ave no use for money where you're goin', he observed callously; 'besides, it 'ud be blowed to bits an' no use to nobody. Look at the bloke at Greenwich, 'ow 'is things was blowed away. 'Ullo! 'ere's two 'aft-crowns an' some tanners. Seven an' thrippence altogether, with the browns. This is the bloke wot and't got no funds. This'll be divided on free an' equal principles to 'elp pay for that beer you're wasted. 'Old up, ol' man! Think o' the glory'.

For Morrison and Fawcett, anarchism is both the future goal of society and the failure of current mainstream politics. Nevertheless, it also represents a future determined only by nihilistic destruction and the end of civilisation alongside the end of capitalist exploitation. For both writers, anarchy represents an apocalypse where Victorian values and the working-class Victorians for whom the politics of anarchism were developed will be blown to bits in the revenge of anarchists in search of the ideal. The late Victorians and Edwardians were obsessed with their own annihilation, precisely because they felt so secure, precisely because the Empire was so big, precisely because the navy was so strong, industry so powerful and the Queen so long-lived, but within a decade everything had melted into air and the fantasies of destruction born of the satisfaction of security started to have very real foundations.

The Greenwich explosion was later reworked in Joseph Conrad's popular novel *The Secret Agent*, and it is this novel that provides the classic picture of a 'dynamitard' of the late nineteenth century:

> And the incorruptible Professor walked too, averting his eyes from the odious multitude of mankind. He had no future. He disdained it. He was a force. His thoughts caressed the images of ruin and destruction. He walked frail, insignificant, shabby, miserable – and terrible in the simplicity of his idea calling madness and despair to the regeneration of the world. Nobody looked at him. He passed on unsuspected and deadly, like a pest in the street full of men.

What scared society the most was not the professor's madness or his peculiar brand of politics, but his social invisibility. He is not a mid-nineteenth-century flaneur observing the crowd with insouciance, but a part of the late nineteenth-century masses, a manifestation of its new sense of totality and power. The professor therefore both embodies the explosive revolutionary spirit of the proletariat and the fickle nature of the individualist within it. He is a contradiction, both invisible and deadly, a theme taken up by Conrad's friend H.G. Wells in his story *The Invisible Man* of 1897. The central figure in this novel meditates on his power to 'strike as I like' in order to begin a 'Reign of Terror'. The story had its last outing, however, in Alfred Hitchcock's 1936 thriller *Sabotage*, which was itself a reworking of Conrad's novel.

TEN

RUSSIA ON THE CLYDE

One figure stood out amongst the radicals and his reputation cast a long shadow. In 1886, Ferdinand Blind, the stepson of a one-time refugee in England, took a pot shot at the German Chancellor, Otto von Bismarck. Bismarck was unscathed and pronounced the dread name of the assassin's mentor – Karl Marx – who had actually died in poverty in 1883. It was true that Marx had known Blind as a young boy, but that was enough for Bismarck to name the real villain, a straw guy trotted out at every outrage. Eleanor Marx and Friedrich Engels laughed at the reference, but it was no laughing matter, for the name of Marx had real caché as the Delphic oracle of socialism and could not be ignored even by those who professed to be socialists but who refused to accept Marxist arguments (especially Marxist economic theory).

Indeed, many revolutionaries of the 1880s thought Marx was already out of date. Neither William Morris nor George Bernard Shaw made much headway with Marxist theory and, being socialists by conviction rather than argument, they effectively joined the anarchists; Henry Hyndman hated Marx but couldn't do without invoking his name, and Edward Aveling made, it seems, only a belated effort to understand the theory even though he was living with Marx's daughter.

There was, of course, a simple reason for the ignorance, for the first volume of *Das Kapital* had not been translated into English and the other parts of the work had not yet been compiled. Samuel Moore, who had an acute mind and an ability to translate Marx's obscurities into readable English, was asked to undertake the translation by Engels, but he became bogged down and had to be assisted by Aveling, with Engels checking everything. Both men had been beaten to the punch by a 'John

Broadhouse', whose translation from the abridged French version was already being serialised during 1885. John Broadhouse was none other than Henry Hyndman. The official translation was finally published in March 1886 to the relief of all. Alongside *The Communist Manifesto* which Engels republished, translated by Moore in February 1888 (it had first appeared in 1850 in an English translation by Helen MacFarlane in George Harney's paper, the *Red Republican*), volume one (and the subsequent volumes) of *Capital* in English reinforced the supremacy of Marxist theory and clearly laid down its methods, aims and frontiers. However, Marxism and Marxist concepts (social democracy) remained only one set of choices out of a dozen varieties of socialist commitment.

Against the more extreme elements of either foreign anarchist clubs, SDF or Socialist League extremists were those whose upbringing and inclination made them assured of the steady growth and ultimate success of the cause of working people and democratic rights for all. The Fabian Society was set up on 4 January 1884 on the foundations of a group called the Fellowship of the New Life, which had been founded by an American called Thomas Davidson in 1852, but the organisation had collapsed over the doctrines of salvation by ethical reform or social change, although a rump continued until 1898. The new group was made up of intellectuals who used meetings as a forum for debate and propaganda on the methods needed to infiltrate collectivist and socialist sociological ideals (quite loosely defined) into the Liberal Party, thereby influencing policy by the slow drip of 'permeation'. It was named after the procrastinating Roman general Quitus Fabius who had frustrated Hannibal by his delaying tactics. The group was influential beyond its small membership of 40 colleagues dedicated to socialism by reform and free from what its members saw as Marxist dogma. At one time or another, the group included Havelock Ellis, Olive Schreiner, Annie Besant, H.G. Wells, Oliver Lodge, George Bernard Shaw and the Bloomsbury Group, including Virginia Woolf. Shaw summed them up as:

A little group of men [sic] who were at that time all under thirty. There was not a single veteran of 1848 in its ranks and not a single person who had ever met Karl Marx ... There were practically no wage-workers: the committee was composed of state officials of the higher division and journalists of the special critical class which produces signed feuilleton, they were exceptionally clever ... They paraded their cleverness ... and they openly spoke of ordinary Socialism as a sort of dentition fever which a man had to pass through before he was intellectually mature enough to become a Fabian. Though at this time the idolatry of Marx by the Socialists was a hundred times worse than the idolatry of Gladstone by the Liberals, the Fabians in restating the economic basis of Socialism, brought it up to date by completely ignoring Marx.

Its leading voices were, however, connected by family ties to most of the intellectuals of Britain. So it was with the pioneer sociologist Beatrice Potter, whose wealthy family included a free-thinking and widely-read industrialist as a father and a mother of unswerving Christianity, but intelligent breadth of interest and eight married sisters, and could therefore boast perhaps the greatest confluence of intellectual power either by marriage or friendship of the nineteenth century, the family's friends including Francis Galton and Herbert Spencer, and cousins of the nature of Charles Booth.

Potter, who admitted to a touch of the 'bluestocking', came from a family habituated to giving 'orders' to the labouring and servant classes, and she recognised that this and the sense of 'power' that orders gave to those above could be used from below upwards – in effect, that the world might be turned upside down to benefit society. She and her fellow Fabians sought to 'reform' society from the bottom upwards by trying to eliminate poverty not by charitable means, but by the new power of social science. She had gone to investigate the poor of the East End to help Charles Booth compile his sociological mapping of poverty and she had taken work as a rent collector and a sewing machinist in a 'sweated' workshop too.

Later, Potter married Sidney Webb, who was one of the 'little folk', his mother keeping a shop just off Leicester Square and he himself leaving school at 16, but a member of a new meritocracy, self-educated at Birkbeck College and then passing all the civil service exams and entering the First Division in 1881. He was to make a lifelong friend in George Bernard Shaw when he met him at the Zetetic or Zetetical Debating Society in Hampstead.

It was in fact Shaw who introduced his friend to a little group of debaters called the Fabian Society based around a middle-class intellectual called Edward Pease, who had abandoned 'thinking' for work as a cabinet-maker and a real livelihood. The Society produced pamphlets and Shaw and Webb, having got on to the executive of the Society in 1885, produced *Facts for Socialists*, the first of a number of pamphlets which were to be the Society's backbone and which continued in print for 65 years.

The target of the Society was the Liberal Party and its policies and the message was 'the inevitability of Socialism and the inevitability of gradualism'. The prizes were the direction of state and municipal enterprise by propaganda and education rather than the piecemeal measures of other radicals or the once and for all revolution of the militant communists. The Fabians were, in effect, a high-powered 'think tank' geared towards influencing rather than taking power. The Fabians had never thought of a 'Fabian Government' coming into existence under that name (nor, indeed, of a 'Labour Government', as before 1900 there was no Labour Party, and even after that it was scarcely worth the Webbs' attention before 1914). The Fabian idea was (if possible) to convert future Liberal government ministers and persons in key positions to Fabianism.

This did not stop electioneering when it was needed and Webb was elected to the London County Council in 1892, a position he held until 1910. From there he was able to influence education policies both in schools and universities. He believed that evolutionary 'permeation' was the key to improvement and might work best and in the most long-lasting manner. Almost nothing existed for the working classes in terms of a university education beyond classes at Birkbeck and an odd class at King's, itself half-populated by black and Asian students desperate for an education. With this in mind and with an unexpected legacy from a Fabian called Henry Hutchinson, he founded the London School of Economics and Political Science, an institution, in the words of Lord Beveridge, who was for so many years its Director, 'where men [sic] should be free to study and teach scientifically, pursuing truth as they saw it in independence of any dogma, whether of Socialism or the reverse'. 'No religious, political, or economic test of qualification', said the Articles of Association of the School, 'shall be made a condition for or disqualify from receiving any of the benefits of the corporation, or holding any office therein.'

Permeation succeeded by slow degrees. By 1891, Fabian ideas had infiltrated the Liberal Party sufficiently to influence conference policy. They even influenced the Conservative Prime Minister Arthur Balfour during the period from 1902 to 1905, himself a friend of the Webbs and an attendee at their gatherings at their home in Grosvenor Road, where Beatrice ran what was effectively a philosophical salon.

Extreme socialists would never be convinced by permeation and had no wish to wait for change. They had been inspired by the Communards of Paris and had seen in their tactics the class war that Marx had predicted and expected. Indeed, both Marx and Engels wrote furiously during and after the Commune in an attempt to raise revolutionary consciousness amongst the members of the International Working Men's Association. Marx wrote letters and pamphlets throughout the summer and autumn of 1870 railing against the 'police-tinged bourgeois mind' and arguing that 'class-rule is no longer able to disguise itself in a national uniform'. 'The national governments', he concluded, 'are one as against the proletariat!' This was an acknowledgement of a state of war across international boundaries. Yet nothing seemed to happen and no revolution loomed, a fact which split the socialists and left them bereft of a clear policy.

Lenin chose to come to London to escape watchful eyes, to organise congresses and to observe the adopted land of Engels and Marx. Many anti-Tsarists lived virtually permanently in London. Alexander Herzen published his revolutionary *Polar-Star* from his home in Westminster in the 1850s and 1860s, and Sergei Stepniak published pamphlets against the Tsar in the 1890s. Lenin transferred the publication of the banned *Iskra* to London, having obtained the goodwill of Harry Quelch of the SDF and the Twentieth Century Press. Tom Quelch, Harry's son, recalled Lenin as 'a small, stocky, ginger-haired young man'.

Lenin came with his wife, Krupskaya, found lodgings in various areas around King's Cross, walked the streets, travelled the omnibuses, read in the British Library, ate fish and chips, visited London Zoo and entertained revolutionary émigrés. Sometimes he went to meetings where he spoke to those assembled in Russian or spoke at great May Day rallies, such as that at Alexandra Park, where international speakers from France, Spain, Poland and Germany united with Hyndman and the union leader Ben Tillett to praise the International.

Lenin's first attempt at a London congress was in 1903, when 57 delegates who had been hounded out of Belgium met in deepest secrecy in a number of halls and pubs across London including an 'anglers' hall in Charlotte Street around the corner to the old Communist Club'. Afterwards, the congress went by bus to Highgate Cemetery to honour Marx's grave, which (before the dubious generosity of the North Koreans in the 1950s) was a small slab set in a row of nondescript burials. The groundsman, nonplussed by the request, could not find the grave.

By 1900, the police were quite sophisticated in their methods and all the delegates were closely watched. One Special Branch detective was Herbert Fitch, who was an expert linguist and had followed the fortunes of the Social Democrats before. It was Fitch who was treated to the perorations of Maxim Gorky, the congress' special guest, and the fiery oratory of Leon Trotsky, some 'fresh-faced girls' who spat blood and fire, and the singing of the red flag. The main congress, which went on for three weeks of interminable argument between the Mensheviks and the Bolsheviks, was held at the Brotherhood Church at the juncture of Islington, Dalston and Hackney. The location had been found by George Lansbury and Henry Brailsford of the SDF as the Church was run on Christian Socialist lines by a Tolstoyan and mystic, Bruce Wallace, upon whose sympathy they could rely.

Lenin returned for the Fifth Congress and this time 336 delegates followed, hounded out of Denmark and Sweden at the request of the Tsar. They had all travelled to Scandinavia under numerous false names and multiple fake passports. They had to find another venue and as Germany was closed to them, it was necessary to telegraph Britain. Someone sent a message to the Liberal John Burns, now an MP and President of the Local Government Board. Amazingly, the Liberal government said that they could come to London as long as they did nothing criminal, and so with a donation of 10,000 marks from the German Social Democrats, they came in their hundreds, arriving at Harwich by continental steamer between 9 and 10 May 1907, transported by train to Liverpool Street Station and thence to their hosts, some at least forced to travel the wholly alien London Underground to their final destination. Others had a short walk to the 'monster doss house' known as Rowton House in Fieldgate Street, the centre of the Jewish-Russian-Polish East End. Thus were Joseph Stalin and Maxim Litvanoff introduced to the joys of poverty in Britain and the weather, which was awful that May. Delegates registered at the Polish Socialist Club round the corner and then at the inaugural meeting at the Workers' Friend Club nearby in Jubilee Street. At the club, Prince Kropotkin noticed a policeman trying to look unobtrusive, but Kropotkin knew Edwin Woodhall from earlier days, went over and introduced his friend Lenin, whom Woodhall thought had an 'intellectual' look.

The Congress, which took place between 13 May and 1 June, was watched by 20-odd police and a multitude of press photographers and journalists. The *Daily Mirror* reported that there were numerous young revolutionary women and that a nondescript female delegate was actually the daughter of a 'governor-general' who 'carried bombs in her muff'. The *Daily Mail*, its journalist watching men in kaftans and high boots mingling with those in Western dress, concluded that this was a 'congress of undesirables'. The *Daily Mail* got it half-right – the delegates had arrived in England under false passports and fictitious names, their purpose was the overthrow of a state, not war with Britain, but the effect of their visit was to energise the British socialist movement.

British police activities sometimes bordered on the farcical, hiding in cupboards and clearly acting like policemen with ludicrous attempts at disguise and making no attempt to really blend in. Indeed, some were known personally to those under surveillance. It was later recalled by Anatoly Lyadov that London itself was porous and many illegal immigrants came permanently or, if inclined towards revolution, for a short respite from the Ochrana, the Tsar's secret police.

By now almost (but not quite) all revolutionaries entering Britain were from the Russian Empire. For the Victorians, Russia was the enemy, even outdistancing France in terms of mutual animosity. Russia's eastward expansion seemed to threaten India and the 'great game' of espionage and diplomacy played across the deserts of Central Asia, and the congresses of Europe only confirmed her aggressive stance; war had narrowly been averted several times since the battles in the Crimea (after diplomatic scares at remote outposts and cities such as Hunza, Pandjeh and Bozai-Gambaz) and all British diplomats were resolutely Russophobes. Victoria herself urged Benjamin Disraeli in the 1870s to go to war with 'those detestable Russians'. Indeed, she felt that 'they [would] always hate us and we can never trust them', an opinion she later repeated to Gladstone in the 1890s.

The 'great game' was the strategic defence of India from Russian invasion and had been played for almost 100 years. Nevertheless, no Russian army had yet massed on India's borders, the disputants finally fixing their differences with the Anglo-Russian Convention which Count Izvolsky and Sir Arthur Nicholson signed at St Petersburg on 31 August 1907. It was not, in the end, Imperial Russia that posed a threat, but the principles of Marx taught in London, Glasgow or Manchester which mixed with the pragmatism of Leninism that would return to haunt Parliament in the shape of MPs dedicated to the independence of India along Bolshevik lines. It was a task for mavericks only and one still fraught with danger, for to speak of independence was effectively to speak treason. Shapurji Saklatvala was one such maverick. Saklatvala was born into the wealthy Tata dynasty in Bombay on 28 March 1874. Although a Zoroastrian, he was educated by Jesuits (but not in religion), moved to Britain and married an ordinary English girl called Sally Marsh, who thereafter took the name Sehri Saklatvala.

In 1893 there was a cholera outbreak in Calcutta and a Russian Jewish doctor called Professor Vladimir Haffkine applied to help and to study the disease. He was a known 'troublemaker', a former member of the revolutionary nihilist Narodnaya Volya Party, and the Russian Embassy sent a warning to the British government. Nevertheless, he finally took up a post as a bacteriologist with the Government of India in 1896 and made contact with Saklatvala, who worked with him for six years. Saklatvala, thereafter working as a geologist, but feeling unfairly treated by his own family went to Britain and to a spa in Matlock, Derbyshire, where he met his future wife. Saklatvala's experience with the very poor and the sick, with Haffkine's revolutionary anti-imperialism and understanding of anti-Semitism, and the background of the Russian Revolution convinced him of the need for pacifism and anti-imperialism. These were the turning points of his political education. Although inclined towards socialism, he first became a Liberal, helping Sylvia Pankhurst and Indian reform, and only later became a communist. He later saw Arthur Field, an Arabist and socialist, espouse the international cause in Manchester to lukewarm interest.

Field recalled that:

> Having come in contact with Manchester Labour Organisations [sic] including the Clarion Movement, from 1909 we may suppose that Saklatvala was trying to influence them, as he had tried to influence the Liberals previously, to take up the matter of organising the workers of India and voicing their claims to justice in the English Labour circles. In 1911 he addressed to the leading men of the Trades Union Congress and the Labour Representation Committee a document outlining the desired activity. He told [Field] the response was disappointing and disillusioning.

Meanwhile, other forces back on the subcontinent were now at work, which put all Indians under suspicion. In the summer of 1909, there began a series of anarchist attacks across India which took the British by surprise. There was a spate of parcel bombings, bomb throwing, shootings, arson, theft and defacement of statues; the Viceroy had been targeted and numerous Indian officials murdered. Then in the heart of Empire, a young Hindu called Madan Lal Dhingra had murdered Sir William Curzon Wyllie, the ADC to the Secretary for India on 1 July. Enough was enough and Scotland Yard, who were particularly bad at tracing the Indian subversives in England, finally began to act. The plot was eventually traced to India House in Highgate, where a number of Hindu revolutionaries under their charismatic leader Vinayak Savarkar had long been plotting bomb campaigns and assassinations to rid India of the British once and for all.

Savarkar was a pupil of the school of anarchist thought that believed in 'propaganda by the deed' and he experimented with bombs and smuggled pamphlets to India in the eventual hope of creating an anarchist republic. Trailed by police, he was arrested in 1910, escaped, was rearrested and banished to exile on the Andaman Islands, a suitable dumping ground for the politically unwanted. Meanwhile, a Sikh called Har Dayal continued to stir up ferment from his home in California, even making alliances with the Germans once war was declared. His own revolutionary army was to cause much trouble, as was his revolutionary paper *Ghadr*, which called for 'revolution' and 'martyrdom' on the 'battlefield of India'.

By 1911, then, Saklatvala was seen as a rich, meddling subversive and was tailed by Scotland Yard detectives. On one occasion, he got lost going to a meeting and went into a police station to ask the way, only to find that the local police already knew of his speech and its whereabouts. For some time, it was hinted that he would be arrested if he set foot back in India. This is hardly surprising as the promise of armed rebellion in the Punjab led by a revolutionary army of 8,000 Sikhs coming from America and Canada came closer with the outbreak of war and the promise of German guns. The Sikh revolutionaries had made common cause with their Hindu brothers in Bengal who had been fighting a terrorist war from 1909 under the leadership of Rash Behari Bose, who claimed to have thrown the bomb at the Viceroy in 1912. The rebellion was set for February 1914, but was infiltrated by a Sikh spy and defused, its leaders being rounded up, executed, transported or imprisoned. It had been a near-run thing and the authorities were nervous of any dissent.

There was therefore an irony in giving shelter to the Tsar's enemies and even his most loyal subjects. What could not be known at the time was that the collapse of this distant empire in 1917 would so wholly infect the body politic of these islands, for Russian émigrés (such as Peter Petroff in Glasgow and Theodore Rothstein in London) were now working tirelessly within British politics to create a revolution in Britain, and Bolshevik money was now financing Sylvia Pankhurst's nascent communist party and would later help pay for the Communist Party of Great Britain and its newspaper, the *Daily Worker*. Meanwhile, British intelligence was employing the Tsar's code-breaker, Ernst Fetterlein, who had fled Russia in 1917 in order to decode Bolshevik messages for the British Empire.

The aim of these Boshevik Russian émigrés was to ferment working-class uprisings, especially in the industrial heartland of Clydeside, where the Scottish revolutionary John Maclean was working tirelessly to bring an orthodox Marxist revolution to fruition. Maclean, born on 24 August 1874, an educated man from a poor background, with the fierce class hatred of Chatterton but with real organisational ability and charisma, was able not only to create Marxist night classes but to do it on the rates! He was only too aware of the power of the Scottish industrial working class and also of the traitorousness of those of its supposed labour and political leaders. The First World War was to be the final battle of international labour against capitalism; instead, it was, according to Maclean, hijacked for national patriotic propaganda to convince working people to enter into capitalist exploitation and death in a 'monstrous war'. Maclean's tough stance gained him a following and many enemies. He was unequivocal: 'nothing but socialism [would] do ... Capitalism ... must be killed ... the only war that is worth waging is the Class War'. On 7 October 1917, Lenin recognised the seeds of the Russian Revolution in the fight on the Clyde and Maclean as one of the 'precursors of the revolution'. Arrested several times, with increasingly tough prison sentences, Maclean was broken by the authorities and died at the age of 44, but not before Lenin had appointed him an Honorary President of the first All-Russian Congress of Soviets alongside Trotsky and others, and had named him Bolshevik Consul in Glasgow, an honorific title not recognised by the British government, however.

Indeed, these revolutionaries had succeeded largely in severing the connection between Hyndman-esque patriotic socialism and full-blown international communism in the various rifts that had split the SDF and isolated Hyndman, who was still the voice of British radicalism. That a particularly Russian revolutionary party, the Bolsheviks, would produce the spur to the amalgamation of various socialist factions and the final creation of Britain's own Communist Party in 1920 organised by Russian dissident internationalists working with Glaswegian dockers and London intellectuals, and operating with one eye on Lenin's socialist utopia would have been unthinkable in 1913, but was now a reality. Russia had finally arrived at the heart of British radicalism, and its infectious presence would not be rendered ineffectual until after the Cold War. It was a supreme irony and a strange type of fulfilled prophecy for those socialists kept at the margins of left-wing politics by the ruthlessness of Hyndman's organisational nouse and his political machine.

When the First World War started, Shapurji Saklatvala became a conscientious objector, but seems not to have been arrested although called up, perhaps because his close relatives all now had knighthoods. The Russian Revolution was the key to Saklatvala's political empathies. By now a member of the Fabians and the Independent Labour Party and a continuing friend of Sylvia Pankhurst, it was a relatively short journey towards the communist utopia, the reality of which he visited in 1923, 1927 and 1934. Rarely encountering racial prejudice, he was, however, blackballed for his adherence to Moscow. Nevertheless, in his bid to become the MP for Battersea, his supporters were many and prominent: J.R. Clynes, Chairman of the Parliamentary Labour Party, Arthur McManus of the Communist Party, K.S. Bhat of the Worker's Welfare League of India, Reverend Herbert Dunnico of the International Christian Peace Fellowship and the prominent feminist Charlotte Despard. Despard appealed:

To Labour, which I have always honoured, to women – women workers and mothers, who are the greatest workers of all, I appeal to my Irish fellow-countrymen and women in North Battersea – support the Party and support the man, Saklatvala – that will be on your side in the great struggle which is bound to come. Saklatvala spoke to us, as a fraternal delegate, in the last Irish Labour Congress, and his courage, wisdom and determination impressed us all.

Saklatvala was an MP for two short periods in 1922 to 1923 and from 1924 to 1929. He died on 16 January 1936, his ashes being buried in the Parsi burial ground in Brookwood Cemetery in Woking, Surrey.

ELEVEN

SMOKED SALMON AND ONIONS

The East End had been the litmus paper of both Christian charity and socialist revolution. Here were the footprints of Octavia Hill, Stewart Headlam, Samuel and Henrietta Barnett, Charles Booth, Eleanor Marx, Tom Mann and Ben Tillett, Beatrice Webb and Charles Bradlaugh. Lenin visited Whitechapel in October 1902 and 1903. In the East End were to be found the origins all those jumbled theories of Christian socialism and of sociology, of anarchism, of social democracy (Marxist communism) and trade union labourism. The area was the poorest in Britain and the strangest, filled with faces that were not merely alien because of race but alien because of temperament, a tipping-out point for everything shunned and benighted in Victorian culture and therefore all the more alluring to the do-gooder and the ardent social experimenter: it was the visible rebuke to the West End and the complacent of 'Society'. When Jack the Ripper was active in the autumn of 1888, George Bernard Shaw sent a letter to *The Star* on 24 September claiming that the killer was actually no more than an ironic social reformer:

SIR,– Will you allow me to make a comment on the success of the Whitechapel murderer in calling attention for a moment to the social question? Less than a year ago the West-end press, headed by the St. James's Gazette, the Times, and the Saturday Review, were literally clammering for the blood of the people – hounding on Sir Charles Warren to thrash and muzzle the scum who dared to complain that they were starving – heaping insult and reckless calumny on those who interceded for the victims – applauding to the skies the open class bias of those magistrates and judges who zealously did their very worst in the criminal proceedings which followed – behaving, in short as the proprietary class always does behave when the workers throw it into a frenzy of terror by venturing to show their teeth. Quite lost on these journals and their patrons were indignant remonstrances, argument, speeches, and sacrifices, appeals to history, philosophy, biology, economics, and statistics; references to the reports of inspectors, registrar generals, city missionaries, Parliamentary commissions, and newspapers; collections of evidence by the five senses at every turn; and house-to-house investigations into the condition of the unemployed, all unanswered and unanswerable, and all pointing the same way. The Saturday Review was still frankly for hanging the appellants; and the Times denounced them as 'pests of society'. This was still the tone of the class Press as lately as the strike of the Bryant and May girls. Now all is changed. Private enterprise has succeeded where Socialism failed. Whilst we conventional Social Democrats were wasting our time on education, agitation, and organisation, some independent genius has taken the matter in hand, and by simply murdering and disembowelling four women, converted the proprietary press to an inept sort of communism. The moral is a pretty one, and the Insurrectionists, the Dynamitards, the Invincibles, and the extreme left of the Anarchist party will not be slow to draw it. 'Humanity, political science, economics, and religion', they will say, 'are all rot; the one argument that touches your lady and gentleman is the knife.' That is so pleasant for the party of Hope and Perseverance in their toughening struggle with the party of Desperation and Death!

The East End was more than a place, it was a living symbol. Arthur Morrison wrote about the East End as a mysterious, endless metropolitan sprawl: 'the street is in the East End. There is no need to say in the East End of what. The East End is a vast city, as famous in its way as any the hand of man has made'; 'but', he continues, 'who knows the East End?'.

The verbal flourish was not merely rhetorical. Charles Booth had gone to find the heart of this 'dark continent' in order to measure its degradation. He had been accompanied by a policeman on his journeys. The anarchist Rudolph Rocker had wished to live amongst its inhabitants; Beatrice Webb (then unmarried) had wanted to taste the experience of 'sweated' labour; Octavia Hill had designed model dwellings for its inhabitants; Stalin had slept in its doss-houses; Jack London had walked its streets unable to persuade a cab to do the journey. The East End remained an enigma of poverty and foreignness into the 1920s. As late as 1925, the journalist H.V. Morton described a bus journey to Whitechapel so his readers might not need to go: 'I caught a penny omnibus back to England with the feeling that I might have spent two hundred pounds and seen less of the East, less of romance, and much less of life.' The East End would be a crucible for the unravelling of Victorian values.

On 1 March 1881, Tsar Alexander II was killed by the Russian anarchist group Narodnaya Voyla. A Jewish seamstress, Jessie Helfman, was only peripherally involved as a courier, but it was enough to bring about the formal persecution of the Jews in Russia, which had started as an informal state policy 100 years earlier and gradually intensified when Russia absorbed Poland. Now it was officially unleashed in the violence of the pogroms, which reached fever pitch in Odessa on 3–5 May. Britain awoke slowly to the crisis and such groups as the International Working Men's Educational Club cranked into belated action. It would, however, take almost ten years for the situation to be recognised and a political response created, and by then the politics of the ghetto would profoundly affect the radical politics of Britain. From the mid-1880s, Jewish immigration began to affect the very make-up of the poorest living in London and in the wake of this deluge of strange, alien creatures into the East End came the tales of what they had had to put up with in Russia – tales of ritual murder, monstrosity and deviance.

The Jewish ghettos in Russia were an exact recreation of the necropolis; the Jews subject to the laws governing the dead. Like the dead, the Jew was beyond slander, outside of the laws which protect life, crowded into the graveyard of the prohibited city quarter or village (where Christians dared not enter). The ghetto was the reminder of proximity and quarantine, and the fear of contagion. Jews, like the dead, were sentient beings but, without a soul, were living and yet 'dead'. They were stubborn, non-rational beings created against nature, parasites whose only craving was supposedly the gold of the living (usury) and the blood of the living (blood libel and child sacrifice). The body of the Jew was the corrupt body of the dead: the decayed body, the chaotic body; the 'soul' of the Jew was black, malevolent and eternally damned.

The mind of the Jew, so it went, was not an individual mind but a collective mind (a ghetto mind) determined by instinct rather than rational consciousness. Like the world of the dead, the world of Jewness was ever growing. Mixing with Jews brought on contagion, which diminished pure blood until one ended up a Jewish Asiatic mongrel, alive but socially dead. As the hallucinatory modes of experience cross or coalesce, they come to rest on the Jewish body both in look and reproductive ability. For the anti-Semite, Jews cannot reproduce normally or naturally. They can reproduce either through interbreeding (producing degeneracy), miscegenation (producing hybrid mongrels or 'mischlings') or financially (usury). In each case the reproductive act produces deformed bodies infected with plague. The Jew was supposedly the carrier of syphilis and leprosy.

There had been a long tradition in Europe which held that the skin of the Jew was marked by a disease, the 'Jedunkratze' or 'parech', as a sign of divine displeasure. By the middle of the nineteenth century, many Western Jews regarded it as one of the signs of difference between themselves and Eastern Jews. Karl Marx, writing in 1861, associates leprosy, Jews and syphilis (with a hint of 'Eastern Jewish' foreignness added in through his use of a biblical reference) in his description of his arch-rival Ferdinand Lassalle: 'Lazarus the leper, is the prototype of the Jews and of Lazarus-Lassalle. But in our Lazarus, the leprosy lies in the brain. His illness was originally a badly cured case of syphilis.'

In the 1780s, the Bavarian Johann Pezzl even described Viennese Jews as monkey hybrids and 'Black':

Excluding the Indian fakirs, there is no category of supposed human beings which comes closer to the Orang-Utan that does the Polish Jew … Covered from foot to head in filth, dirt and rags, covered in a type of black sack … their necks exposed, the color of a Black, their faces covered up to the eyes with a beard, which would have given the High Priest in the Temple chills, the hair turned and knotted as if they all suffered from the 'polica polonica'.

The Jews' 'black' skin looked back to the Black Death and the blackening of victims, as well as forward to contemporary nineteenth-century racial debates in which blackness was the absolute mark of inferiority and the most dangerously contagious of colours (because, like Judaism, it could be worn 'inside'). The Jews, apparently according to anti-semitic historians, crossed the boundary between whiteness and blackness to become 'mongrels' when they interbred with black people during the Alexandrian period, or so the anti-Semite Houston Stewart Chamberlain thought. The Polish nobleman Adam Gurowski arrived in America during 1850 and actually thought mulattos were 'Jewish'. Russian Jews felt helpless against such insults and inferior and quiescent because of them. What was needed was an injection of confidence in future times, an assurance that could no longer be supplied only by the rabbi.

Believers in the potentialities of Edward Bulwer Lytton's Vril power saw in his 'discovery' racial, prehistoric, Darwinian and political issues. Yet it was a vision that came from a darker place altogether and one that was connected with the new philosophical arguments around Christian origins. The most significant revision of mainstream ideological Christianity was 'Aryan Christianity'. Such a revision of belief also had at its core an occult, mystical anti-Semitism that became important to radical romanticism, white supremicism and pan-Europeanism. For Arthur Schopenhauer, Judaism was a perversion of a morality that Christians had originally shared with or actually borrowed from Buddhism.

Even more direct was Schopenhauer's belief that Judaism was a creation of the Babylonian captivity, with the tribal Hebrews swapping the worship of Baal and Moloch for the single god of the Babylonians. New Testament ideas remained firmly Indian (Aryan) in origin. Christ was therefore not Jewish at all. Where Jewish ideas coincided with Aryanism, this was because the 'Hellenised' Jews in Alexandria had been supposedly exposed to the Brahmin Indian theology. Thus, Christianity was 'de-Judaified'. Richard Wagner intended to base his opera *The Victors* (1856) on this philosophy and Chamberlain was quite clear that the composer's *Parsifal* (1877–82) was a renunciation of Judaeo-Christianity from the perspective of a purer Aryan Christianity.

The Eastern esoteric belief in a common mind was detached by its Western adherents so that it only applied to the elect. The elect were naturally Aryan and through the idea of a 'universal mind' they were linked across time and space to the ancestors of the Aryan race. Belief in reincarnation meant that the romantic Aryan-Christian could link to noble ancestors and to future generations with what they reconstituted from Vril energy. The occultist Madame Blavatsky, whose visit to London in 1887 was an incalculable influence on Annie Besant and other leaders of Britain's intellectual elite, thought the Jews were 'a tribe from the Chandalas of India ... outcasts'.

Thus, the Jews who arrived in Britain came already tainted with a rhetoric of mumbo-jumbo social Darwinism, theological prognostications and plain anti-Semitism derived from the most advanced Germanic esoteric thought. The Jews who came to Britain and settled in the East End of London were the poorest of the poor, ragged, ignorant, superstitious and talking Yiddish. They came in their thousands and settled in Whitechapel and its surroundings, forming a sort of ghetto as they did so, many involved, as William J. Fishman points out, with the sweated labour of the textile industry:

> Formerly in Whitechapel, Commercial Street roughly divided the Jewish haunts of Petticoat Lane and Goulston Street from the rougher English quarter lying in the East. Now the Jews have flowed across this line; Hanbury Street, Fashion Street, Pelham Street, Booth Street, Old Montague Street, and many other streets and lane and alleys have fallen before them; they fill whole blocks of model dwellings; they have introduced new trades as well as new habits; and they live and crowd together, and work and meet their fate almost independent of the great steam of London life surging around them.

Karl Marx called them 'the smeariest of all races', but his daughter was attracted to these reminders of her ancestry and worked amongst them, while Annie Besant, working at her sociological statistics with Charles Booth, concluded that the alien exploitation so abhorred by those wishing to bring in immigration controls was a fantasy. 'Jews', she concluded, were 'untiring and thrifty' and even 'if every foreign

Jew resident in England had been sent back ... the bulk of the sweated
workers would not have been affected'. Her argument did little to sway
public opinion with regard to the universal 'Jew'. How were attitudes
to be changed? As the immigrants streamed in, so too did ideas about
how to alleviate the lot of those newly arrived, who not only faced the
disapproval of the indigenous East Enders but also the active hostility
of those Jews already established in England, those whose roots lay not
with the Ashkenazi Russians and Poles, but in the Sephardic-Dutch
tradition.

The problem, as the small caucus of revolutionaries saw it, was that
the Jewish immigrants were so poor that mere survival was all most
could think of; they were too embedded in an alien language (Yiddish)
and its culture, and they were indoctrinated in a quietist religion. Jewish
socialists were happy to discourse in Yiddish but were unhappy about
the religious scruples and poverty of the mass of their brethren. They
could do something about religious scruples by showing that God had
yet again abandoned the Jews, perhaps for good, and that it was time to
turn to other means to help themselves; secular leaders might 'preach'
socialism to those few who would listen and do it, moreover, in the
native language of European Jewry. To alleviate poverty, Jewish socialists
argued for the salvation of unionisation, even if that unionisation met
with the passive hostility of gentile trade unionists.

Jewish socialist veterans of the Commune and the European revolutions
came to the East End to organise poor Jewish labour. They had made a
start at unionisation in the 1870s, but it had petered out subsequently.
Nevertheless, in 1875, Aron Lieberman arrived in London. Lieberman
was a linguist and a Talmud expert, a Hebraist and a revolutionary who
had tasted the various versions of Russian activism and had worked on
the secret revolutionary paper *Vperyod,* having left the Vilna seminary
an atheist and militant. A crackdown by the police saw him flee
to Germany and thence to England, where he joined up with other
exiles and continued to produce the paper whilst teaching Judaism at a
religious school! The revolutionaries in London put him up at a house in
North London until he moved in with a friend in Spitalfields. Here he
formed (with ten others) the second Jewish union, but the first Hebrew

Socialist Union. The Union stood on the anti-capitalist principles and internationalism of most of the various forms of socialism (the exception being Hyndman's SDF).

The East End Jewry, whether Zionists, Bundists, socialists or anarchists, all found themselves under the surveillance of the rabbinate, whose emissaries were themselves the victims of socialist ire. It was not unknown for rabbis and others to be assaulted and insulted.

Lieberman had a nucleus of an organisation and a paper in which he could air his views (if only sporadically as the press was always in debt), but he had not made an impression on his sponsors, who saw him as a rather childish, posturing lightweight. He had defended Bakuninist and Marxist ideologies even though they were opposed, but he had become a friend of Johann Most, in whose Third Section of the Communist Workers' Union most Jewish socialists had joined against the wishes of the Narodniki, itself having split into a 'Black Section', which looked to a spontaneous uprising, and Narodnaya Volya, which looked to the immediate destruction of society in Russia by fire and flame. This was too heady a brew for a revolutionary who could see some good in both sides and who was burdened with a personality that was sliding into despair. Whatever he was, Lieberman proved a tragic figure at the last. Having fallen in love with a colleague's wife, he followed her to the United States where, his love being unreciprocated, he blew his brains out in a lodging house in Syracuse, New York State on 18 November 1880.

Lieberman's absence put another revolutionary in the spotlight. This was L. Winchevsky, who had been born L. Benzion Novochvitch in the village of Yanova in Lithuania in 1856. Making his way to the East End via Paris, he adopted his pseudonym as a political convenience and took a job at a bank under the name Leopold Benedikt. These were dangerous times and multiple names were used by everyone to cover their tracks. In Whitechapel he brought out a socialist paper in Yiddish called the *Poilishe Yidl* in which he played down intra-faith argument, instead addressing his reader as a 'man [sic], as a Jew and as a worker'.

By the late 1880s, there was real movement towards organisation, education and unionisation in the Jewish community of the East End. In 1884, the Society of Jewish Socialists expanded into the International

Workers' Educational Club with its meeting hall at 40 Berner Street, and with the new club came a newspaper, the *Arbeter Fraint*, a socialist propaganda vehicle which continued printing on and off until the 1900s. Here every exiled revolutionary turned up to read the papers, to talk, to smoke and relax and to hear William Morris, old Russian Narodniki, Kropotkin and others in the old rickety hall, which could hold 200. They might also buy the *Arbeter Fraint*. In 1892, the premises were shut down for health and safety reasons following agitation by a hostile police force and a suspicious Jewish middle class. By a quirk of fate, the club is best remembered now for one of Jack the Ripper's murders, which happened near the entrance. The revelation nearly caused an anti-Jewish riot partially incited by the *Church Times*, which took a dim view of Christ-killing alien nihilists. In 1889, during the fight for unionism, those at Berner Street helped organise a mass rally against the sweating system in the garment industry. The march was banned, went ahead and was harassed with inevitable arrests, but the Jews of the East End had shown their teeth.

By the end of the century, not all anarchists were hell-bent on destruction. The East End Jewish anarchist groups were humiliatingly small and politically divided, poor (it was an unwritten rule that an anarchist did not have a bank account and that all money was shared) and undecided what action to take for the better (for the most part, this was syndicalist anarchism). Most of their co-religionists would have nothing to do with political madmen who believed in free love and did not go to synagogue. Into this Yiddish-speaking world came a new voice. Rudolph Rocker was a German gentile, born in 1873 to a family of typesetters from Mainz. Hating arbitrary authority, he was drawn to social democracy and away from the Catholicism drilled into him at the orphanage where he went to live after his parents died. As he wandered through Europe a homeless journeyman printer, he became drawn to libertarian politics, which appealed both to his rational side as well as his 'romantic imagination'. In 1893 he was in Paris and fell in with a group of radical Jewish anarchists. Instead of being repelled, he was deeply drawn to their plight as well as being intrigued by their Yiddish culture and attracted to their open and egalitarian attitude towards women. In the same year, he was invited by the West End Autonomie Group based off Tottenham Court Road to help smuggle literature into Germany. Once he arrived, he was introduced both to Louise Michel and Errico Malatesta, and also went exploring in the East End, where he discovered another group of activists, this time Jewish and poor, but anarchists like himself.

Such anarchists were shunned by the West End group of social democrats whose attitude was patronising. They were also disliked or treated with suspicion by East End non-Jewish radicals like Ben Tillett, who considered them scum in terms little different from Hitler: 'a Socialist government would … have to think of ways to get rid of this scum; false pity for them would harm the Socialist cause'. Indeed, these Jewish aliens were nothing but the 'hyenas of the revolution'.

It was not a good start, but Rocker felt an affinity with these oppressed, highly intelligent, but impoverished idealists. He found lodgings in the East End, learned Yiddish and courted a Jewish girl called Millie Witkop, who agreed to live with him, a situation that caused an immense stir when the two travelled to New York to meet the anarchist union leaders of the Knights of Labour in 1897. At Ellis Island they were stopped by an official, who asked them for their marriage certificate: 'We have no marriage certificate. Our bond is one of free agreement between my wife and myself. It is a purely private matter that concerns only ourselves, and it needs no confirmation from the law.' The immigration officers were less than impressed and continued their questioning, to which Millie answered: 'Do you suggest that I would consider it dignified as a woman and a human being to want to keep a husband who doesn't want me, only by using the powers of the law? How can the law keep a man's love?' 'This is the first time I have heard a woman speak like that' was the reply. 'If everyone ignored the law in respect of marriage, we should have free love.' 'Love is always free', Millie answered. 'When love ceases to be free it is prostitution.'

The visit was at least a partial success and with the fundraising of Emma Goldman and an injection of American cash in 1898, the *Arbeter Fraint* was relaunched to continue the job of proselytising on behalf of libertarian anarchism. The paper also advertised educational and entertainment events as well as engaging in debate with Social Democrats and the newly emerging Zionists, whose work in the East End was opposed by Rocker as a perceived retreat from the international battle with European capitalism. By 1901, the anarchist Jewish East End was both anti-monarchist and pro-Boer, a combination guaranteed to alienate most of the British Jewry (both new arrivals and old assimilationists) and indigenous Christians.

Rocker really became the anarchists' 'rabbi' when he founded the Workers' Friend Club in Jubilee Street in 1906, where debate and discussion could take place, where entertainment would be regularly offered and where subsidised meals might be procured. One of those chewing his herring and brown bread was Lenin, while another was Peter the Lett, better known as Peter the Painter. Whether you were a Zionist, a Bundist, a Social Democrat, an anarchist or a communist, and whether you were for expropriation (theft from the capitalist class) or keen on 'propaganda by the deed' (bombs) or were for unionisation and more peaceful means of affecting the revolution, all were welcome, although fighting and rioting sometimes broke out amongst rivals.

Guy Aldred, who professed anarcho-communism and who was living with Millie Wirtkop's sister Rose, saw the extremist advocate of 'terrorism' Arnold Roller talk at the club one night, a celebrity figure with a strange, almost mystical attraction to some of his listeners:

> He spoke more than once at the Jubilee Street Club. He did not spend all his time in London but often disappeared mysteriously and as mysteriously reappeared in his old London haunts. I often saw him leave the club and turn into the Whitechapel highway, attended by a group of admiring supporters. His violent speech entranced them … He was arrayed in black, and wore an overcoat with a cape after the style of Edward VII. On his head was a kind of black sombrero. He carried himself with a swagger and strode towards Aldgate like a king, guarded by his retinue, and disdaining all who passed him. He had all the flamboyant grace of the traditional highwayman and might have been named Claude Duval … His case for direct action was sound, but what constituted direct action was menacing and absurd. It included every possible kind of social outrage under the heading of sabotage.

Rocker himself, although categorised as an anarcho-syndicalist, remained an open-minded believer in the goodness of human endeavour and the possibilities of change through peaceful and practical libertarian politics:

> There is never an end to the future, so it can have no final goal. I am an Anarchist not because I believe Anarchism is the final goal, but because I believe there is no such thing as a final goal. Freedom will lead us to continually wider and expanding understanding and to new social forms of life. To think that we have reached the end of our progress is to enchain ourselves in dogmas, and that always leads to tyranny.

This socialist-atheist and communalist future might be the anarchists' grand aim, but their organisation was tiny and impoverished, almost totally Yiddish in outlook and speech, and conflated with the idea of chaos in the daily press. How could Jews work internationally if they were unable to work for themselves or even to talk in the language of their host country? The dilemma was significant. Should Jews work exclusively for their own salvation rather than make alliances with those who appeared to be in the same economic situation but whose hostility was intractable? For Lieberman, Jews were in essence anarchists from Bible times. Was the answer less about internationalism and more about socialism and the rescue of the ideology of a homeland in Zionism?

TWELVE

IMAGINED WORLDS MADE REAL

A ll the foreign revolutionaries who floated in and out of Victorian London were searching for societies which only existed as imagined places inside their heads, universal utopias not yet quite realised and Jerusalem in the clouds. National revolutionaries such as the Hungarians, Italians and Poles looked upon Britain as a very temporary home until their return to their own lands. One group fell between the universalists and nationalists, and it was the genius of a visionary revolutionary coupled with the very fact that Britain had an empire which turned the trick of creating an imaginary homeland whose centre might actually be the real geographical Jerusalem. Political Zionism was born out of the misery and pogroms of Russian oppression.

The old Jewish saying 'next year in Jerusalem' was just that, a matter of meaningless words, no one believing that a return to a homeland once occupied centuries ago could possibly occur, not least because there was no impetus from the millions of mittel European Jews who lived lives of grinding poverty or from those assimilated Jews in the West whose positions in society offset any anti-Semitism. Benjamin Disraeli had been, after all, the leader of the party of the social elite and had risen to become Prime Minister, and, whilst a Christian convert, was always depicted in cartoons as a Jewish stereotype and referred to by European diplomats such as Otto von Bismarck as 'the Jew'; the Rothschilds, nouveau riche as they were, were always too trusted to offend; Sir Moses Montefiore was a friend of Queen Victoria; Karl Marx was a Jewish apostate living in Soho. The Jews of Russia were too hidebound by their close ghetto-like existence and their close association with their rabbis, whilst their richer counterparts in Britain and the United States were too spread out and wore their religion largely without conviction.

Things changed as the nineteenth century waned, as the situation in Russia worsened and as the plight of the refugees could no longer be ignored. As so often in the revolutionary world of nineteenth-century London, the troubles started far away, but became a problem for British diplomacy to unravel. Chaim Weizman was born in Pinsk in 1874, the son of an enlightened merchant who was determined that his children would escape the claustrophobic world of Russian bigotry and Jewish self-preservation. Weizman grew up to get a good education and escape the trap of only knowing Yiddish, and was to learn Russian, German, English and French. He studied chemistry at university. He was a 'Maskil', a follower of the Jewish and Hebrew renaissance centred on Odessa. The assassination of Tsar Alexander II dashed these hopes and forced Jews to dream other dreams. One group who emerged from such dreams was called 'The Lovers of Zion', which Weizman was drawn to as a youth. The Lovers of Zion were secularists, seeing religion as the obstacle to reform and rebirth; they thought that the rejuvenation of Jewish life had to come from culture and education.

By the age of 19, Weizman was studying with Carl Liebermann at the chemical organic laboratories in the Charlottenburg Technical College in Berlin. Liebermann had become famous for his synthesis of the dye base alizirine. Meanwhile, the Lovers of Zion had gained a leader in Menahem Ussishkin, who saw Odessa as the home of the East European Jewry. He was succeeded by Asher Ginzburg, who called himself Ahad Ha'am or 'One of the People' and who extended the organisation with a self-help and secret group called B'nai Moshe ('The Sons of Moses'). Ha'am preached spiritual regeneration and a type of quietism that was rapidly losing its hold. There was a need for practical solutions. Weizman was by this point collaborating with Christian Deichler on synthetic dyes and original research into naptha derivatives.

Another mind had also been troubled by the idea of the future of the Jews. He was the Viennese journalist Theodor Herzl, the French correspondent for the *Neue Freie Presse*. Herzl formulated a radical break with the thinking of the Lovers of Zion. He proposed that only one solution was viable and that was the creation of a nation state. It was a leap of imagination and audaciously far sighted. Herzl called the first Zionist conference at Basle in 1897. Later he claimed that 'at Basle I founded the Jewish State'. It was certainly a bold claim as nothing at all, either philosophically or really historically, existed anywhere to support this statement. Jews were divided, the Jewish Bund was cold about the idea and the Lovers of Zion were split, while the neutral Jewish world remained largely indifferent. Nevertheless, Herzl had already written a pamphlet called 'Der Judenstaat' ('The Jewish State') and began contacting prominent Jewish leaders. A bank account was set up to purchase land in Palestine and negotiations began with the Ottoman Empire. Weizman was elected on to the steering committee. The key, however, lay not with the East but in the heart of London, to which Herzl travelled next.

Herzl's next congress, like that of Lenin later, was to be in London, the centre of world trade and an empire that might have a corner worth settling. The congress met in the Queen's Hall near Oxford Circus in 1900, followed by a tea party in Regent's Park. Despite the fact that delegates were delayed by faulty Underground trains, the congress was successful enough to gain new and important followers. Herzl soon travelled to the East End to recruit the ordinary mass of poor Jews likely to be swayed by his rhetoric, speaking to large crowds on Mile End Waste. Such rhetoric about a 'promised land' appealed both to the possible aspirations of poor Jews as well as to the wishes of British anti-semites hoping that such immigrants would leave Britain. Previously, Herzl had declared at the London Congress that: 'England [sic] the great, the free, with her eyes fixed on the seven seas, will understand us!' The British Empire was the key to the puzzle of Jewish liberation, not the internationalism of the Bund or communism. It was an idea that Weizman came to understand only three years later once Herzl was long dead. Nevertheless, Herzl had ignited a fire and the speeches by Max Nordau and himself did nothing to dampen the impatience of many who wanted immediate land purchase and settlement in Palestine, where there were already 800,000 Jews (or ten per cent of the Palestinian population), most of whom lived in Jerusalem. Many of Herzl's followers owed allegiance to the Bolsheviks and so added a vehemence as well as a secularism that was without the religious zealotry often ascribed nowadays to Zionist thought. Indeed, Zionism continued to be socialist in outlook until the founding of the state of Israel, and Stalin as well as Truman backed its foundation.

The Alien Immigration Bill was now being proposed and the anti-immigration propagandist William Evans-Gordon of the 'British Brothers League' had travelled to the Pale of Settlement to see conditions there. Here he met Weizman, who easily convinced him of the need for a Jewish homeland. Evans-Gordon became an ironic Zionist just as Jewish help faltered. No one wanted to upset the Turks and Edmond de Rothschild suggested facetiously that the Jewish state might as well be founded in Uganda, a suggestion taken literally for some time. Everyone wondered about Herzl's ambitions, including Weizman. 'I suppose', mused Weizman, 'all the synagogue politicians imagine that with Edward the Seventh's illness Herzl has been invited to rule England for a while.'

On 4 July 1904, Herzl died and it was left to Weizman to unite the various Jewish factions and argue for a new homeland in his leisure at night. He was now living in Manchester, as had Engels before him, this time to work in the chemical industry. At the British Congress of 1905, Weizman had to argue for a reaffirmation of the Basle proposal 'to create for the Jewish people a home in Palestine secured by public law'. It was a curious and illogical ideal, but one that caught the imagination of the Prime Minister Arthur Balfour, then fighting for his political future at a general election. Balfour met Weizman in a hotel suite at the behest of Charles Dreyfus, who was one of Weizman's Jewish co-workers and campaign manager for the election:

> 'Mr. Balfour, supposing I was to offer you Paris instead of London, would you take it?' He sat up, looked at me, and answered: 'But Dr. Weizmann, we have London.' 'That is true,' I said, 'but we had Jerusalem when London was a marsh.'

In a moment of weakness, fatigue or enthusiasm, Balfour was convinced. 'He explained', Weizman recalled years later, 'that he sees no political difficulties in the attainment of Palestine, only economic ones', an extraordinary statement of political hubris at the time, considering that no war had been declared between Britain and the Turks. The coming of war changed both the possibility of a Palestinian Jewish state and the need to erase the influence of Herzl's 'German' Zionism (the Germans and the Turks also actually declared for a Jewish homeland, but had pronounced a jihad against the British Empire during the First World War). Weizman had to rethink the Jewish state through the eyes of British aspirations in the region. 'I have no doubt', he said one day to the novelist Israel Zangwill, 'that Palestine will fall within the influence of England. Palestine is the natural continuation of Egypt and the barrier separating the Suez Canal from Constantinople, the Black Sea, and any eventuality that may come from that direction.'

It was the problem of Ugandan settlement which was the cause of the letter sent from Balfour, at that point Foreign Secretary, to Baron Rothschild and the Zionist Federation of Great Britain and Ireland that led to the Balfour Declaration which was issued on 7 November 1917. It stated that:

> His Majesty's government view with favour the establishment in Palestine of a national home for the Jewish people, and will use their best endeavours to facilitate the achievement of this object, it being clearly understood that nothing shall be done which may prejudice the civil and religious rights of existing non-Jewish communities in Palestine, or the rights and political status enjoyed by Jews in any other country.

'Messianic times had arrived' indeed, with both the pro-Zionist Prime Minister David Lloyd George and former Home Secretary Herbert Samuel (who was himself Jewish) promising that 'together we shall rebuild the Temple as a symbol of Jewish Unity'. It would, of course, clash with another equally powerful and parallel ideology – Arabism.

In its apparent easy attitude to drugs and homosexuality and its appeal to personal 'freedom', Orientalist Islamism was part of the decadent's persona from the eighteenth century. It was hardly new. There were the numerous Islamophiles who for 100 years played the 'Great Game' in high Asia and who made up the many missions, embassies and diplomatic visits to the Khanates and Emirates of the region dressed in native dress and burnished faces disguised as holy men, doctors and horse traders, speaking fluent Persian or Afghan and all to stop the Russian armies marching on India. George IV and William IV had Sake Dean Mahomed, and Queen Victoria enjoyed the company of Abdul Karim, who waited on her at table at the Golden Jubilee on 20 June 1887, taught the Queen the rudiments of Urdu and was accused of prejudicing her against Hindus by working for the Muslim Patriotic League (an accusation she dismissed as racial prejudice). Sir Richard Burton had gone disguised to Mecca and Orientalists had long fantasised about the joys of the harem. Byron had visited the 'east' and, like Thomas Phillips, who sponsored Richard Dadd's visit to Jerusalem, had dressed up in the exotic costumes of the Arabs (Albanian costume to be exact) and was painted in them as a dashing 'Oriental'. Painters flocked to the Holy Land in the 1840s and 1850s in search of biblical authenticity. It was to the Dead Sea that Holman Hunt travelled to paint his Christian allegory *The Scapegoat* (1854) and Dadd had painted Jerusalem in rosy hues in *The House of Herod* (1842). The Middle East or 'Levant', with its deserts and souks, biblical place names and associations with the Crusaders, was a well-trodden path and one that seemed to mesmerise its travellers.

Nevertheless, what emerged at the end of the nineteeth century from dreams of the Orient was the 'invention' of political 'Arabism', quite a different matter from the ideas of harems and wild horsemen, which was encapsulated by an outright rejection of Ottoman Europe and the discovery of the 'subjugated' peoples of the Ottoman Empire and of that 'barbaric' Eastern culture centred in the area then known as the Hiyaz of the Arabian peninsula. It was a world that was especially attractive to those who rejected the stultifying Englishness of their birth, but who had not yet found a 'psychic' place for themselves in which the 'self' could develop freely. Thus, the East was both the rejection of an old self and the acceptance of a future new self, more alive and real than before.

Into this new world on 16 August 1888 stepped T(homas) E(dward) Lawrence, the illegitimate son of a governess who lived with his father Thomas Lawrence, who had long since abandoned a harridan of a wife obsessed with Jesus and interested only in converting Catholics in the neighbourhood. Thomas Lawrence was comfortably and professionally middle class and conservative in taste. Despite his unusual family circumstances, both his parents craved quiet respectability and rebuked their son when he once mentioned Oscar Wilde. The couple were, however, intelligent and rational, and rejected organised religion and that muscular Christianity that came from the athleticism of playing public school games. Thomas, the father, reminded Thomas junior that games were not necessary, whilst at the same time Lawrence himself developed a secular religiosity which later became his 'creed' of mankind, in material form, political Arabism. Yet, Lawrence was also brought up in the world of the Crusaders, warrior knights, gentlemanly chivalry and honour. The virtues of Christian knighthood led him to pursue an archaeological interest in the Middle East. It was not enough and did not satisfy him:

> I am not going to put all my energies into rubbish like writing history, or becoming an archaeologist … I would rather write a novel … or become a newspaper correspondent.

Lawrence grew out of his own platonic ideal of self. He was always theatrical, taking on a role for the self to act out, finally and triumphantly 'strutting about the [Versailles] Peace Conference in Arab dress'. Standing aloof, but seeking recognition, he created a self-image that was part artist and part charlatan. For him, it was always that 'fiction seemed more solid than activity', but this did not mean that fiction was inactive. He dreamed in fiction:

> I had had one craving all my life – for the power of self-expression in some imaginative form … At last accident, with perverted humour, in casting me as a man of action had given me place in the Arab Revolt.

Thus, Lawrence knew himself as the expression of his own fiction. Yet what, in T.S. Eliot's terms, would be his 'objective corollary'? It would be a devoted interest in the Crusades, but twisted into a fascination with the heroics of 'Saladin' rather than Richard the Lionheart: 'Super Flumina Babylonis (Psalm 137), read as a boy, had left me longing to feel myself the node of a national movement ... [creating] the new Asia.' It was, as he recalled, 'fantasies', but with such power that they imposed themselves on reality. Lawrence took the narrative features of fiction and turned them into action. Such fictions as he might turn on the real world were of the romantic type in an age where romance was exhausted. He concluded that 'the epic mode was alien to me, as to my generation [as] fantastic [as] old Mallory'.

It was the knight errant that fascinated, the Christian hero leading Muslim followers in a crusade. Interestingly, Lawrence was always weary of actual Arabs, their endless indecisiveness and bickering, and of semitic people generally, and never contemplated becoming a Muslim himself. The Arab Revolt, Arabs themselves, were for Lawrence a type of 'manufactured' reality, a type of plastic or malleable space onto which one might impose one's will in creating the thing one needed most – a sense of self-worth:

> To invent a message, and then with open eye to perish for its self-made image ... the self-immolated victim took for his own the rare gift of sacrifice; and no pride and few pleasures ... were so joyful as this choosing voluntarily another's evil to perfect the self.

Lawrence liked the 'barbaric' nature of the people he led and the war he fought. It had the appeal of the olden days, but was thoroughly modern. He wore Arab dress when he could and now felt uncomfortable in his uniform. It was all part of his 'imaginative vision' which was measured against the rational slaughter or 'murder war' of Foch's Western Front. In so doing, Lawrence became a revolutionary through and through, leading 'Arabs [who] fought for freedom' and who also 'became revolutionary' when they realised that they had no 'constitutional rights'. The mode of a revolutionary suited Lawrence, who understood that:

> To live in the dress of the Arab, and to imitate their mental foundation, quitted me of my English self, and let me look at the West and its conventions

with new eyes: they destroyed it all for me ... and then madness was very near as ... it would be near the man who could see ... through the veils ... of two customs.

Thus, Lawrence was not only alienated from his home, but was also in the heart of an alien culture. This double alienation gave him the ability to express himself, but also to discover another self, unknown to himself until his encounter with the Middle East, and masked from childhood. It manifested itself in a type of relish for nihilist revolutionary terrorism where, after becoming familiar with 'high explosive[s]' and 'dynamite', he was confident enough to decide 'to revive the old idea of mining a train' which he had toyed with since the beginning of the war. The effect of these technical lessons in death was to make him immune to violence and to revel in its consequences, where execution and massacre became life-renewing acts: 'Blood was always on our hands: we were licensed to it.' It was a terrible acknowledgement and one that accompanied his strange attraction to 'voluntary slavery' and humiliation, precisely because it liberates the will:

I liked the things underneath me and took my pleasures and adventures downward. There seemed a certainty in degradation, a final safety ... True there lurked always that Will uneasily waiting to burst out.

However, this self was in turn a mask and Lawrence merely an actor of a strange sort, one who could manipulate his superiors and fascinate his audience because he appeared ephemeral and unfixed. He recalled that '[General] Allenby could not make out how much was genuine performer and how much charlatan'. To the Arabs, he was 'El Aurrens' whilst, bored after the war, he enlisted in the Royal Air Force as John Hume Ross until his discharge, whereupon he returned to enlist a further time as the raw recruit 352087/A/c Ross, in which name he wrote *The Mint* about his experiences between August and December 1922. This was the stance he needed in order to be what he wanted to be, 'a celebrity', merging his public and personal personas in subtle and disturbing ways:

There was a craving to be famous and a horror of being known to like being known ... the eagerness to overhear and oversee myself was my assault upon my inviolate citadel.

It was the power of the will that allowed Lawrence to vanish and reinvent himself, but it was a will wholly dedicated to martyrdom and a deep and peculiar self-hatred. Yet it was only this that would allow the final victory of Lawrence's personality over that material reality which he saw as debasing and disgusting (he had a horror of being touched), but which was absolutely necessary for the will to triumph: 'the lone hand had won against the world's odds'.

Yet the lone hand needed an identity, whether in the army, the RAF or the press. Lawrence sought that identity after the war in the Tank Corps and in the RAF, where he recorded in excoriating prose the life of an ordinary recruit down on his luck. The book has the feeling of George Orwell's *Down and Out in Paris and London*, recording the sordid conditions of barrack room life, the bland food, the overtight uniforms, the constant swearing and the continuous farting of his sleeping comrades. The story of Lawrence's reinstatement in the RAF begins not in the playing fields of Eton or in Henry Newbolt's famous paean of praise to cricket, but in a lavatory, the hero wracked with fear and trembling:

> God this is awful. Hesitating for two hours up and down a filthy street … Try sitting a moment in the churchyard? That's caused it. The nearest lavatory, now … My right shoe is burst along the welt and my trousers are growing fringes. One reason that taught me I wasn't a man of action, was this routine melting of the bowels before a crisis.

The journey is fraught with danger, a wilful return to the repressed; an officer half-recognises his writing style and nearly blows his cover. *The Mint* is harsh, abrasive and entirely modern in its concerns with the visceral and unpleasant (popular editions published were censored and abridged). It was also an attempt to escape from Lawrence's 'coffin-body' and allow him to live life in the public gaze not as a celebrity, but as a type of flagellant, whose very presence disturbed and nauseated:

> Could a man, who for years had been closely shut up, sifting his inmost self with painful iteration to compress its smallest particles into a book – could he suddenly end his civil war and live the open life, patent for everyone to read?

Accident, achievement, and rumour (cemented equally by my partial friends) had built me such a caddis-shell as almost prompted me to forget the true shape of the worm inside. So I had sloughed them and it right off – every comfort and possession – to plunge crudely amongst crude men and find myself for these remaining years of prime life. Fear now told me that nothing of my present would survive this voyage into the unknown.

Lawrence's chameleon nature was exactly why he needed to abase himself in both anonymity and order and why, in the final moments of his life, his actual impatience and frustration with that very anonymity and order led him to assert his individuality once more and to ride his motorbike too fast, ending his life not in oblivion, but in that legendary fame and post-mortem celebrity he craved but repressed.

Out of the milieu of foreignness that was the East End, Zionism had taken shape, and out of the heated imagination of a latter-day crusader, Arabism had been formed. Both were intimately connected with Britain. It was the very nature of the Empire as an internal place, a place in the mind as well as in geographical space, where geography would comply with imagination, which allowed Lawrence, Herzl and Weizman to help create the modern world of the Middle East, a world that emerged from the perfectly satisfactory working empire of the Ottomans. It was a rewriting of the map according to ideologies which slowly split apart; a consequence of imaginative play, the triumph of the conquest of Damascus by Lawrence and the vision of Jerusalem by Herzl.

THIRTEEN

PLAYING CRICKET IN THE CORRIDORS

A s nineteenth-century radicals called for more collectivism (more trade unionisation and more class solidarity) to protect the individual from the unregulated free-for-all that was capitalism, other radicals were preaching the exact opposite, fearing that individualism itself was under threat. These two pulls came to dominate the early twentieth century and have proved irreconcilable. Victorian Britain was getting too large and too complex to leave unregulated the power structure that had existed in Georgian times, and the concept of the importance of the state in public and private affairs came to dominate discussion of politics. Slowly the meaning of the 'state' evolved and the role of government changed, and with these changes the nature of the 'private' person and the sense of one's own personal space changed too. Society, seen in the mass, seemed to threaten to extinguish the singularity of the self that was the cornerstone of Victorian sensibility.

Writing in 1869, the critic Matthew Arnold had considered the state itself to be sacred, threatened by the onslaught of ill-educated democracy and the votes of the ignorant masses. Only a 'remnant' of cultured survivors would be left after the deluge of ignorance about to swamp civilisation – anarchy would be the inevitable and unstoppable result:

The very framework and exterior order of the State is sacred; and culture is the great enemy of anarchy, because of the great hopes and designs for the State which culture teaches us to nourish. But as, believing in right reason, and having faith in the progress of humanity towards perfection, we grow to have clearer sight of the ideas of right reason, and of the elements and helps of perfection, and come gradually to fill the framework of the State with them and to make the State more and more the expression, as we say, of our best self ... with what aversion shall we then not regard anarchy, with what firmness shall we not check it, when there is so much that is so precious which it will endanger.

Things moved so rapidly during the nineteenth century and opinions changed so dramatically that constitutional experts and those of a legal bent, like the political theorist Albert Venn Dicey, felt compelled to record the relationship between the changes in public taste and the concomitant changes in legislation. Dicey was born in 1835 and did not die until 1922, so was in a unique position to record the flow of constitutional history. In essence he was a Liberal, but a Liberal whose leanings were essentially conservative. More enlightened than his peers, he nevertheless vehemently opposed Irish Home Rule when it became an issue, refused to countenance votes for women and believed that bad laws were better than no laws. His idea of democracy was straightforward and clear: the sovereignty of Parliament; the importance of the common law; the intelligence of educated voters; and the impartiality of the court system. This was as far as the British constitution need go, but he recognised that it had gone much further over the course of the nineteenth century.

Dicey crystallised his thoughts in a series of lectures first given at Harvard during 1898 and thereafter published in 1905 as the jauntily titled *Lectures on the Relation between Law and Public Opinion in England during the Nineteenth Century*, with a second edition appearing in 1914. By the time of the First World War, it was clear which direction British politics had taken. Dicey saw the changes to the constitution as three distinct movements coinciding with the overwhelming changes in public opinion and tolerance. The first stage simply catalogued the period of inertia from the Glorious Revolution of 1688 to the first great Reform Act of 1832, and for this period William Blackstone was the apologist. This was followed, so Dicey suggested, by a short period of unequalled change and democratisation following the ideas of men like Jeremy Bentham and John Stuart Mill, whose creed of practical happiness was summed up in the ideas of Mill's essay *On Liberty* in 1859, where the liberty of the individual (a mantra since the days of the Civil War) was again asserted against the background of uncertain times. The argument was both a justification and the legacy of liberalism and laissez-faire attitudes.

The object of his essay, wrote Mill in 1859, was:

> to assert one very simple principle, as entitled to govern absolutely the dealings of society with the individual in the way of compulsion and control, whether the means used be physical force in the form of legal penalties, or the moral coercion of public opinion. That principle is, that the sole end for which mankind is warranted, individually or collectively, in interfering with the liberty of action of any of their number, is self-protection ... There are good reasons for remonstrating with him or reasoning with him, or persuading him, or entreating him, but not for compelling him, or visiting him with any evil in case he do otherwise ... The only part of the conduct of any one, for which he is amenable to society, is that which concerns others. In the part which merely concerns himself, his independence is, of right, absolute. Over himself, over his own body and mind, the individual is sovereign.

Yet it was clear that something momentous had changed. Looking back from 1914, Dicey concluded:

> Contrast now with the dominant legislative opinion of 1859 the dominant legislative opinion of 1900 ... The current of opinion had for between thirty and forty years been gradually running with more and more force in the direction of collectivism with the natural consequence that by 1900 the doctrine of laissez faire ... had more or less lost its hold upon the English people. The laws affecting elementary education, the Workmen's Compensation Act of 1897, the Agricultural Holdings Acts, the Combination Act of 1875, the whole line of Factory Acts, the Conciliation Act, 1896, and other enactments ... to which I have referred, though some of them might be defended on Benthamite principles, each and all if looked at as a whole prove that the jealousy of interference by the State which had long prevailed in England had, to state the matter very moderately, lost much of its influence, and that with this willingness to extend the

authority of the State the belief in the unlimited benefit to be obtained from freedom of contract had lost a good deal of its power. It also was in 1900 apparent to any impartial observer that the feelings or the opinions which had given strength to collectivism would continue to tell as strongly upon the legislation of the twentieth century as they had already told upon the later legislation of the nineteenth century.

Such changes were exemplified by laws passed almost continuously from 1906 onwards, including:

The Old Age Pensions Act 1908, the National Insurance Act 1911, the Trade Disputes Act 1906, the Trade Union Act 1913, the Acts fixing a Minimum Rate of Wages, the Education (Provision of Meals) Act 1906, the Mental Deficiency Act 1913, the Coal Mines Regulation Act 1908 and the Finance (1909–10) Act 1910. These provisions of government interference had, to all intents and purposes, through the intensification of protectionism and socialism, broken the belief in laissez-faire and greatly enlarged the role of the state in everyday affairs.

To Dicey, the coming of absolute 'universal suffrage' would make the British system equivalent to that of America, whilst the tendency and tenor of changes in the law drew Britain nearer to the situation in the France. Either way, it was revolution from the top which now privileged (rather than equalised) trade unions and the working class, and was to be accomplished by greatly increased taxation on those of the middle class neither in the trade unions nor in the working class:

The main current of legislative opinion from the beginning of the twentieth century has run vehemently towards collectivism … Revolution is not the more entitled to respect because it is carried through not by violence, but under the specious though delusive appearance of taxation imposed to meet the financial needs of the State … Collectivism or socialism promises unlimited benefits to the poor. Voters who are poor, naturally enough adopt some form of socialism.

It seemed that endless reform was in the air by the late nineteenth century. In 1888, the Liberal MP Sir William Harcourt exclaimed that 'we are all socialists now', a comment somewhat more facetiously echoed by the

Prince of Wales in 1895, and although the two actual socialist parties, the SDF and the Socialist League, were tiny, everyone thought of themselves as a socialist or, at least, 'an unconscious socialist' as Sidney Webb put it, as long as they supported the vague ideals of reform and its implication: collectivism.

Herbert Spencer, apostle of those liberal virtues so necessary to men of his individualist creed, saw in the Liberal Party those actions which were the very destruction of the principles which it stood for in the first place. These were the principles of that Manchester-style capitalism which put self-help, laissez-faire, low taxes, non-conformism and individualism as the greatest social virtues, and which were now being eroded in the dictatorship of 'pathological' collectivism. For Spencer, whose idea of society was that of a living organism, this amounted to a terminal illness:

> Dictatorial measures, rapidly multiplied, have tended continually to narrow the liberties of individuals; and have done this in a double way. Regulations have been made in yearly growing numbers, restraining the citizen in directions where his actions were previously unchecked, and compelling actions which previously he might perform or not as he liked; and at the same time heavier public burdens, chiefly local, have further restricted his freedom, by lessening that portion of his earnings which he can spend as he pleases, and augmenting the portion taken from him to be spent as public agents please ... Thus, either directly of indirectly, and in most cases both at once, the citizen is at each further stage in the growth of this compulsory legislation, deprived of some liberty which he previously had.

Spencer was deeply perplexed. 'How is it', he asked, 'that Liberalism, getting more and more into power, has grown more and more coercive in its legislation?'

Nowhere was the move towards centralisation and consequent bureaucratisation more obvious than in central government departments, especially the Home Office, which turned from a small government office (albeit an important one) with very few officials who were chosen because of their position in society into one of the largest government departments, professionalised and bureaucratised in equal measure and served by a very large network of trained expert inspectors with a remit to pry into many aspects of life that were once thought of as private.

The origins of the Home Office go back to the seventeenth century, where the 'principal secretary' sorted out the monarch's affairs. By the eighteenth century, the duties of the secretary were split, but by 1782, this had proved unworkable and all the functions were combined into a small department of state with a secretary, two under-secretaries, a chief clerk, ten other clerks and some domestic servants. The whole department existed to keep the internal peace of the realm. Yet the duties soon proved enormous, as legislation for prisons, police and alien naturalisation took up all the available time and enormous amounts of correspondence clogged up the workload. The 1833 Factory Act was decisive in making the role of the Home Office different from before. Whereas private enterprise and local authority (usually the same thing with the same people) had the final say, now central government could order, hector, persuade or even punish those local worthies who thought central government was there to be ignored. The Whig taste for Benthamite utilitarianism and a dislike of the landed interests made the 'experts' who were now influencing the Home Office and the department itself a truer servant of central government's wishes.

Nevertheless, the core of the duties remained firmly in the hands of those men whose families were used to being in power and whose qualifications for the job were a family pedigree, regal connections and a classics degree. In the middle of the century, this was sufficient to run the country without too many mishaps if all the unsolvable problems might be left to non-governmental individuals. In essence, the department was both conservative and Tory. Nepotism, waiting in line for promotion and a private income were the qualifications for a good clerk and when entry by exam – and therefore a meritocratic culture – was introduced, it was hotly opposed by the old guard. Indeed, for most of the century, snobbery meant that the clerk dealing with crime and the law was considered to be at the bottom of the pecking order, even though his position required real expertise and even though law and order were central to the business of the secretary.

In the early 1850s, attitudes began to thaw at the edges as the work of controlling the country began to fray. In 1854, civil service reformers finally began work on a report into the permanent organisation of the Home Office from the principle that there was a new concern with growth because of the realisation that 'the Government of the country could not be carried on without the aid of an efficient body of permanent officers ... possessing sufficient independence, character, ability and experience to be able to advise, assist, and to some extent, influence, those who are from time to time set over them'.

Testing for this new breed of civil servant began in April 1856. Further internal reorganisation meant that in 1870 there were 33 officials working centrally. This was a small rise, but one that had the Treasury in a spin over costs. It would be the tension between efficiency and costs that would mark many of the Home Office's future tussles with the Treasury. The Colonial Office also went through a continuous period of restructuring between 1868 and 1872. The necessary extra staff that both departments accrued were not so busy as they might have expected and passed their time making bets on passing vehicles, playing corridor cricket, writing books of poems or kicking their heels. It would be another 20 to 30 years before staff were fully employed in the domestic, criminal or general divisions set up in 1876, when there were still only 36 central staff in Whitehall.

'Rationalisation, examination and competition' really entered the Home Office in the period from 1876 to 1896 and it was to radically change the outlook and actions of its members. L.N. Guillamard recorded his own reminiscences of working at the Home Office during this period of change in his memoirs, written in 1937. He recalled 'a ferment was at work owing to the introduction of the democratic system of entry by competitive examination, which paid no heed to family trees and recognized no aristocracy but that of brains'. It was a revolution from which a large expert cadre of professional bureaucrats would emerge, centralised, controlled and organised as an arm of the new idea of 'big' government. Interestingly, the older civil servants noticed that the new system robbed successful candidates of their 'humility'; many new recruits were 'cocksure' after having fought their way competitively into their positions. The older uncertainty and moral hesitancy was lost and replaced by a domineering and patronising attitude to the public whom they served. Yet they worked hard too. An average of 47,000 letters were received in 1886, each one needing a handwritten reply and giving each clerk 75 letters to deal with a day.

One of those irksome issues which needed urgent attention was the relationship of the police service to the Home Office; a final vicious tug of war with the Commissioner Sir Charles Warren in 1886 established the direct control of the department over a force that believed itself an 'independent' arm of domestic imperial policy. Another was the collection of statistics and data, which had become increasingly important to MPs and which the Home Office, in charge of prisons and overseeing industry, should have been able to provide. It was not until the 1890s that the rather lackadaisical attitude towards number crunching was finally tackled. The age of the new man who was an expert and a professional was about to dawn. In 1894 Herbert Asquith wrote impatiently to Gladstone:

> We shall never get the thing right, until we have two or three men at headquarters with the same kind of expert knowledge and ability in industrial matters, which clerks in the Criminal Department have in regard to their special work.

Civil servants in their vast new buildings in Whitehall (completed in 1909) were backed up by a very large number of regional inspectors who were the brains and the brawn behind most executive decisions.

The growth of the truly modernised and bureaucratised Home Office belongs to the period from 1896 to 1914, a period when much new legislation came to dominate the statute books, not the least of which was the Aliens Act of 1906, which, together with licensing, shop hours and the overview of the employment of children at work, meant new sub-departments would be required. The continuous revision of the Acts relating to factories, work compensation and coal mining had doubled workloads and increasing agitation amongst the workforce would add urgency to neurosis. It was a department at breaking point. In 1899,

46 clerks in the department dealt with over 50,000 letters, and by 1909, 60 clerks dealt with over 71,000 pieces of correspondence. The work grew to meet department expansion, which was never enough to meet demand and never increased in anticipation of demand. Railway strikes, the suffragettes and general rioting across Britain in the years before the First World War caused further tensions.

The department was still an old boy's club, but of a different sort, not one made up of the sons of the landed gentry, but one where expert opinion informed men whose minds had 'exactitude [and] impartial ability, bred by an English classical education'; in short, the higher up the ladder you were, the more you were required to have 'imagination', discrimination and humility. A type of class system remained firmly in place as the new aristocracy of the civil service gathered to exclude the 'lower clerks', who were to be recruited from the 'clever boys' of the lower middle classes, and no working men were to rise above the inspectorate, which was outside the department anyway. This ushered in further crises when dealing with a mass of legislation dealing with working men's problems and the radicalism of the Liberals.

To get up to date in order to cope, the Home Office was forced to become part of an emergent technical bureaucracy, obtaining a calculating machine in the 1890s and an addressograph in 1907. In 1908 a new electrical adding machine had replaced its predecessor and there was a duplicating machine too. Thus, the department entered the machine age through the pressures of the workload, actually becoming one of the first automated offices. The future had arrived willy nilly under the pressures of modernisation, itself the result of centralisation, professionalism and the rise of the technical expert.

However, there was no revolution in government, despite the fact that until the twentieth century, most people thought that government should be small and should not interfere with private matters. The evolution of industrial society had changed the social fabric and brought tensions and threats which suggested that what appeared robust was actually fragile. The modern world that emerged as Victoria aged meant that, almost without noticing, a new person was required by the rise of democracy. The 'expert' would be less and less interested in public opinion and tied increasingly closer to the unapproachable scientific expertise of technocrats and processed data.

For the Fabians, it was Gladstone's administration of 1880 to 1885 'which may fitly be termed the "no man's land" between the old Radicalism and the new Socialism', as Beatrice Webb saw it. Indeed, the Liberals seemed to have stumbled into collectivism in a fit of 'absence of mind'. The political field, it appeared, had forever shifted out of Parliament, collectivisation (and its possible consequence, socialism) had become an extra-parliamentary imperative, the one force greater than everyday political business, collectivism its practical application of all political theory. Parliament would from now on, it was supposed, be forced, whether it liked it or not, to follow the inevitable path of historical progress. Those who aligned themselves with labour and the masses were now in the advance guard of political debate if not actual power. Gladstone felt the inevitable pull of new forces, a point he made to Lord Rosebery in 1880 at the beginning of his administration. Gladstone rightly saw that what was 'outside Parliament' was now as significant as what went on inside.

Gladstone hated extra-parliamentary collectivist socialist pressures, of which 'he radically disapprove[d]'. Even the Conservatives, led by new men like Joseph Chamberlain or Lord Randolph Churchill, the inventor of 'Tory Democracy', felt a chill. It was clear to both parties that the extension of the franchise in 1884 removed any pretence that the government was not interfering in local affairs: laissez-faire was dead. Nevertheless, the change of franchise did not mean the overturning of the old order by any means and overt socialists were defeated wherever they stood for election. In 1885 the SDF candidates, Harry Quelch, H.H. Champion, H. Burrows and 'Mrs' Hicks, were all soundly thrashed at the polls, despite a programme offering free school meals for the poor. There simply was no opposition able to stand against the two main parties.

FOURTEEN

THE COLLECTIVE DREAMS
OF BEES

It was, however, in the last quarter of the nineteenth century that something occurred which could only be explained as an historical and moral watershed, equivalent to a change in human nature. Before the 1880s, individualism reigned supreme as the central tenet of political life; after 1885, the whole idea was a busted flush. The change was accounted for by a belief that those in power had lost their nerve. This was not, so the Fabians thought, the result of pressure from underneath, but a spontaneous breakdown of nerve amongst those in 'Society': 'panic fear of the newly enfranchised', following an overwhelming concentration on the poor by books, investigators, journalists and artists during the period, forced the ruling elite to reassess its right to rule, leading to a wave of philanthropic endeavour and parliamentary enquiry.

This did not, of course, force those in power to disappear, but to reorganise on different, less aggressive and therefore less overtly capitalistic lines; model dwellings and ideal villages such as Port Sunlight and Bourneville thrived through a benevolent paternalism designed, with all good intent, to turn the masses away from unionisation, atheism, drink, pleasure and collective action. The old artisanal working-class elite were not by inclination collectivistic or socialist, but the new unskilled had to be turned away as well, some, at least, living through the grace and favour of the new class of industrial magnates, living not in slum conditions, but in the primrose-strewn prisons of model industrial towns and purpose-built dwellings. Beatrice Webb's socialist idealism based upon her sociological and scientific approach was still confronted with the grim truth of a big sister's rebuke:

> My dear child, working men just don't count; it's money that counts, and the bankers have it. Not brains, but money … Credit; credit, Beatrice; it is credit that rules the world.

Yet things had changed. At the heart of the constitutional debate which raged between 1829 and 1832 was the nature of the voting public, the new middle classes. Thomas Macauley, then MP for the borough of Calne, a constituency in the gift of Lord Lansdowne, was a leading voice calling for reform because, if it were not granted, 'it would drive to the side of revolution those whom we shut out of power'. Thus, the reform would prove a tactical move through which Parliament 'may exclude those whom it is necessary to exclude'. When the Bill passed into law in 1832 amidst much riot and disorder, the Whigs thought that they had answered the constitutional crisis once and for all. Macauley, writing in the *Edinburgh Review* in October 1829, recorded his own fear of a democratic future. Democracy was something forced upon Parliament and was not encouraged.

Despite her own personal hatred of democracy, Victoria's reign saw a continuous widening of the franchise. The Chartist demands may have been resisted (demands for universal political rights went back to the time of Major Cartwright and the Constitutional Clubs in the eighteenth century), for their immediate demands could not have been admitted without permanent upheaval, but change there was, and more and more men from every class found themselves with a say in politics, both locally and nationally. Such widening of political participation was accompanied by a belief that the governance of Britain was becoming more complicated and specialised as the population grew, the economy developed, the Empire expanded and the working man organised.

It soon became not merely desirable but necessary to widen the vote to all those who might prove to be 'active' citizens. This was an urgent issue because the masses were often considered moribund and apparently socially inactive by their social 'betters', or, more worryingly, were seen as having a taste for organisations hostile to representational democracy based on capitalist lines. It was vital to 'control' the democratic urges of better-off workers by offering a property franchise which would give the vote to respectable working men. This was the franchise adopted in 1867. By the time of the debates on the Reforms Bills of 1866 and 1867, therefore, the nature of what was at stake had changed. The question was one couched in binary terms, which were incompatible with laissez-faire capitalist democracy. The two opposing terms were social democracy or collective democracy. The new electorate would be working class by default, so the question was how to create 'democracy' and not allow in the disease of socialism. The nature of representational government was the prize. Government as envisaged by John Stuart Mill was now incompatible with the very people who would soon gain the vote.

Change came when it was inevitable, the weight of public opinion balanced against the self-preservation of politicians whose interests were increasingly pooled within the emerging modern political machine. From the legislation of 1867 onwards until the end of the century, ordinary people took an inordinate interest in political issues by attending debates and educational political groups, cheering meetings, joining parties, voting and decorating their homes with the portraits of politicians.

Why this happened as it did is not entirely clear. It may be partially explained by talking about a newer and freer sense of public opinion, but it may be more selfish than that. What is clear is that the political machine replaced not only aristocratic patronage but also churchgoing as a means both to material and spiritual advancement. Participation in politics was, as before, a road to betterment, but now it was also seen as a particular moral duty. In the boroughs, there was a feeling that there should be inherent rewards built into the system. To give such rewards was a way of keeping loyalty amongst supporters who were felt by the 'grandees' (of whatever party) to be of particular local use. Thus, this new party loyalty would prove to be a boon to local advancement into the type of positions admirably suited to obedient party members. These might include postmasterships, roles as magistrates (which were difficult to obtain without party patronage), jobs in the civil service and ultimately perhaps a mayoralty in a borough. This system remained largely unchanged until 1914, with only the exception of the meritocratic civil service reforms, which themselves could be 'rigged'.

National politics quietly replaced the politics of the local parish and national issues replaced local problems in the mind of voters. After 1888, elected county councils finally replaced the antiquated system of quarter sessions run by local magistrates, and by 1894, parish councils came into existence, thus completing 'democracy' from the local village parish to Parliament at Westminster. In the 1890s, newspapers started to note gains and losses not by personality, but by party. The party machine had replaced aristocratic oligarchy. What did the rise of 'American democracy', as it was called, mean in practice? The verdict was difficult to calculate, the ends far exceeding, yet also far short in some ways, of the Chartists' demands of the 1830s and 1840s.

Nineteenth-century parliamentary reform meant increasing popular participation in politics, but popular participation may be viewed from different perspectives. From one point of view, popular participation meant the achievement of a sense of personal and social fulfilment in politics. The extension of the franchise gave men human dignity. The style of the best popular leaders of the period – Richard Cobden and Gladstone in particular – added to this a certain elevation of the mind and spirit, a changed attitude to the world achieved almost entirely by the force of political rhetoric. But there was another side to the picture. Popular participation also meant 'social control' – the incorporating of men outside the conventional structure of society into its fabric so that they had no choice but to be interested in its preservation.

For many people, now made politically aware by the continual agitation for franchise reform of the previous 100 years, democracy had proved to be a trap. They saw themselves as only enfranchised to vote, but not to participate, something they were rigorously excluded from by the party machinery that was more centralised and controlled than before and less amenable to change, reinforcing the power of capitalism and the power of an aristocracy now wearing the guise of plutocracy. Instead of power, the populace had the vote. The vote had apparently only empowered the ill-educated. Real power remained elsewhere. The system seemed a sham to perpetuate injustice and it was for this reason that anarchism as a political creed continued to fascinate writers and thinkers into the early twentieth century.

Anarchist philosophy stood for cooperatve individualism, anti-statism, anti-capitalist and enlightened 'socialist' values, but other forms of socialism were determined by collectivism, statism and technocratic rule. The two branches of socialism would both be dedicated to the future. Anarchism was one branch of the general social democratic tendencies of which communism was the other, and the victory of one strand or the other was going to destroy the Victorian and Edwardian world and usher in future times. All politically advanced thinkers were assured of it. Lenin, writing in January 1918, was in no doubt of the final victory of socialist ideals; it was the logic of international modernity itself. 'That the socialist revolution in Europe must come, and will come, is beyond doubt', he predicted, 'all our hopes for the final victory of socialism are founded on this certainty and on this scientific prognosis.' Before the victorious armies of the Red Guard, international capital would surely fall; the revolution in Soviet Russia would be merely the prelude to pan-European revolution.

Yet in the 1880s, collectivism and socialism were the last things on the minds of the leaders of Britain's unions. The unions had now gained respectability by defending the rights and gaining privileges for their memberships of skilled artisans. Here there was no talk of collective action, brotherly solidarity or democracy. All was quietist and defensive, defending the gains made for the craft workers. Yet the change that Gladstone detected was also a change that the old unions could not resist either.

In Britain the rise of collectivism separated from the concomitant idea of socialism early on, although both continued on parallel and occasionally convergent paths. Collectivism started almost by accident in the workplaces of East London. It happened simply enough. Three matchgirls working in the Bryant and May factory had spoken to the socialist journalist Annie Besant about their dreadful working conditions. They had been sacked and the workforce, which mainly consisted of young Irish girls, had turned out to protest and seek out journalists to hear their point of view in Fleet Street.

The young female workers at the Bryant and May factory in the East End of London (now fashionable apartments) had by default changed the horizon, for they had proved the collective power of the unskilled labouring person. It was a lesson learned and, soon after, Ben Tillett formed the Tea Operatives and General Labourer's Union to challenge the owners of the new docks in Tilbury for an extra penny on the hourly rate. Tillett recalled the elation of the strike and negotiations, and the fact that it was the 'beginning of the social convulsion which produced the "New Unionism"'.

More disturbances followed in 1889 when the gas workers at Beckton Gas Works in the East End (situated next to the docks as well as being the largest gasworks in the world) were forced to work with heavier, more difficult machinery, which effectively stopped them being able to take a break. One of their workers, Will Thorne, down from Birmingham after losing his job for insubordination, tried unsuccessfully to organise the unionisation of the labourers and to use the power of the new union to fight for the right to fair and equitable breaks and working conditions. His annoyance at his failure created sufficient frustration to call a meeting at the nearby Canning Town Public Hall on 31 March, where, assisted by Tillett and others, he persuaded 800 men to join the National Gas Workers and General Labourers Union. This momentous outcome was followed by many thousands joining in the next two weeks. Thorne recalled that:

> The formation of our union was the definite establishment, and the beginning of what has been termed 'New Unionism'. It was the culmination of long years of socialist propaganda amongst the underpaid and oppressed workers. Politics had been preached to them, vague indefinite appeals to revolution, but we offered them something tangible, a definite, clearly lighted road out of their misery, a trade union that would improve their wages and conditions; that would protect them from the petty tyranny of employers ... They came in [their] thousands, within six months we had made over 20,000 members in different parts of the country. We showed the way to the dockers and other unskilled works; our example and our success gave them hope. Within a short time the 'New Unionism' was in full flower.

On the Thames, over 150,000 men worked in the docks and in the many factories that bordered it. Most were unskilled dock labourers working on an antiquated system, whereby they queued for work at the dockyard gate and were randomly chosen by a 'sweater'. One observer noted the humiliation and misery of these 'human rats' fighting to get work. Less than 20 per cent even had the vote in the areas near the docks. And yet it was not lost on the workers that, powerless as they were, if they banded together, they would close the whole of the docks and thus effectively paralyse the heart of the Empire.

A strike on the docks on the south side of the Thames had been resolved by negotiation with Tillett's organisation early in August 1889, but the trouble on the northern bank over pay and conditions had reached a stalemate. Tillett was joined in the fight that was now inevitable by the leader of the stevedores, Tom McCarthy, and by Tom Mann and John Burns of the SDF. Their demands clearly showed that the poor had had enough of unfair piece work, but the implications were huge. The demands were for the abolition of plus and contract systems, a minimum half-day period of employment, the taking on times to be reduced to two per day, overtime to be penalised by raising the rate of difference from one to two pennies per hour and, crucially, the basic hourly rate to be raised to 6d.

By 22 August, all the various groups who kept the port functioning – and there were many, both skilled and unskilled, on the water and on land – had banded together and brought Thames traffic to a halt. The Joint Committee of the dock owners, however, stood defiant and the strikers waivered. They needed stiffening, by leafleting, by the actions of mass-picketing organised by Tillett, and by street-corner oratory, rallies and marches. Tillett recalled one great march:

First came a posse of police, behind whom the marshals of the procession, with axes and scarfs, reserved a clear space for the leaders ... Next came the brass band of the stevedores, following which streamed the multitude whose calling lay at the docks and riverside. Such finery as they boasted in the way of flags and banners had been lent by friendly and trade societies ... there were burly stevedores, lightermen, ship painters, sailors and firemen riggers, scrapers, engineers, shipwrights, permanent men got up respectably, preferably cleaned up to look like permanents, and unmistakable casuals with vari-coloured patches on their faded greenish garments; Foresters and Sons of the Phoenix in gaudy scarfs; Doggett's prize winners, a stalwart battalion of watermen marching proudly in long scarlet coats, pink stockings and velvet caps with huge pewter badges on their breast, like decorated amphibian huntsmen; coalies in wagons flashing aggressively for coppers with bags tied to the end of poles.

John Burns, attending the Trades Union Congress (TUC) in Liverpool in 1890, gives us a picture of these newest union members and contrasts them to the 'aristocracy of Labour' whom they had now joined as equals:

> The 'old' delegates differed from the 'new' not only physically but in dress. A great number of them looked like respectable city gentlemen; wore very good coats, large watch-chains and high hats – and in many cases were of such splendid build and proportions that they presented an aldermanic, not to say a magisterial, form and dignity.

> Among the 'new' delegates not a single one wore a tall hat. They looked workmen. They were workmen. They were not such sticklers for formality or Court procedure, but were guided more by common sense.

The older unions still sneered at the new 'Londoners' in the organisation and disregarded or belittled their demands. This was because traditionally the union membership was clustered in the towns of the north, divided between coal miners, engineers and cotton workers, who made up 750,000 votes, or one-half of the whole TUC. Such concentration led to regional and vocational snobbery, a snobbery which infuriated Will Thorne, who recalled:

> Stung by the boorishness of the old school, I jumped to my feet and hurled this rebuke at them, when they jeered and laughed at one of the general labour representatives: 'A firewood cutter is as good as an engineer. Are you only going to listen to engineers, and not to unskilled workers?' I was wild with rage, but my reprimand went home, and the speaker that I had interceded for was from then onwards given a fairer hearing.

The peaceful and disciplined demeanour of the marching strikers impressed many who watched and also may have given some pause for thought about the new strength of the masses. Engels, watching on the sidelines, looked on with awe at the risen masses and saw in their solidarity the first flickers of the revolutionary spirit that he and Marx had predicted:

> The people are throwing themselves into the job in quite a different way, are leading far more colossal masses into the fight, are shaking society more deeply, are putting forward much more far-reaching demands: eight hour day, general federation of all organizations, complete solidarity. Thanks to Tussy [i.e. Eleanor Marx] women's branches have been formed for the time – in the Gasworkers and General Labourers Union. Moreover, the people regard their immediate demands only as provisional although they themselves do not know as yet what final aim they are working for. But this dim idea is strongly enough rooted to make them choose only openly declared Socialists as their leaders. Like everyone else they will have to learn by their experiences and the consequences of their own mistakes. But as unlike the old trade unions, they greet every suggestion of an identity of interest between Capital and Labour with scorn and ridicule, this will not take very long.

The optimism shown by Engels was based not only on what was going on in the London docks, but also on the fact that socialism seemed to be rising unstoppably. Two congresses, one socialist and one on behalf of labour, had been held in Paris during 1889; Engels, Eleanor Marx, James Keir Hardie and William Morris had attended the socialist convention, whilst the labour wing had been attended by Henry Hyndman and the SDF, by the Fabians and by the older trade unions. Very soon, both groups would make an uneasy alliance during the Second International. The forces of opposition, resistance and revolution may have been split, but there was the feeling that a wind was stirring that would soon turn into a cleansing gale, a gale led by the gathering force of new unionism. Watching a march on 4 May 1890, Engels remarked that, finally, 'the English working class [had] joined up in the great international army ... the grand-children of the old Chartists [were] entering the line of battle'.

Yet the dock strikes inevitably had to be settled by negotiations over wages and working conditions, not the dictatorship of the proletariat, the relatively restricted demands of the workers had to be negotiated and a living had to be resumed. Limited and specific demands would not bring about the revolution after all. Most of the strikers had Irish origins, so it made sense for Cardinal Manning to agree to bring the two sides together for what proved to be difficult and protracted talks. Manning was of the establishment and was trusted by the owner's committee, but he also tried to have compassion for the workers (mostly Catholic and Irish) who were his flock and who would be steered away from revolutionary thoughts by some compassionate Catholicism. He was heard to remark that there was 'no justice, mercy, or compassion in the Plutocracy', but he advocated little more than general compassion. Agreement was found and the strike was halted at a mass rally in Hyde Park on 14 September 1890. A march through the East End followed the next day, whilst a few days before, on 9 September, John Burns had stood on Tower Hill and declared: '[I] can see a silver gleam – not of bayonets to be imbued with a brother's blood, but the gleam of the full round orb of the docker's tanner.' In his socialist history of the strike, John Charlton has suggested that the workers' actions were such a resounding victory because of:

> The energy, determination and organisational skill of Ben Tillett, the physical strength and tactical sense of Tom Mann and the rhetorical power, flamboyance and daring of John Burns [who] were a formidable combination, perhaps the most powerful in the whole of British labour history.

What it resoundingly proved was the collective power of the unskilled and the pressure they could bring to bear, even without the vote. Such collectivism would provide the model for governmental measures which reflected the collectivist ideas of approximately 39 million subjects who provided the luxuries for a middle class of approximately 4.1 million and an upper class of only 1.4 million. Simple numbers had tipped the balance.

Engels may also have taken heart from the wave of school strikes in 1889. Banners were emblazoned with 'NO CANE' and other libertarian slogans, and schoolboys had worn red 'liberty' caps and flown the red flag. Moral outrage followed with the educational press in apoplexy. In its edition of October/November 1889, the *Educational News* declared that 'schoolboy strikers ... are simply rebels. Obedience is the first rule of school life ... School strikes are therefore not merely acts of disobedience, but a reversal of the primary purpose of schools. They are on a par with a strike in the army or navy ... They are manifestations of a serious deterioration in the moral fibre of the rising generation ... They will prove dangerous centres of moral contamination'.

There was little change in the situation for schoolchildren in the following century. During September 1911, many working-class pupils saw school as little more than legalised prison for the children of labouring families. The previous summer had seen protracted and bitter trade union action; it was these disturbances that ignited the resentments of those schoolkids whose parents were already striking. The pupils almost universally came from slum families, driven to a bare subsistence because of unemployment. The children looked at their parents' plight and, imitating their actions, organised pickets and marched. It would be a lesson in political action for the future.

Such actions proved the power of mass movements, but for many middle-class observers, it also showed the importance of the herd mentality which had permanently suppressed individual free will. Social science 'proved' that men were impelled by the general laws of instinct and the species, and inner compulsions were relegated to impulses formed at birth. Determinism became the watchword of Social Darwinists and sociologists, the individual crushed beneath the weight of group decisions and social circumstances. The viciousness of poverty was innate, born of the very nature of its environment.

In May 1901 Gustav Maeterlinck, the occultist author of *Der Golem*, published a little book on the life cycle of the honey bee. Called *The Life of the Bee*, it went through 25 editions between its publication and 1935, and reportedly sold over 100,000 copies. Why did anyone queue to get a book that was purportedly a work on the nature of an insect?

Maeterlinck's book seemed to contain a secret code: a commentary on the complex nature of bee behaviour and an essay on contemporary life. In studying bees, Maeterlinck seemed to find the perfect metaphor for the 'loneliness' and isolation of the individual when outside or excluded from the masses, but also a means to explain the need of the controlling queen to return at regular intervals to the masses to 'breathe [in] the crowd' dwelling in 'the city'; the queen may be the hub of the wheel of society, but the whole was animated by the selfless effort of the 'workers'. The workers worked not merely towards turning into lived experience the political principle of state sovereignty that had been the backbone of republican government since Jean-Jacques Rousseau first enumerated it in *The Social Contract* in 1762, but towards a principle of sovereignty *embodied* in an actual queen. Such a society was a microcosm of Spartan republicanism 'where the individual is entirely merged in the republic, and the republic in its turn invariably sacrifices to the abstract and immortal city of the future'. Such sacrifices as are made by all the organs of the community are aimed at racial improvement and are at the 'cost of the liberty, the rights and the happiness of the individual', for 'as a society organizes itself … so does a shrinkage enter the private life of each of its members'.

The fears and dreams of late Victorian society are here enumerated as the necessary conditions for the future: collectivism based on the effort of the workers; centralisation and the growing complexity of urban life; the subordination of the individual and individual freedom to race survival, all set against an unchangeable social hierarchy with a queen ensconced at the head of the 'republic', immobile, immured, secret and magical. At the end of it all comes the inevitable apocalyptic crash of the cosmic-historical cycle rounding in decadence, abandonment and destruction as the swarm moves on and into a new era once the 'old queen stirs' and the city is finally abandoned, not in panic but deliberately and with forethought, all the bees 'patriotically' gathered round an ageing queen:

[The bees] will not leave at a moment of despair; or desert, with sudden and wild resolve, a home laid waste by famine, disease, or war. No; the exile has long been planned, and the favourable hour patiently awaited. Were the hive poor, had it suffered from pillage or storm, had misfortune befallen the royal family, the bees would not forsake it. They leave it only when it has attained the apogee of its prosperity ... Restlessness seizes the people, and the old queen begins to stir. She feels that a new destiny is being prepared. She has religiously fulfilled her duty as a good creatress; and from this duty done there result only tribulation and sorrow. An invincible power menaces her tranquillity; she will soon be forced to quit this city of hers, where she has reigned. But this city is her work; it is she, herself. She is not its queen in the sense in which men use the word. She issues no orders; she obeys, as meekly as the humblest of her subjects, the masked power, sovereignly wise, that for the present, and till we attempt to locate it, we will term the 'spirit of the hive'. But she is the unique organ of love; she is the mother of the city.

FIFTEEN
THE WAY OF THE EGO

As collectivism gained ground, what remained of individualism? The French Revolution with its ideal of the 'rights of man' had confirmed the absolute equality of individuals and had effectively destroyed any arguments for the concept of superiority by class or caste. What it substituted was a different type of inequality: that of each individual's mental capacity. Citizens could only be differentiated through the strength of their individual inner compulsions, an idea which soon became the ideology of the imagination, something considered unique, powerful and infinitely creative; an inner voice and an inner vision capable of being imposed on the world. It was this sense of the imagination and therefore the 'essential' inner and inexpressible self that meant that the centralist, socialist and communalist ideals of Victorian Britain were complemented by a set of ideals centred on the self-contained and autonomous individual who might be angelic or satanic by turns.

Romantic ideology turned the idea of the imagination into an idol. Imagination was attached to nature and nature was not only linked to man's moral vision but also to God through the sublime. Yet such a formula soon faltered as it was discovered that the self could reach the sublime without God and that, indeed, the self and its surroundings were permeable and crossed by dark instincts and desires that could not be controlled by conscious will alone. Dark forces might define the self as dark forces might warp society. To surrender to the self was also to release forces that might actually threaten the nation and predict its destruction. The dreamers of the future unleashed the dark desires of the self, desires of violation, derangement, fear, murder and drug addiction in order to release the destructive but revitalising forces that would sweep away the old order and bring renewal.

What was barely thinkable at the start of the nineteenth century was intellectual orthodoxy and common gossip by its end. The French Revolution, and its aftermath in Romantic thought, changed the political as well as the imaginative landscape so that those born after the cataclysm in France could not think as their forefathers had done before the coming of the Terror and every attempt to return to a settled past was thwarted by novel and unseen agitations.

The execution of Louis XVI may have been a political consequence of practical actions, yet it was also a profound shock in which new ideas of the 'person as citizen' flourished alongside the new politics that would embody the new rights and obligations of selfhood. This was an ontological as well as political revolution whose ideas infiltrated Britain and infected the brains of a few who needed to be quarantined for the good of the many. The disease of self-expression, individualism, of dreams of the triumph of the people or of the proletariat, and of that republicanism of the self that marks the advanced thinkers of the period could not be put back in the bottle – the genie of revolution was out for good and in the manure of Victorianism the seeds of change sprouted.

The embodiment of rights was already compromised by the possibility of its divisibility. 'Despondency and melancholy' were from now on, if one is to believe William Wordsworth, the lot of those poets and others too sensitive for the world. Dorothy Wordsworth, Mary Lamb and Samuel Taylor Coleridge were amongst British victims of this new sensitivity to life.

Coleridge became increasingly obsessed with the relationship between mental, imaginative, emotional and physical states. In May 1801, he told his friend Thomas Poole his self-diagnosed problems in great detail, whilst in a letter of 1804, he could write that 'I was heart-sick and almost stomach-sick of speaking, writing, and thinking about myself'. Such morbid interest in the ego led him to invent a word for his woes: 'psychosomatology'. His interest in the imagination, which he explored in great detail in *Biographia Literaria*, also led him to formulate a theory that equated the 'I' of self with the self-contained 'I' of God. Yet this equation was riven with anxiety. Coleridge had begun taking laudanum (opium in solution – usually with wine) as early as 1796; a decade later he was an opium addict and by December 1813 was so deranged by the addiction that he feared the sort of mental collapse that might confine him to a straitjacket:

> An indefinite, indescribable, TERROR [sic], as with a scourge of ever restless, ever coiling and uncoiling SERPENTS drove me on from behind ... From the sole of my foot to the crown of my head there was not an inch in which I was not continually in torture.

It was an age of madmen during the reign of that Hanoverian George III who was himself a mad king. The old 'history' of theological conflict ended in the American and French republican experiments. From now on, 'history' would be about the conflict of political ideologies. Yet 'post history' was also the age of modern psychology and existential aloneness. The new political and imaginative landscapes blended and merged until one was unthinkable without the other, the social world now encompassing an inner world of the self every bit as important as the world of action. A radical change of human consciousness had occurred whose consequences would reverberate throughout the next 200 years.

The Byronic personality which was one consequence of the French Revolution's influence outside France had unwittingly discovered the path to Hell alongside the path to Heaven, and no one knew that road better than the Marquis de Sade, whose *Justine* was published in 1791 and was reissued continuously until 1801, when the orders of Napoleon put a temporary end to its career. In *Justine*, the heroine does not win through on virtue alone or enjoy a virgin's peace at the novel's happy ending; instead, she is debauched, sodomised, raped, crucified and branded for the sake of her virtue and finally cut to pieces by a lightning strike. At the heart of the novel, however, is not sex, but nature and the impulses of nature, a survival of the fittest in a nightmare world. 'Is this existence other than a passage each of whose stages ought only, if he is reasonable, to conduct him to that eternal prize vouchsafed by Virtue?' asks the deluded Justine. 'Who will avenge us if not God?' she cries in despair; 'No one ... absolutely no one', answers one of her torturers. Another villain makes it quite clear that nature is cruel and blind and actually opposed to Christianity: 'The doctrine of brotherly love is a fiction we owe to Christianity and not to Nature', exclaims one of the monks in the Abbey in which Justine is incarcerated.

The forces unleashed by the concept of equality amongst autonomous individuals living in a material world also destroyed the idea of an all-powerful and invisible God whose presence regulated morals. What was left was a free-for-all where the only drive was that of the 'will to power'. Yet this drive had as its goal only destruction, both social and personal. Here democratic 'man' was spurred on by the quest for forbidden, occult and arcane knowledge, where he became a 'moral' aristocratic. In rising above the mass of mankind and in experiencing the exquisite tortures of destruction, the adventurer in arcane realms rises to a transcendence of feeling denied to the rest of us, in the gutter but looking at the stars, as Oscar Wilde had it.

'The puddle of voluptuousness', as one revolutionary moralist put it in the eighteenth century, was not extinct by the nineteenth century, nor was the cleansing of the Augean Stable ever completed by the moralists. It just took on a new life, now epitomising the revolutionary stance of individualists. One such was the essayist Thomas de Quincey, lowly born, a runaway from his school in Manchester, a tramp, a dosser on floors in London, a friend of prostitutes and Jews and a self-styled 'opium-eater' at the age of 17. London would be de Quincey's haunted city, a city where he first obtains opium from a druggist near the Pantheon on Oxford Street, where he sleeps on the floor of an attorney's house in Soho, which he shares with a servant girl who believes a locked room contains the secrets of Bluebeard and where he encounters 'Ann' the 'streetwalker', whom he falls in love with but never learns her last name or even if she really existed.

Through the haze of drug memories, London became a fluid form, now clear and close, now receding. London was de Quincey's visionary city at once present and imagined or 'recalled' in the way Romantic poets had imagined such things might be recalled in the mind's eye. Just before sleep each night and in his mind's 'theatre', de Quincey would first project the waking visions that would haunt his dreams, dreams that were enhanced by opium.

De Quincey is best known as the author of *Confessions of an English Opium Eater* (1821 and revised in 1856), in which he explored the dark corners of an addiction he relished both for its popular and its 'wicked' appeal. In many ways it is a Victorian book produced in anticipation of the Victorian era and reissued during the period. De Quincey was one of the first to recognise the significance of the inner world of the imagination, 'that inner world – that world of secret self-consciousness – in which each of us lives a second life apart and with himself [sic] alone'. What comes with this inner world is the idea not only of the public mask but also of the schizophrenic personality. Dorothy Wordsworth once commented that '[De Quincey's] whole time and thought are employed in deceiving himself, and seeking to deceive others'. He would nevertheless start a trend in which masks, make-up and deception – the very surface of things – would for some become the exact and only truth to existence, the very age itself a simulacrum of emptiness which needed to be filled with yet more lies from inner space in which murder lurks and drugs accommodate. The man who made drug taking respectable in Victorian Britain was also the man who ushered in the very British, very Victorian version of perversity. Murder replaced de Sade's sexual power as the key to epicurean living. And murder was closely related to the mysteries of drug addiction, as de Quincey reminded his readers:

> The original etymology of the word Assassins itself, as the name of the community, is not so certain. Skeat sets it down as simply the Arabic hashishin, 'hashish-drinkers', from the fact or on the supposition that the agents of the Old Man of the Mountains, when they were detached on their murderous errands, went forth nerved for the task by the intoxication of hashish, or Indian hemp.

Drugs and murder, and ghastly good taste. De Quincey was the inheritor of that perverse Sadeian epicurianism first made public by the likes of William Beckford, the millionaire author of the gothic Arabian tale *Vathek*, a tale in which the exhausted physical indulgence of the main character and an ennui produced by being able to afford everything without challenge gives way to the only deal left on the table – that with Satan himself.

De Quincey, not being a millionaire, could only enjoy the fantasy of that epicurean taste in which the wealthy Aleister Crowley was to indulge so successfully and Oscar Wilde so disastrously later on in the century. De Quincey 'invents' the epicureanism of those who cannot afford to be epicurians, whose pockets are not deep enough, but whose imaginations are sufficient to make up the deficit. Like Wilde and Crowley, de Quincey sees perversity as the basis of all good taste, or at least the taste that matters in the nineteenth century. Thus having indulged in drugs, he ventured into murder, humorously admittedly, in the style of the satires of Jonathan Swift, but with enough edge of curiosity and indulgence to make the reader quite wonder if the joke isn't, in the end, his own blunted desire rather than repulsion.

De Quincey's *On Murder Considered as One of the Fine Arts* was serialised in *Blackwood's Magazine* beginning in 1827. In the following extract, published in *Blackwood's Magazine* in November 1839, the author pretends to be a connoisseur of murder as others are connoisseurs of fine wine or objets d'art:

> A good many years ago … I came forward in the character of a dilettante in murder. Perhaps dilettante is too strong a word. Connoisseur is better suited to the scruples and infirmity of public taste. I suppose there is no harm in that, at least. A man is not bound to put his eyes, ears, and understanding into his breeches pocket when he meets with a murder. If he is not in a downright comatose state, I suppose he must see that one murder is better or worse than another, in point of good taste. Murders have their little differences and shades of merit, as well as statues, pictures, oratorios, cameos, intaglios, or what not.

The club which our dilettante creates for those of similar interests holds annual dinners at which the members eye each other as potential victims, even if murder as such is scrupulously avoided, at least by the

'President', de Quincey himself, as a fictional central character in his own concoction:

> As to murder, I never committed one in my life. It's a well-known thing amongst all my friends. I can get a paper to certify as much, signed by lots of people. Indeed, if you come to that, I doubt whether many people could produce as strong a certificate. Mine would be as big as a breakfast tablecloth. There is indeed one member of the club who pretends to say he caught me once making too free with his throat on a club night, after everybody else had retired. But, observe, he shuffles in his story according to his state of civilization.

Unfortunately, the President has a pushy nephew whose ambitions offend the exquisite taste of the patrons. The members send a petition:

> President, we would do much to serve a relative of yours. But still, what can be said? You know yourself that he'll disgrace us. If we were to elect him, why, the next thing we should hear of would be some vile butcherly murder, by way of justifying our choice. And what sort of a concern would it be? You know, as well as we do, that it would be a disgraceful affair, more worthy of the shambles than of an artist's atelier. He would fall upon some great big man, some huge farmer returning drunk from a fair. There would be plenty of blood, and that he would expect us to take in lieu of taste, finish, scenical grouping. Then, again, how would he tool? Why, most probably with a cleaver and a couple of paving stones: so that the whole coup d'oeil would remind you rather of some hideous Ogre or Cyclops than of the delicate operator of the nineteenth century.

The eye would be offended by such oafish behaviour, for murder to be done properly must be done tastefully, must, above all, be artistic. It became the mantra of detective writers at the end of the century, but it was also the formula for a certain perversion of taste and decadence in feeling which made the hideous and grotesque palatable and enjoyable. Charles Baudelaire once announced to a friend in the middle of the century that:

> [He] intend[ed] to write a novel in which my hero will be a scoundrel, I mean a real scoundrel, a murderer, a thief, an incendiary and a buccaneer,

and who will conclude my book with the following little speech: 'And in the soft shade of this tree planted by my own hands, surrounded by a loving family, by children that adore me, a wife that dotes on me, I savour amidst peace and tranquility the fruits of my crimes.'

Such sentiments started to 'infect' revolutionary art and nihilist thought in writers such as Fyodor Dostoevsky and Mikolai Gogol, in Edgar Allan Poe and poets such as Robert Browning. And, of course, it shaped the way in which Jack the Ripper was perceived and why he remains an icon of late Victorianism.

Victorian morality was essentially based on personal and social restraint and a personality determined by restriction and guilt. If such restrictions were breached, they might lead merely to indulgence and vulgarity, but – and it was a big but – where those morals were determined by false values and a distorted vision, the breaking of that compact might lead instead not to mere sensuousness, but to a type of personal or social rebellion made legitimate by its activities precisely because it was defined and contrasted against falsity and mere appearances.

Thus, two types of rebellion occur in the fissure between conformism and doubt. Anarchist, Marxist or social democratic revolutionaries were usually conformist and conservative in their personal habits and lifestyles, but radical in their political demands, whereas personal or 'egotistic' rebels were often deeply politically conservative, but at the very same time broke the very norms of acceptable behaviour and did so in ever more extreme and bizarre ways. The rebellion of the ego against the centre and against the mass was determined by a feeling of superiority based on self-exclusion. It was also effectively open-ended as it measured itself against the false social premises and norms which blinded everyone else to the truth of their situation. Thus, having broken with society, both in terms of personal and mental habits because they were exposed as false, the ego has nowhere to go except inward into a solipsistic and ever-neurotic search for the values 'beyond good and evil'. Such was the case with Wilde, who was both the toast of society and its secret enemy. Wilde's decadence shows in such of his works as the banned play *Salome*.

Salome was originally written to cash in on Parisian bohemia's fashionable interest in the perverse as an expression both of artistic integrity and of revolutionary self-expression. Many others, including Gustave Flaubert, Joris Karl Huysman, Stephane Mallarmé and even an American called J.C. Heywood, had tackled the theme since the 1860s. Gustav Moreau had already worked the subject in paint, which in turn had influenced Huysman's *A Rebours* (1884), which itself had a huge influence on *The Picture of Dorian Gray* (1890). Wilde intended to shock audiences in the theatre, but the prose play was in fact a play unintended for the British stage and was written in French during 1891 and 1892 and published in that language in 1893. An English translation intended for the stage was produced in 1892, but the Lord Chamberlain forbade the play on the grounds of blasphemy (there was a ban on stage representations of biblical events), so it was published as a book in 1894 with plates by that most decadent of decadents, Aubrey Beardsley, whose own illustrations had to be toned down for fear of prosecution for pornography.

Wilde concentrates on the intense erotic atmosphere surrounding the meeting of Jokanaan (John the Baptist) and Salome, the daughter of Herodias and step-daughter of King Herod (actually an amalgamation of three historical Herods). In the play, Salome develops a sadistic erotic attachment to Jokanaan, which he rejects and which may only be slaked by Salome dancing the dance of the seven veils before Herod, who himself has a morbidly voyeuristic attachment to his step-daughter. The dance demanded by the epicurean Herod is, of course, the first theatrical striptease (although her body is meant to be bejewelled rather than naked at the end – a rather moot point), the outcome of which is that Herod offers Salome anything she wishes, a trap set up by Salome's jealous mother Herodias, for Salome demands the head of Jokanaan, which is brought bleeding onto the stage.

Salome is a femme fatale, a type of lunatic prostitute of an extreme type. She is, perhaps, borrowed from Walter Pater's description of the Mona Lisa in *Studies in the History of the Renaissance* (1873), a book

Wilde cherished as his 'golden book' and possessed in prison. In Pater's description, the Mona Lisa becomes a vampire:

> The presence that rose thus so strangely beside the waters, is expressive of what in the ways of a thousand years men had come to desire. Hers is the head upon which all 'the ends of the world are come', and the eyelids are a little weary. It is a beauty wrought out from within upon the flesh, the deposit, little cell by cell, of strange thoughts and fantastic reveries and exquisite passions. Set it for a moment beside one of those white Greek goddesses or beautiful women of antiquity, and how would they be troubled by this beauty, into which the soul with all its maladies has passed! All the thoughts and experience of the world have etched and moulded there, in that which they have of power to refine and make expressive the outward form, the animalism of Greece, the lust of Rome, the mysticism of the middle age with its spiritual ambition and imaginative loves, the return of the Pagan world, the sins of the Borgias. She is older than the rocks among which she sits; like the vampire, she has been dead many times, and learned the secrets of the grave; and has been a diver in deep seas, and keeps their fallen day about her; and trafficked for strange webs with Eastern merchants: and, as Leda, was the mother of Helen of Troy, and, as Saint Anne, the mother of Mary; and all this has been to her but as the sound of lyres and flutes, and lives only in the delicacy with which it has moulded the changing lineaments, and tinged the eyelids and the hands. The fancy of a perpetual life, sweeping together ten thousand experiences, is an old one; and modern philosophy has conceived the idea of humanity as wrought upon by, and summing up in itself all modes of thought and life. Certainly Lady Lisa might stand as the embodiment of the old fancy, the symbol of the modern idea.

Salome's eroticism is that of the necrophiliac and castrating Medusa, but it is also touched with homoeroticism; her intense sexuality a matter of disgust, abjection and polymorphous perversity:

> Jokanaan, I am amorous of thy body! Thy body is white like the lilies of a field that the mower hath never mowed. Thy body is white like the snows that lie on the mountains, like the snows that lie on the mountains of Judaea,

and come down into the valleys. The roses in the garden of the Queen of Arabia are not so white as thy body. Neither the roses in the garden of the Queen of Arabia, nor the feet of the dawn when they light on the leaves, nor the breast of the moon when she lies on the breast of the sea … There is nothing in the world so white as thy body. Let me touch thy body … Thy body is hideous. It is like the body of a leper. It is like a plastered wall where vipers have crawled; like a plastered wall where the scorpions have made their nest. It is like a whitened sepulchre full of loathsome things. It is horrible, thy body is horrible. It is of thy hair that I am enamoured, Jokanaan. Thy hair is like clusters of grapes, like the clusters of black grapes that hang from the vine-trees of Edom in the land of the Edomites. Thy hair is like the cedars of Lebanon, like the great cedars of Lebanon … Let me touch thy hair… I will kiss thy mouth … I will kiss thy mouth.

Salome does not ask, she demands the head of the Baptist as both a sexual favour and an aesthetic requirement, for she is the embodiment of antinomian desire and what she demands is that which dare not be surrendered, 'the head of Jokanaan', whose surrender will effectively destroy the old decadent order and usher in the future with the coming of the Messiah. Herod is surrounded by babbling fools (the Jews of Jerusalem) and barbarism (the negro slave who decapitates the prophet) and steeped in madness and voluptuousness, his every mental image bathed in the light of crazy sexual distortion:

The moon has a strange look to-night. Has she not a strange look? She is like a mad woman, a mad woman who is seeking everywhere for lovers. She is naked too. She is quite naked. The clouds are seeking to clothe her nakedness, but she will not let them. She shows herself naked in the sky. She reels through the clouds like a drunken woman … I am sure she is looking for lovers. Does she not reel like a drunken woman? She is like a mad woman, is she not?

Herod knows of and fears his future, for he is a prey to the same auditory hallucinations as Jokanaan; he too hears 'the beating of the wings of the angel of death'. The end of the old order begins when Herod inadvertently slips in the blood of the Captain of the Guard who has killed himself for love of Salome and whose body has not yet been removed. The past and the future are held in suspense as Salome is finally smothered to death. She, rather than Jokanaan, is the prophetess of future times; after all, what Herod fears most is that Jokanaan can raise the long dead, not the yet to be born.

Salome is not the prophetess of salvation, but of the coming of the end of a civilisation and of a specific era (the classical age). Nevertheless, she does not usher in the Christian era; rather, she foretells the post-Christian era where desire and self-gratification are all. The Sadeian framework suggests that death and sexual perversity are the ruling passions rather than the revelation of God. The play is therefore a nihilistic work and one that ends in the vacuum of utter meaninglessness. Salome is certainly one of the first characters to live beyond the 'law', but her death does not reinstate the old order; instead, it designates the beginning of the new order bereft of moral guidance beyond the self that seeks.

Wilde's egotistical sublime allowed him (or required him) to see himself as:

> a man who stood in symbolic relations to the art and culture of my age. I had realised this for myself at the very dawn of my manhood, and had forced my age to realise it afterwards. Few men hold such a position in their own lifetime, and have it so acknowledged.

In his stance as symbolic icon, Wilde took as his role model the poet Lord Byron, but unlike Byron, Wilde saw himself related to (rather than detached from) the late Victorian age as someone 'more noble, more permanent, of more vital issue, of larger scope' than that of his predecessor. Wilde realised that Byron's personal circumstances were the key to his 'celebrity' status in an age when the act of living was to be turned into the supreme art form and where the artist was inseparable from his 'condition': the life and the art were indivisible, the private and the public as one, lived in the glare of (late Victorian) international journalism. As the 'captain of [his] soul', Wilde allowed pleasure to dominate, but finally:

> Tired of being on the heights, [he] deliberately went to the depths in the search for new sensation. What the paradox was to [him] in the sphere of

thought, perversity became to [him] in the sphere of passion. Desire, at the end, was a malady, or a madness, or both.

That Wilde had such a supreme belief in personal destiny also allowed him the compensation of martyrdom ('absolute humility') when it was offered at the prosecutions he brought against the Marquis of Queensbury. His foolish attempt to corner the vicious Marquis and his refusal to escape to France during the trials were all a part of his complex and perverse personality, in which he was not only the perpetrator of 'vice' (he was well aware of the risks of 'feasting with panthers'; he enjoyed the danger), but where he also took on the role of self-created victim and martyr.

When confronted with the inevitable destruction if he continued his legal battle with the Marquis, Wilde adopted a typical pose – 'one can't keep going abroad', he quipped, 'unless one is a missionary, or, what amounts to the same thing, a commercial traveller'. Yet the humour and apparent insouciance had a darker significance which signalled a type of situation filled with inherent danger. It was this inherent danger that also suggested imminent personal metamorphosis: 'they beg me to be careful'. But Wilde would be careful of nothing: 'Careful? But how can I be careful? That would be a backward step. I must go on as far as possible … Something is bound to happen … something else.'

Imprisonment led to bankruptcy and bankruptcy led to further hounding by the Marquis (who was himself dangerously psychopathic), resulting in the final indignity of Carey Street and the Court of Bankruptcy, where Wilde was flanked by two policemen. He was now left 'completely penniless, and absolutely homeless', a true moment of existential crisis.

'Would you like to know the great drama of my life? It is that I have put my genius into my life – I have put only my talent into my works', Wilde confessed to André Gide. Despite the humiliation, Wilde was able to compensate for the situation by accepting his new role of the martyred Christ. This personal compensatory sublime replaced the more aggressive position taken up before his imprisonment – invulnerability had been replaced by eternal 'suffering' and the search for 'holy ground'.

He had turned from the perpetrator of 'crimes' into a veritable 'Man of Sorrows', the victim of Poe's 'imp of the perverse' where his position of 'pariah' was a result of the fact that he finally recognised that '[he] had ruined [himself]'.

Yet in that ruin was a rebirth, although one again outside the parameters of normal conduct in which supreme individualism is the only goal: 'Neither religion, morality, nor reason can help me at all. Morality does not help me. I am a born antinomian. I am one of those who are made for exceptions, not for laws.' Freed from 'reason' and from the 'religion which does not help [him]', Wilde turned to 'symbols' of '[his] own creating' where 'everything to be true must become a religion', but which must become a personal, rather than a social, faith.

Such a faith makes martyrdom the only recourse for the egotistical sublime where reversal is the model of artistic existence. Wilde saw his former life as one dominated by the age itself (which, of course, he epitomised, at least in his own head) and in which he was a 'typical a child of [his] age, that in my perversity, and for that perversity's sake, I turned the good things of my life to evil, and the evil things of my life to good'. His new incarnation as the martyred Christ was to be brought about by degradation as a vocation. 'There is not a single degradation of the body', he mused, 'which I must not try and make into a spiritualising of the soul.' From a personal 'state of rebellion', Wilde turned to the 'new life' of 'grace' offered to the contemplative self. Yet here also there had to be an absolute refusal of social norms, for, to Wilde, the thoughts of most people are the thoughts of all: meaningless mass thoughts of no consequence. 'Their thoughts are some-one else's opinions, their lives a mimicry, their passions a quotation', he mused.

For Wilde, this movement represented an advance into the altruistic ego rather than the self-obsessed and selfish ego, but nevertheless retained the core of the belief in the supremacy of the self over its social determinants, for the individual who followed the 'Christ-like life must be entirely and absolutely himself [sic]', because 'Christ is the most supreme of individualists ... not merely the supreme individualist, but ... the first individualist in history ... for [whom] there were no laws'. In aligning himself with the Christ figure, Wilde was able to 'abolish' the notion of historical social forces and reinvigorate the concept of personal destiny, thereby reinstating his own personal sublime: 'Since [Christ's] coming the history of each separate individual is, or can be made, the history of the world.'

In following this philosophical route, Wilde was able to defeat the 'middle-class mind' of 'the British Philistine'. He thus placed himself alongside those who live the law-beyond-the-law and with the 'sin and suffering' of Christ, and by attacking those middle-class values that he hated most, he was again able to take on that revolutionary position which 'seems a very dangerous idea'.

Wilde's death did nothing to diminish a reputation that might have been extinguished at the end of the century; in fact, his reputation grew. The cult of epicurean living became the absolute condition for Edwardian (and twentieth-century Georgian) avant-gardism and Wilde was its god. Extremes of hedonistic living could be found in the new night clubs such as the Cave of the Golden Calf, Cave of Harmony and Café Royale, where crème de menthe, cross-dressing and lesbianism were expressions of the new freedom. Paganism in all its forms, and occultism in its strangest form, mixed with Vorticism, Futurism and Imagism, and the ragged Bohemias of Fitzroy Square and Soho rubbed shoulders with country-house decadence, champagne and drug addiction amongst the children of the rich.

Foreign influences and an economic boom changed tastes and allowed those who could to pursue forbidden fruits. Where *The Times* merely saw 'a corrupt society', others sought explanations. The author Stephen McKenna in *Sonia,* his bestselling novel of 1917, suggested that there was:

A spirit of unrest and lawlessness, a neurotic state not to be disassociated from the hectic, long-drawn Carnival that ... may be traced from the summer of the Coronation [1911] ... The new money was spent in so much riotous living, and from end to end there settled on the country a mood of fretful, crapulous irritation. 'An unpopular law? Disregard it!' That seemed the rule of life with a people that had no object but successive pleasure and excitement and was fast becoming a law unto itself.

This was the first of the 'live fast, die young' generations whose kicks came from sex, drugs and fast living. For their parents, their world already appeared to be finished, their responsibilities and duties stripped away by the new democracy. In 1908, the Duke of Norfolk was convinced that 'our ancestors kept the political power in the hands of those who had property ... but their successors had destroyed that system, and placed political power in the hands of the multitude, and we must take the consequences'.

For the children of the old landed aristocracy now left without civic or political responsibility, there was nothing left except to live for the moment. They would dance to the tune of new money with artists, actresses of dubious repute, émigré aristos of even more dubious background, dancers, cross-dressers, Jews, Blacks and drug fiends. Drug-themed books and plays were everywhere and Lady Diana Cooper recalled years later that cocaine was served in salt cellars at smart set dinner parties. Indeed, it was only with the availability of drugs flowing in from America during the First World War and the effect that they were starting to have on morale that any effective legislation was brought in at all. Philip Hoare points out in his book of the period that:

From 28 July 1916, Regulation 40b forbade, for the first time, possession of opium or cocaine by other than authorised persons. In June 1918, it was announced in *The Times* that soldiers would henceforth require a doctor's prescription to obtain twelve named drugs: 'barbitone, benzamine lactate, benzamine hydrochloride, chloral hydrate, coca, cocaine, codeine, diamorphine, Indian hemp, opium, morphine, and sulphonal and its homologues, and any salts, preparations, derivatives, or admixtures prepared from or with any these drugs'.

It was the erotic conjunction of sexuality and necrophilia of *Salome* rather than the slick verbal duels of *The Importance of Being Earnest* that fascinated the literati of the early twentieth century and *Salome* found its expression in the bisexual and promiscuous Canadian actress Maud Allan (born Beulah Maud Durrant in Toronto in 1873), whose own family background included insanity and alleged sex murder. Maud's father was subject to weird 'fugues' and had once been robbed by drug fiends, at least according to her brother Theo, who had a history of strange beliefs until the day he was arrested for hacking to death two girls at a local church and the arranging their bodies in the style of Jack the Ripper; Maud's mother was said by the press at the trial to be 'perverse'.

When Maud came to London, she therefore trailed a personal history every bit as peculiar and perverse as the play she would be associated with. She was a femme fatale in the mode of Loie Fuller, Sarah Bernhardt, Mata Hari or Theda Bara and was received by her followers as a 'vamp' in the style of Dracula's wives and every symbolist female at the time. She was the epitome of sex; the first sex symbol for a decadent age. At first, *Salome* was banned in Britain after its notorious revival by Aurelian-Francois Lugné-Poe at the Theatre d l'Opera on 11 February 1896, but after performances in Berlin, Paris and Vienna, Maud's Salome arrived in London in 1908. The actress had plenty of publicity before her arrival. She danced, it was said, 'in naked sensuality', 'a delicious embodiment of lust'. In *The Vision of Salome*, Allan set London on its head. One review enthused in true decadent fashion:

> One moment she is the vampire ... next she is the lynx. Always the fascination is animal-like and carnal ... Her slender and lissom body writhes in an ecstasy of fear, quivers at the exquisite touch of pain, laughs and sighs, shrinks and vaults, as swayed by passion ... She kisses the head and frenzy comes upon her. She is no longer human. She is a Maenad sister. Her hair should be dishevelled, her eyes bloodshot. The amazing crescendo ceases, she falls to the ground a huddled yet wondrously beautiful mass ... London has never seen such a graceful and artistic dancing. It is of a magical beauty. But the beauty is magic; and the magic is black and insidious.

At her height, Maud also became an icon for homoeroticism, but others were emerging from the shadows.

Aleister Crowley was the man who took on the mantle of those who lived to *épater les bourgeois* and it was his form of antinomian revolt that marks a major theme in late twentieth-century thought: 'Do what thou wilt shall be the whole of the Law', the slogan of the abbey life which Crowley stole from the seventeenth-century novel *Gargantua*, became the rallying cry for the generation brought up on Timothy Leary. In Crowley is at once the fag end of nineteenth-century decadence and the beginnings of twentieth-century individualism. Crowley begins his career as a posh philander and self-proclaimed and self-published poet, but he ends his career as an occultist, showman, decadent (a bisexual absinthe drinker), drug taker (he took opium, cocaine, anhelonium and ethyl oxide) and prophet whose theatricality may often have been mere cockamany antics, but whose message of an absolute individualism based on magic, the supremacy of the self, sexual liberation and drug hallucination became the anthem for the all those succeeding decades which have led into the twenty-first century. Crowley is in the tradition of de Sade, Byron, de Quincey and Wilde, from whom he borrows, distorts and synthesises, adding as he does so a blend of Orientalism, Theosophy and Indian mysticism, duly eroticised and filtered through an essentially Symbolist imagination tempered by a revolt against all things Victorian.

It was a revolt against the self and against society that was always close to mental breakdown, to which G.K. Chesterton attested:

> I had reached that condition of moral anarchy within in which a man says, in the words of Wilde, that, 'Atys with the blood-stained knife were better than the thing I am'. I have never indeed felt the slightest temptation to the particular madness of Wilde [homosexuality]; but I could at this time imagine the worst and wildest disproportions and distortions of more normal passion ... I had an overpowering impulse to record ... horrible ideas and images; plunging deeper and deeper as in a blind spiritual suicide.

What Crowley craved was an apocalyptic debasement of the body from which all things might be born anew. His ideas were to some extent based upon the arguments of Max Stirner, whose *Der Einzige und sein Eigentum* was published and distributed in 1844 (although the title page states 1845), but appeared in an English edition only in 1907. Stirner, whose cause was disparaged by Marx and Engels and whose arguments were largely ignored as revolutions swept Europe and as organised communism came to the fore, was nevertheless an advocate of personal, rather than social, revolution. He argued that the concept of the liberal state had taken the place of both the Hellenic and later Christian concepts of the higher good. Where once one sacrificed the self for a higher moral or religious ideal, the nineteenth-century person sacrificed themselves on behalf of 'Man', the new religion of mankind declared in such statements as the 'rights of man'.

To regain the total self, the unique self, one had to withdraw obedience both to the concept of 'Man' and to the self-sacrifice required by the modern state. Only then could one have a real sense of who one was without the false morals of higher good, then embodied in the idea of liberalism which, having denied religion and effectively killed off belief in God, replaced these beliefs with 'humanity', a concept that had robbed individuals of their 'true' freedom by proclaiming it as the only freedom. Anything else was to be seen as 'slavery'. This freedom apparently now created competition or egotism, but actually produced the homogeneity of the liberal state which actually stifled the freedom of the individual. Only by discovering the 'un-man', the property that is the inviolable true self which is one's only property, can the unique individual regain his or her 'ownness'. Whether Crowley ever read Stirner is not recorded, but he lived out his philosophy.

Crowley's vision was essentially Satanic and theatrical: obsessed with the anti-matter of Victorian respectability, obsessed indeed with what was forbidden, abject, strange and distorted, a discoverer of what the will was capable of bringing forth from the perverseness of unconscious desire. His theatricality was at one with his magical practice and as he rose through the ranks of the Golden Dawn, or staged his occult rituals or even had sex, each was an act, an exteriorisation of the self. His interest was in that personal revolt which may be criminal in the eyes of society; his focus was the unmentionable bodily functions and natural mechanics of the anus from which the 'new' might be magically 'born':

The anus: locus of decay, death, the repulsive and forbidden – the antinomian journey is linked, surely, to all Faustian exploration of dark spaces, the Unknown and not just the high but the low. Curiosity is the motive force here: the Pandora function on man [sic], which motivates his pact with Satan.

Edward Alexander (Aleister) Crowley was born on 12 October 1875, the only son of a wealthy brewing family who were also fanatical and rather fearsome members of the Plymouth Brethren, his father prone to converting strangers and predicting the collapse of the Church of England and the coming of the Antichrist, his mother dour and complacent. Crowley was brought up a gentleman, became a self-proclaimed poet, was an accomplished mountain climber and a rather better than efficient chess player.

The Book of the Law emerged after Crowley's new wife Rose (his first 'Scarlet Woman') began to have visions in a house in Cairo between 8 and 10 April 1904. She was visited by an entity who was the minister of Hoor-paar-kraat, a messenger from 'the forces ruling this earth at present'. Here apparently was a spirit who possessed both power and knowledge and was able to predict 'events which had not yet taken place'. Rose was no medium, so to test her, Crowley took her to the Boulak Museum, where she was able to identify a funerary stele depicting Horus, the number of which was 666! The little 'book' that was afterwards dictated directly to Crowley from a dark man with a 'savage' face, who was called Aiwass, the minister of Horus, was Crowley's signature work *The Book of the Law*. The work that went on in a dark room over the two or three nights was no less than the explanation of the universe set out in recondite and occult Egyptian symbols such as the Goddess Nuit and Hadit or 'the winged globe at the heart of Nuit' who was Horus and whose age we had now entered. Although the book would form the essential heart of Crowley's thought, he took many years to return to it, instead developing a magical practice around what he had learned.

In *The Book of the Law*, all events were explained as part of a monadic system which is made up of numerous other monads. Thus, everybody is a 'star' or singular monadic entity unattached to his or her neighbours. What attaches us (to each other and thence to the universe) is the repetition in everyone of personal experience which turns this community of experience into a single entity or monad joined to the universal or cosmic system. This implies the extension of consciousness to include all other consciousness. If, however, we are stars in a solipsistic system, it holds that we must act for ourselves alone: 'Do what thou wilt shall be the whole of the Law … there is no law beyond Do what thou wilt', but it is a law tied by 'love under will'; 'love is the law'. This 'law' of the universe is set against 'Restriction', which is 'Sin'. Indeed, Crowley exhorts his readers and growing band of followers to seek enlightenment through the new spirit guides to 'tear down the lying spectre of the centuries'. In so doing, hypocrisy will fall away and so, Crowley tells us, 'veil not your vices in virtuous words', but let vice show itself for what it is as the virtue that has been hidden and is alone real. As everything in his life tended towards the dull and dreary, Crowley was always on the lookout for a means to 'dynamite the morass of mediocrity'. And so in these short phrases and well beyond his ability to predict the future, he initiated the 1960s and began the party.

As with Theosophy, from which Crowley borrowed as he borrowed from Buddhism, Hinduism and the Kabbala, the aeons turn until 'this present period [which] involves the recognition of the individual as the unit of society' and thus annihilates all social-based theories. To enter the new 'Aeon of Horus', as he explained in his appended preface of 1919, the old world must be abandoned:

The prevalence of infantile cults like Communism, Fascism, Pacifism, Health Crazes, Occultism in nearly all its forms, religions sentimentalised to the point of practical extinction.

Consider the popularity of the cinema, the wireless, the football pools and guessing competitions, all devices for soothing fractious infants, no seed of purpose in them.

Consider sport, the babyish enthusiasms and rages which it excites, whole nations disturbed by disputes between boys.

Consider war, the atrocities which occur daily and leave us unmoved and hardly worried.

We are children.

Crowley considers evolution to be essentially anti-social, because against the absolute freedom of the will, desire and personal choice untempered by social habit:

> Liberty stirs once more in the womb of Time. Evolution makes its changes by anti-Socialistic ways. The 'abnormal' man who foresees the trend of the times and adapts circumstance intelligently, is laughed at, persecuted, often destroyed by the herd; but he and his heirs, when the crisis comes, are survivors.

For Crowley, society at the end of the nineteenth century stood on the edge of an apocalyptic change. The period of the banal was finally ending and the age of the liberated individual was about to dawn, and with this individual the certainties of the old world and those of the new (which were only the outdated and outmoded expressions of past thinking) would also pass away. This new world would be an age that had outgrown conventional politics, democracy, censorship and modern consumerism. 'Abnormal' man would set history free from convention as the world 'Democracy dodders' in war, consumerism, 'shops acts, the motoring laws, Sunday suffocation and censorship'. Fascism and communism were merely the political symptoms of mass society, but 'the herd will be destroyed in mass … to assure the future of the race'.

Crowley was always an artist, and sometimes, at his best, an artist manqué, a symbolist and then later a surrealist in execution if not in intent ('Homard a la Thermidor destroys the digestion', he comically interposed in one of his most serious books, *The Book of Lies*). The system of occult law he developed and synthesised was called by him 'magick' and it consisted of finding ways to impose the individual will on a 'passive' universe and, by so doing, to go beyond material experience or give immaterial experience material form. It was, in one sense, the rediscovery of a system old as the hills, but it was also a very modern application of the Romantic ideal of the self-creating imagination of genius.

Crowley's identity was also protean, as he reinvented himself as AA, Master of Thelema, Frater Perdurabo or the numbers 666. He was also a contrarian, an antinomian through and through, often masking ideas in gobbledygook, cooking references or popular culture. The contrarian *The Book of Lies*, which he published in 1918, is subtitled:

WHICH IS ALSO FALSELY
CALLED
BREAKS
THE WANDERINGS OR FALSIFICATIONS
OF THE ONE THOUGHT OF
FRATER PERDURABO
(Aleister Crowley)
WHICH THOUGHT IS ITSELF
UNTRUE
BOOK OF LIES

It is a title at once reminiscent of Dadaist jokes and psychoanalytic investigation. In its preface, Crowley explains that he alone 'held in [his] hands the key to the future progress of humanity'.

Yet Crowley was no would-be messiah. Instead, his message – if it is a message at all – is how to live without externalities, how to create a spirituality that is of the body united with the mind in which all things are possible because all things are subject to the dictatorship of the will. The universe is, in effect, inside ourselves and matter is subject to it. 'Let us', says Crowley, 'create nothing but GOD', for 'the universe is insane' and 'pure chance ... rules the universe'. Because there is no intentionality in the manner of things or of matter, there can be no guilt or sin attached to actions which are good or bad according to how they affect the 'equilibrium' of the cosmos. The good sense of all other 'religions' is false because, based on the false consciousness of 'mythopoeia', Crowley is the progenitor of all modern occultism.

Crowley's contrarian attitude took him beyond Wilde. All Crowley's antinomian aphorisms are witty, but they are intended to be neither clever nor true, precisely because the universe contains its own contradictions and dualisms. Thus, all his sayings are negations wilfully intended to be meaningless and therefore unrecoverable within the logic of those trying to tie him to the common-sense perspective of society. In a section called 'Onion-Peelings' in *The Book of Lies*, he wrote that:

> The Universe is the Practical Joke of the General at the Expense of the Particular ... those disciples nearest to him wept. Then certain laughed. Others next wept. Others next laughed. Next others wept. Next others laughed ... But though FRATER PERDURABO laughed ... He also wept ... He neither laughed nor wept. Nor did he mean what he said.

By proceeding in this way, Crowley continued to maintain the mystique of a master adept, while also retaining a mask of inscrutability under which he worked. His persona was precisely a masquerade where the surface appearance substitutes for a 'deep' personality. This is de Sade reborn. In some senses, Crowley was always trying to escape that classification that would halt the 'exploration' he wished to undertake on behalf of his 'will power', where the deep mental strata somehow 'gives away' the man. Instead, he used the technique of externalising his will, allowing his 'personality' to express itself externally. He even owned a magic cloak that he thought imbued him with invisibility. He was invisible in the sense that he could not be seen by humanity en masse, hence when he went out with his cloak on, he was truly invisible. The fascination with invisibility was in his ability to warp the laws of physics by applying the mind to his existence.

For a man who wanted authenticity, Crowley was always masked. Indeed, a paradox of the mask was that it was indeed the true self with nothing below, nothing that suggested an unconscious or repressed sensibility, nothing, that is, that was available to the burgeoning world of pyschoanalysis. Everything was oddly on the surface. In his guise as 'MYSELF [sic]', he took on the political establishment as a revolutionary: 'I am not an Anarchist in your sense', he tells us; indeed, '[he] is against Anarchy, and for Feudalism', because, 'every "emancipator" has enslaved the free'. It is a statement too close to fascism to ignore, despite Crowley's rejection of all political discourse. The fascist 'will' rises above the mass and force social and psychic obedience, which in turn restores order, natural law and harmony, and in so doing brings that 'freedom' which is the return of individualism. 'It is the combination of his poetry, his personality and his life which makes him the most extraordinary figure of his age', thought the twentieth-century occultist Charles Cammell.

Collectivism was a type of liberation for many, bringing economic prosperity and social stability, while for others it was a disaster, creating a more bureaucratised society in which the factory system and its new 'experts' as well as capitalism were supreme and in which the experts and the new bureaucracies were stultifying the life of the individual, whose body was cared for but whose soul was starved. The answer for those less adventurous than Crowley and less foolhardy than Wilde was not to turn to drugs, magic, sex or the cosmos, but to confront collectivism and urban modernity with communalism and return to the land in order to deal with the spiritual malaise.

SIXTEEN
VEGETARIAN
REVOLUTIONARIES

The 'back to the land' movement, which began in the 1880s and has lasted in some form or other until recently, was a reaction to the industrialisation and urbanisation that threatened to swallow the very last field, tree and tradition. It was tied, as so much was, to the regeneration of the self as a social being. Its ideology was therefore socialist in the broadest sense. In his book *Merrie England* (1893), Robert Blatchford was quite clear on a return to 'primitive' socialist values:

> First of all, I would restrict our mines, furnaces, chemical works and factories to the number actually needed for the supply of our own people. Then I would stop the smoke nuisance by developing water power and electricity. Then I would set men to work to grow wheat and fruit and to rear cattle and poultry for our own use.

People wanted to return to a simpler life and reinvent themselves in natural surroundings, less in terms of a Wordsworthian sublime and more in terms of a cabbage patch one could call one's own. John Ruskin, who had taken a lead in these matters, wanted workers to return to a healthy life of toil. In his monthly published letters, which he started in 1871 under the title 'The Workmen and Labourers of Great Britain', he urged a spiritual renewal through clean air, water and earth:

> We will try to take some small piece of English ground, beautiful, peaceful and fruitful. We will have no steam engines upon it and no railroads; we will have no untended or unthought-of creatures upon it; none wretched,

but the sick; none idle, but the dead … we will have plenty of flowers and vegetables in our gardens, plenty of corn and grass in our fields – and few bricks. We will have some music and poetry; the children shall learn to dance to it and sing it.

Both Ruskin's social experiments and those of William Morris a little later were attempts to revive the feudal guild system either as a gothic Christian community or as an atheistic modern commune; both were essentially attempts to revive a mythical way of life. Ruskin founded communities, workshops and workers' education schemes, but most failed. Nevertheless, they inspired others towards handicraft and rural pursuits. Morris' ideas were not Christian – indeed, they were, in his eyes, communist – but were a decentralised communism which had 'evolved' from 'state communism' (to use his phraseology) into a localised anarcho-communalism based, of all things, on a return to a fourteenth-century past where well-made handicrafts, mutual aid and beauty had replaced urbanism, industrialisation and exploitation.

In Morris' *News From Nowhere*, the narrator goes home after a night's discussion at the Socialist League, the organisation Morris had founded with Eleanor Marx, Edward Aveling and others in December 1884, only to wake up in the future, which has been transformed into a socialist utopia after an uprising in '1952' following the suppression of a demonstration in Trafalgar Square. Morris, it appears, was still musing over the defeat of the radicals on Bloody Sunday in 1887! Thus, wish fulfilment would fill the gap that reality stubbornly would not. This new world is one of haymaking, conversation, beautiful ('comely') women, unpolluted rivers, gothic architecture, thatched houses and bright home-made clothing where happiness seems universal, 'centralisation', 'manufacture' and the 'gambling market' all having withered after being found valueless; Parliament is now a repository for 'dung' and Britain, having given up its empire, is a contented 'republic', the bain of 'cockneyism' having finally been defeated. For Morris, this utopian dream was a 'vision' of future times and future possibilities. Others looked to the past for their vision of the future.

Men like Edward Carpenter, Albert Fearnehough and Charles Fox revived the sense of the seventeenth-century 'Diggers' and became ardent followers of the advice in Henry Thoreau's *Walden,* which was published in Britain in 1886. Carpenter threw away his everyday clothes, denoting, as they did, class and social propriety, and devised a simple garb of Indian sandals, a woollen shirt and trousers. He also avoided meat to save money, all of which gained him admirers, although his advocacy of free love and open-air sex was more difficult to accept. Nevertheless, his example led both to the Guilds of Handicraft and the new school movement with its liberation of the schoolchild from the tyranny of the classroom. E.M. Forster recalled:

> The two things he admired most on earth were manual labour and fresh air and he dreamed like William Morris that civilisation would be cured by their union. The Labour movement took another course and advanced by committee meetings and statistics towards a state-owned factory attached to state-supervised recreation-grounds. Edward's heart beat no warmer at such joys. He felt no enthusiasm over municipal baths and municipally provided bathing-drawers. What he wanted was *News From Nowhere* and the place that is still nowhere, wildness, the rapture of unpolluted streams, sunrise and sunset over the moors, and in the midst of these the working people whom he loved, passionately in touch with one another and with the natural glories around them.

Yet where were the unspoilt wilds of 'England'? Apparently they were to be found in Surrey and in the Cotswolds (or along the Thames or in Oxfordshire for Morris and in the Lake District for Ruskin), where artists flocked to find the last remaining remnant of 'Ye Oldie England'. There was Gertrude Jekyll and Helen Allingham of course, William Sargent and Guy Dawber, and unknowns like Edith Holden and numerous others who might hire a cottage or commute from the town by railway and stay a weekend. Natural scenery and natural peasantry were what was wanted. England had to be saved from any more physical or spiritual degeneration. Octavia Hill began the Society for the Protection of Ancient Buildings (which later became the National Trust) in 1877 and everywhere there was an upsurge of indignation against ancient byways being blocked and commons being closed to the public or built upon. The National Footpaths Preservation Society was formed in 1884 as a result of the campaigns by Henry Allnutt (a man with a gift of an unfortunate surname to his detractors).

For men like George Sturt, who hated the wealthy, and for those who wished to find serenity in country living, the old idea of ignorant peasantry would no longer wash. Instead, in a remarkably short time, the rural bumpkin was transformed into the noble shepherd and village craftsman. The bumpkin was gone, replaced, in part, by the village idiot, but the idea of village life as idiotic and ignorant was swept away too. The elevation of the simple countryman found its apotheosis in the First World War, in which millions of the rural poor fought in France. Maurice Hewlett, for instance, changed the name of his published poem from the derogatory *Hodgiad* to *The Song of the Plow* in 1916 and A.E. Housman created the myth of the tragic nameless countryside in his elegiac and wholly imaginary series of verses called *A Shropshire Lad*, which he published in 1896 and whose themes are early death, vague patriotism, loss, melancholy and a wistful pastoralism which all seemed to represent a world passing, but one which had never truly existed:

> Into my heart an air that kills
> From yon far country blows:
> What are those blue remembered hills,
> What spires, what farms are those?
>
> That is the land of lost content,
> I see it shining plain,
> The happy highways where I went
> And cannot come again.

How could one recover a world that never really existed or that existed only in the imagination? Everything was apparently vanishing and many enthusiasts were precisely enthusiasts for the lost or the nearly lost traditional world they wanted to inhabit. Cecil Sharp was one, collecting folk songs from the aged of the rural scene. He was joined by W.A. Barratt and Frank Kidson, Lucy Broadwood and J.A. Fuller

Maitland. The Folk Song Society was founded in 1898 to combat 'our terribly overgrown towns' and the growth of 'pawnshops and flaming gin palaces', as Sir Hubert Parry, the man who would put William Blake's *Jerusalem* to music, remarked. The term 'folk song' was a new coinage of the period, now seen not as mere rural doggerel, but as our 'national music'.

This national music was an invention of a particularly potent kind. It fitted a mood of nostalgia and patriotism. Sharp published *Folk Songs from Somerset* (1904) and rearranged Sabine Baring-Gould's collection of songs, which were republished as *Songs of the West* (1905). Finally, in 1905, both collectors published *English Folk Songs for Schools*, the standard work until the 1960s and the basis of English folk music ever since.

Music was accompanied by dance and so 'Morris' dancing was also 'revived'. In 1907 Mary Neal, who wished to see women involved with what until then was a male preserve, called a meeting between Sharp, herself and other ruralists, who between them formed the Association for the Revival and Practice of Folk Music, which became the Esperance Morris Guild. However, Sharp established a rival group in the school of Morris dancing he founded at Chelsea Part-Time College in 1909. Two female enthusiasts, Maud and Helen Karpeles, also formed the Folk Dance Club in the spring of 1910. In 1911, the English Folk Dance Society was created to complement the world of village-made music.

Why dance? The answer was not traditionalist at all. Dancing was for the 'recreation of the workers of the world'. It was a 'team' or communal activity for working people created 'to take their minds off the daily drudgery which must fall to their lot', as the *Folk Song Society Journal* pointed out in 1899. England was now filled with May Queens, Morris men and olde worlde tea shoppes catering for the new craze of cycling.

All this was not really enough. The trick was to live a simple rural life, which was sustained by the individual and cooperative manual labour in a community. Such experiments had been tried throughout the nineteenth century and Pantesocratists, Spencians, Owenites, Chartists and Ruskinites had gone their own way to utopia and back via the bankruptcy courts. It seemed impossible to live apart from the global economy which had already arisen and the free-booted capitalism that all despised. The whole affair was complicated by its appeal, which was to city workers who could not cope with the realities of rural living and soon gave up hope. Agrarian communes were a dream rather than a sustainable reality and the early ones were socialist and Christian utopian in character.

The arrival of Prince Kropotkin in Britain in 1886 and the writings of Tolstoy created a new taste for anarchist politics and revived the notion of communal existence. The anarchist paper *Freedom* addressed the issue with a rallying cry:

> To the Anarchist, who places the happiness of men, women and children above all other aims ... from bad surroundings, bad conditions and hard and uncongenial work, there can be no cry more fascinating and so full of hopes as 'Back to the Land!'

This was a strange proposition – to go backward to find the future – and the contradiction showed. For the most part, the call to take up one's shovel was a cruel deception, if based on honourable ideals. City folk could not live as country folk and they soon realised the difficulties of crop seasonality, poor harvests and dreadful accommodation. Communes were founded near Sheffield and in the Cotswolds, while others were founded by workers and intellectuals near Maldon in Essex and by a group in Croydon created by the remnants of two previous rural movements, the Brotherhood Movement and the New Fellowship. Not one of them could sustain itself either in terms of food, money or clothes and each folded, often amidst bitter arguments and near-starvation. What was needed was another idea and it came in the garden city movement.

There had been utopian building schemes before, such as the pantisocratic dreams of the Romantics and the model villages of the Owenites and Chartists, but by the Edwardian period, the swing of anti-Victorian influences (if they may be called such) had allowed such plans, all of which had failed at first, to have a second, more successful flowering. It was true that very successful communities had been developed by the likes of Cadbury, Rowntree and Lever, but these were industrial in origin, philanthropic in motive and authoritarian in practice, benevolent ghettoes for privileged workers who forfeited their right to live in their grace-and-favour cottages when they left their employer.

Ebenezer Howard was born on 29 January 1850 to a shop-keeping family in London and, after schooling, went to work as a clerk until he decided to emigrate to the United States, where he got a job as a reporter in Chicago and met Walt Whitman and Ralph Waldo Emerson, whose ideas influenced his growing utopianism. Having returned to England, he was hired by *Hansard* to report on Parliament, but his reading of radical 'socialist' novels and treatises convinced him of the need to rethink the urban experience, which was almost entirely alienated from living in and with nature.

In order to succeed, Howard turned his attention to the city and attempted to rationalise its essence; his ideal city would combine the urban and the country, would be rational but organic (actually circular) and would do away with the growing blight of suburbanism altogether.

The urban regeneration that Howard dreamt of was a community of cooperation and artisanal communal work based around the reworking of the concept of the agrarian and the metropolitan, around the bucolic and the newly established idea of the suburban garden. To achieve his aims, he founded the Town and Country Planning Association in 1899, but he first put his ideas in print in *Tomorrow: A Peaceful Path to Real Reform* (1898; reprinted 1902) and then revised the book and republished it as *Garden Cities of Tomorrow*, in which, following the Digger ideology of the seventeenth century, he exalted his readers to get a 'new life' and found a 'new civilization', his slogan being 'Go Up & Possess the Land'.

The inaugural meeting of the Garden City Association was at Bourneville in 1901, where around 300 guests debated the value of the new life; at its second meeting in Port Sunlight, there were 1,000 attendees. Having industrial and Quaker links transformed the Association from one of cranks to that of visionaries advocating low-density housing for industrial workers in an 'experimental community seeking a novel environmental order'. Howard's vision was to unite the best aspects of the town and country into something that he called the 'town-country', where 'the people 'would find the best expression of their talents'. It was an ideal taken partly from the religious 'communistic' radicalism of the seventeenth century, partly from the socialism of William Morris and partly from the anarchist politics of Prince Kropotkin.

The socialist architect Raymond Unwin, who was a member of Morris' Socialist League, believed that:

> In the squares and quadrangles of our Garden City dwellings the spirit of co-operation will find congenial ground from which to spring, for there association in the enjoyment of open spaces or large gardens will replace the exclusiveness of the individual possession of backyards or petty garden-plots.

However, Howard's own original vision, which he was forced to modify, was to create revolutionary living space in which to found 'a new commonwealth'. His utopias did get built, starting with Letchworth in Hertfordshire in 1903. The towns that followed (Henrietta Barnett's Hampstead Garden Suburb, Welwyn Garden City, etc.) did not attract the proletariat; instead, they attracted freethinkers, utopians and agrarians looking to live out their ideologies of reform and 'the simpler life'.

Yet people did respond to this utopian call. The Garden City movement *did* include cooperative housing facilities like communal kitchens and halls, new forms of children's education and inclusive spaces for people with disabilities, and was renowned for attracting avowedly political residents like feminists and suffragettes, socialists, anarchists, simple lifers, vegetarians, anti-vivisectionists and the entire panoply of highly interesting and extremely intelligent people who usually went under the generic soubriquet of 'cranks' – the kinds of people attacked for 'fanaticism and crankiness [which] have caused them to take up freak science, freak religions and freak philanthropy', as one (female) critic would express it in the 1920s.

In England, the ideal was taken to the hearts of the liberal middle classes, who took to wearing 'rational' artisanal smocks and sandals and practising the virtues of those craft guilds advocated by Morris; in Germany, Howard influenced Weimar architects, while in Russia, his ideas were rethought in terms of urban regeneration and proletarian power. As such, he became an unacknowledged hero of Soviet reconstruction. George McKay points out that:

> Ebenezer Howard's brainchild, the collective house at Homesgarth, would become the unacknowledged basis for a new kind of city-block. The most famous prototype for this was built in 1929 in a Moscow park, the Narkomfin building, designed by Moisei Ginzburg – as in Homesgarth, there were no kitchens, while the glazed part of the block would house a library, gymnasium, laundrette, kitchens and cafes for the tenants. Family life was to be phased out in the Narkomfin and the other 'vertical garden cities' that were supposed to follow it, in favour of the collective rearing of children, leaving men and women to devote themselves to building a new society.

The unwritten rule of all 'back to the land' progressives was the refusal to take animal life and the belief in peaceful coexistence. It followed that alongside pacifism, one would find vegetarianism as the lifestyle choice of many. The movement in Britain had begun in the mid-eighteenth century, when people such as Charles and John Wesley, the founders of Methodism, their friend George Whitefield and the prison reformer John Howard decided to embrace the 'Pythagorean' way. Abstemious ways were seen as both rational and godly. In 1809, a vegetarian church coalition was formed in Manchester and William Lambe produced a report on *The Effects of a Peculiar Regimen in Sirrhous Tumors and Cancerous Ulcers*. His argument was that a healthy diet of distilled water and vegetables and nuts would prevent serious illness. He, in turn, influenced John Frank Newton, whose book *The Return to Nature* influenced both Byron and Shelley, both of whom became vegetarian for short periods, as being both rationally sensible and radically rational at the same time. Both believed meat eating led to a propensity for violence and war.

By 1847, the word 'vegetarian' had been coined and vegetarian restaurants began to appear in London. One vegetarian society was formed under the leadership of a charismatic called Joseph Brotherton and in September 1847, the British Vegetarian Society was formed in

Northwood Villas in Kent. This in turn was influenced by women's rights leaders such as Anna Kingford who had been forced to study medicine in France because she was barred from doing so in Britain, and who had returned to petition Parliament for the protection of married women's property. The daughter of well-to-do London parents, Kingford rode to hounds until a revelation turned her into an animal rights campaigner and vegetarian. She went on to publish a book, *The Perfect Way: A Treatise Advocating a Return to the Natural and Ancient Food of Our Race*, and to found the Victoria Street Vegetation Society, whose ideals overlapped with those of the Theosophical Society.

Annie Besant herself was a convinced socialist, atheist and Theosophist, something that led George Bernard Shaw to suggest she'd gone bonkers! Shaw himself was a famous vegetarian, influenced by his reading of Shelley and by personal inclination. He turned to a meatless diet in January 1888, visiting a vegetarian restaurant in Fitzrovia, the fashion then at its height for vegetarian places to eat. At the same time, Shaw embraced sexual abstinence as both healthier and more morally appropriate to his new lifestyle. All this was too much for his fellow socialists and meat eaters, who felt that he was somewhat of a prig. William Morris would abstain for good form when Shaw called, but Shaw's irritating eating habits (which were so pronounced that he sent cards to places he was visiting to avoid embarrassment) were too much for (Mrs) Jane Morris.

It was not Shaw's socialist views or eccentric clothes that alienated Jane Morris, but his meatless diet. Shaw later remarked that 'to refuse Morris's wine or Mrs Morris's viands was like walking on the great carpet with muddy boots'. William Morris, on the other hand, was sympathetic to vegetarianism, maintaining that a chunk of bread and an onion was a suitable meal for any man, but he insisted on a bottle of wine to wash it down. Mrs Morris, on the other hand, was indifferent if someone drank water or wine, but a meatless diet was to her a suicidal fad. Thus, Shaw succeeded in alienating both Morrises. Years later, H.G. Wells and Shaw got into a tiff when Wells suggested that Shaw was not a proper vegetarian because he took liver pills, described by Shaw as those 'chemicals'. It was a row that smouldered for years.

Pacifism went hand in glove with vegetarianism. In 1898, at the height of the Spanish–American War, George Bernard Shaw commented in the magazine *M.A.P.* (*Mainly About People*) that:

A critic recently described me as having 'a kindly dislike of my fellow creatures'. Dread would have been nearer the mark than dislike; for man is the only creature of which I am thoroughly and cravenly afraid. I have never thought much of the courage of a lion tamer. Inside the cage he is at least safe from other men. There is less harm in a well-fed lion. It has no ideals, no sect, no party, no nation, no class: in short, no reason for destroying anything it does not want to eat. In the Mexican war, the Americans burnt the Spanish fleet, and finally had to drag wounded men out of hulls which had become furnaces. The effect of this on one of the American commanders was to make him assemble his men and tell them that he wished to declare before them that he believed in God Almighty. No lion would have done that. On reading it, and observing that the newspapers, representing normal public opinion, seemed to consider it a very creditable, natural, and impressively pious incident, I came to the conclusion that I must be mad. At all events, if I am sane, the rest of the world ought not to be at large. We cannot both see things as they really are.

The question of political and moral certainty was posed in terms of insanity: either me or them and they are the deluded multitude. Shaw's well-known certainties were themselves based upon contrariness and his whole system was based precisely upon this dichotomy. The world was out of step and only one man was marching to the rhythm of the future – Shaw himself.

Here Shaw expresses himself in a 'new' creed: pacifism, one peculiarly suited to radicalism and especially tailored to understanding yourself as an outsider. Although the word itself was not invented until 1901 and did not gain general currency until the twentieth century, the idea had arisen after the Napoleonic Wars when a 'federating bond' between European nations had been mooted to end conflict forever on the Continent. This had failed and had been replaced by various peace societies mainly based on the American model, itself based around Noah Worcester. The London Peace Society, which later became the British Peace Society, was formed at the same time but independently of its American sister organisation and it held congresses on the model of the anti-slavery congresses. The British organisation gained prominent supporters such as Richard Cobden, but an attempt to hold an international congress in Paris was ironically frustrated by revolution. Nevertheless, in 1849 another successful attempt was made and 600 delegates turned up, including Victor Hugo.

After this date, the international organisation petered out, but the legacy remained. Cobden and his colleagues had hoped to persuade nations to make peace for rational economic reasons rather than pushing a moral agenda, despite its numerous Quaker and Christian members, but as the concept of pacifism crept into the radical imagination, it transformed into a moral hatred of imperialism and capitalist-led war, rather than revolutionary (and atheistic) war, which was seen as 'moral' and cleansing.

Pacifism was often implied in internationalism and the two ideas did duty as stand-ins for each other. These ideas themselves were absorbed into the holy trinity of socialism, international-pacifism and atheism that all radicals had to proclaim at the end of the nineteenth century as part of their protest against the past and their espousal of the future.

The most important conjunction of vegetarianism with pacifism and anti-colonialism was articulated by Mohandas Karamchand Gandhi, who was born on 2 October 1869 into a wealthy and religious family whose head became 'Prime Minister' of Kathiawar. In his search both for Indian independence and personal salvation, Gandhi embraced a deeper Hinduism that he had actually learned, in part, from Europe, being influenced both by Leo Tolstoy's *The Kingdom of God is Within* in 1893 and John Ruskin's *Unto This Last*, which he found in 1904. He also read Edward Carpenter's *Civilisation: Its Cause and Cure*, which proved highly influential. In 1889, however, having trained as a lawyer, he came to England dressed as a European. It was a burden soon lost and he settled down in West Kensington dressed in Indian clothes, eating vegetarian meals and drinking cocoa (having long before suffered agonies over eating meat). Here he met and was influenced by the idea of Helen Blavatsky, who had 'borrowed' ideas from Hinduism and Jainism and who introduced or reintroduced him to the *Bhagavad Gita*. As his ideas developed, he would improve on his personal ascetism, which included avoidance of sexual relationships (he remained married), disavowal of his sons, adhering to a strict saltless vegetarian diet mostly of nuts, not speaking on a Monday and self-abasement in order to focus the mind on the way in which the self could contact the masses and become one with them.

Gandhi borrowed the ideas he found in Ruskin and Tolstoy, as well as the New Testament and the Koran, in order to synthesise his lifestyle with a universalist set of beliefs that might be applied to social and industrial conditions, nationalism and anti-imperialism. Like the English ruralists whom he admired, he abandoned his own home for a communal ashram (with particularly puritan rules) and his formal clothing for a simple spun dhoti, turban, cloak, scarf and sandals; his main followers in India were, to the end, European intellectual émigrés of one sort of the other, who, having lost faith in communism or anarchism, looked to him to fill the spiritual void.

The spiritual void was partially filled by vegetarianism, a central plank of Gandhi's theories By the time of his death, Gandhi was living on a most meagre diet. Nevertheless, whilst in London, his time was often spent wandering the streets in search of sustenance. He recalled:

> I would trot ten or twelve miles each day, go into a cheap restaurant and eat my fill of bread, but would never be satisfied. During these wanderings I once hit a vegetarian restaurant in Farringdon Street. The sight of it filled me with the same joy that a child feels on getting a thing after its own heart. I saw among them [Henry] Salt's *Plea for Vegetarianism*. This I purchased for a shilling and went straight to the dining room. This was my first hearty meal since my arrival in England ... From the date of reading this book, I may claim to have become a vegetarian by choice. I blessed the day on which I had taken the vow before my mother. I had all along abstained from meat in the interests of truth and of the vow I had taken, but had wished at the same time that every Indian should be a meat-eater, and had looked forward to being one myself freely and openly some day, and to enlisting others in the cause. The choice was now made in favour of be vegetarianism, the spread of which henceforward became my mission.

Gandhi's vegetarianism and Hindu dislike of killing was at one with his pacifism and his belief in non-violent resistance, which he turned from a personal philosophy into a social movement known as civil disobedience in the anti-colonial international struggle. Effectively, he learned to make pacifism a weapon of political struggle. From his readings, he came to a rather legalistic conclusion: one must attend to the law as it is and decide after due deliberation whether it is just or unjust – if it is judged unjust, then one may 'resist'. Thus, he developed Satyagraha, something he had first used in South Africa during an industrial dispute, but which he further developed once he had understood the methods of the suffragettes. Satyagraha was the means of 'exerting moral force' to gain an end result, of imposing the will on behalf of a truth that could not be resisted. Hence, his pacifism was an active form of civil disobedience undertaken to humiliate or embarrass the opposition.

But this in itself was attached to an economic ideal of 'local development, self-sufficiency, and appropriate technology' based on the handmade guild system of those like Tolstoy, Ruskin or Morris. It is hardly surprising then that Gandhi's communalistic vision of 'economic equality' had to tackle the twin evils of money and class. This meant:

> Abolishing the eternal conflict between capital and labour … levelling down … the few rich in whose hands is concentrated the bulk of the nation's wealth … and the levelling up of the semi-starved naked millions … A non-violent system of government is clearly an impossibility so long as the wide gulf between the rich and the hungry millions persists.

No socialist would have disagreed. The ends were clear enough, but the means still remained shrouded in controversy.

SEVENTEEN
ON THE FRONTIER

For the more adventurous, the atmosphere of the late Victorian period and the Edwardian twilight was so much suffocating conformism, individuals hobbled by rules of social etiquette, social division and racial superiority which seemed not merely the artificial cant of a dead legacy but also the mask covering ignorance, brutality and dogma. It was in this atmosphere that the children of the 1870s and 1880s felt they had grown up and it was from this atmosphere that they had to escape, both psychologically and physically. This break with the past required the escapee to reinvent himself or herself as he or she thought he or she should be rather than as he or she was expected to act. For some, this meant nothing less than a rebirth into something altogether more exotic and intoxicating than an English lady or gentleman. It was, in essence, an adventure undertaken as an escape from self and country, an adventure undertaken without God or guidance and directed under the willpower of the participant alone.

In a sense, this took individualism to its ultimate frontier where a new type of beauty was discovered and a new sort of heroism was to be found in the face of the overwhelming presence of modern technological ugliness and imperial rapaciousness. For some individuals, the problem of how to live at the end of the nineteenth century required nothing less than a leap of existential faith, partly physical in undertaking and partly imaginative and moral in scope in order to escape from the banality of old England which had become, by degrees, some sort of comfortable pastiche of itself.

Nothing less than a new language would suffice to express this new communal vision. Ebenezer Howard took to lecturing in Esperanto, the international language invented by a Jewish opthalmoligist called

L.L. Zamenhof, who under the name Doktoro Esperanto published his new language in the book *Unua Libro* in 1887, the word itself meaning 'one who hopes', a book and a language designed to unite nations through non-aggressive speech.

Howard had advocated a new model of the urban environment, but this too was merely a bandage on the period's faults. For some people, nothing would do but to set out for the frontier, the very edge of the white man's civilisation, not in the pursuit of imperialism, as so many young men and women had done and were still doing, but in the quest to find a truer self through escaping the imperial regime altogether. This meant travelling further into the imagination than before and venturing into unknown territories.

In every case, the participant seems to have been energised by an imaginative and romantic dream of an elsewhere, more perfect, more exotic, more strange than that which could be found at home in the cosy shires, county towns or seaside resorts of England. Each in his way was a loner, living essentially in the dream world that he carried with him as a type of personal talisman, proof of his individuality, but which in time became other peoples' dreams too, so much so that the original individual quest was lost in the general myth surrounding it.

Archibald Belaney was born on 18 September 1888 to George Belaney and his wife Kittie in the seaside resort of Hastings, then a mixture of fishing town, middle-class gentility and working-class holidaying. Either way, it appeared the epitome of dullness and sobriety as Archibald grew up and increasingly he retreated into his fantasies. His father was born in 1857 and had a promising career ahead, but waywardness took him to America after a secret marriage in which his bride had suddenly died, as did a son after George deserted them. In America George appears to have settled in Florida during 1885 and had dealings with William Cody, better known as Buffalo Bill, with whom he may have travelled. What is known is that he arrived in Bridgeport with two women, his wife Elizabeth and another woman called Katherine.

After two years, Elizabeth escaped this odd ménage and 'moved' to New York, where she was reported by George to have died. He then married Katherine, who seems to have become his third wife. Returning to England with 'Kittie', whose maiden name was Kittie Cox whilst she was in America but who became Kittie Morris in England, they settled again in Hastings to the chagrin of his sisters and mother. For Archibald, his mother's origins were never part of this strange and perhaps sordid triangulation, but instead carried the romance of the American frontier. For him, Kittie was an Apache woman called Katherine Cochise, something that added to his growing obsession with all things Native American, which his father's stories must have excited. Nevertheless, his father's growing waywardness meant that eventually George drifted back to the United States, having abandoned both his wife and their children. Archibald grew up amongst spinster aunts and a loving grandmother and never saw his father again.

Whilst at Hastings Grammar School, a modest middle-class establishment whose uniforms were modelled on Eton, Archie, as he was called, developed his life-long obsession with being a frontiersman. This was not the schoolboy obsession with all things relating to the 'Wild West' that was the staple of bedtime reading and schoolyard games, but a genuine fascination with the lives of Native Americans and their life of resistance in the face of Western progress and rampant imperialism. A boy who essentially lived through his active imagination, Archie was someone who did not cultivate friends and was not interested in company, much preferring to go 'stalking' in the woods alone. Once when asked about this obsession with the frontier, not something easily accessible from Hastings, he curtly answered: 'No … I am going to become an Indian, and if I fight anyone it will be the white man who has been so cruel to the Redskins.' He told his uncomprehending mother:

Oh, Mother, you don't understand. It isn't the clothes. It's what they stand for. All this pokiness and stuffiness. I hate it. I was never meant to live like this. I was meant to be free, just as Father is. I swear I am going to Canada just as soon as I leave school. I am going to live with the Indians and become an Indian. I am going to forget the ways of white people.

The opportunity to escape came when Archie was 16 and, after protracted family negotiations, he boarded the *SS Dominion* for Canada to the freedom he craved and as far away from the Englishness that had come to suffocate him. Here he might be able to reinvent himself as what he felt he truly was – an American Indian.

By slow and painful degrees, Archie lost his English accent and took on the Canadian drawl, mixed with trappers and guides along the northern frontier, became tanned, lean and tough, learned to carry rifles, canoes and equipment, adopted native clothing, grew his hair long, tied it with a leather thong and took to native ways. He learned Ojibway and ingratiated himself with local tribespeople, and by degrees felt he had sloughed off the old life of England and reinvented himself as a 'half breed'; the frontier was not an escape perhaps, but a coming home. He now peddled a story of high adventure where his origins took him to an Apache village on the Mexican border. It was a lie, but oddly it was also a higher truth and it was to that truth that he lived his life. He was also developing an ideology of the self that would sustain his sense of homecoming:

> White men, redskins, and half-breed ... they belonged to that fraternity of freemen of the earth whose creed it is that all men are born equal, and that it is up to a man to stay that way. For in this society the manner of a man's speech, where he comes from, or even his name are matters of small moment, and are nobody's business but his own.

Indeed, by now, Archie had an existential vision, one which was not interested in the afterlife but which was filled with the experience of the here and now, with sunshine and fresh air and the joy of living in the wilderness. For the would-be native, this was to become his life's 'pilgrimage', although he had not realised it yet as he still had to earn a living taking a growing number of tourists on fishing trips or beaver trapping.

During the First World War, Archie joined up to serve in the Canadian forces and went dutifully to Flanders, where he was wounded and repatriated to Hastings to the family he hadn't seen in years. Flanders had been a terrible psychological shock and Hastings was an equal disaster. He married on a whim, abandoned his wife and returned to

Canada, his father's waywardness pulsing in his veins. Indeed, in some sense, he was always in search of the myth that was his father, his actions replicating that sexual flippancy and familial disregard for which his father was notable. He married and abandoned four women, of whom two were Native American with whom he had two children, but he was essentially a loner who along with his abandonment of Hastings had also abandoned the sense of family life, which was replaced by the wilds of his hut in the wastes of the north.

The cabins that Archie lived in were shelters perhaps, but they were the visible signs of a life made by deliberate decision, for alongside the native dress, this was a return to and commitment to the land of 'pilgrimage':

On all sides from the cabin where I write extends an interrupted wilderness, flowing onward in a dark billowing flood northward to the Arctic Sea. No railroad passes through it to burn and destroy, no settler lays waste with fire and axe. Here from any eminence a man may gaze on unnumbered leagues of forest that will never feed the hungry maw of commerce. A painted warrior stands post in his appointed place, his eagle bonnet spread in brave array; the paint work, the emblems, they have all been reproduced. The tokens are all here. Atavistic? Perhaps it is; but good has come of it. Every wish has been fulfilled, and more. Gone is the haunting fear of a vandal hand. Wild life in all its rich variety, creatures deemed furtive and elusive, now pass almost within our reach, and sometimes stand beside the camp and watch. And birds, and little beasts and big ones, and things both great and small have gathered round the place, and frequent it, and come and go their courses as they will, and fly or swim or walk or run according to their kind. Death falls, as at times it must, and Life springs in its place. Nature lives and journeys on and passes all about in well-balanced, orderly array. The scars of ancient fires are slowly healing over; big trees are growing larger. The beaver towns are filling up again. The cycle goes on. The Pilgrimage is over.

By the end of the First World War, Archie Belaney, who was proficient in Ojibway and was friends with various influential tribal members, was about to change his name and his identity. This led to his adoption in the tribe as Wa-Sha-Quon-Asin, Shining Beak or Grey Owl, the name he adopted from then on. He later married a French-speaking Indian girl called Anahareo whose hatred of white men and love of nature he shared:

> And that's something to be proud of in a country filling up with bohunks and dagoes out to the scrounge enough out of it so a lot of foreigners in Europe can be supported in a state of comfort new to them. You Indians have owned this country since God made it, but you had to leave it to a lot of immigrant Europeans to show what a rich place it is.

With Anahareo, Grey Owl set out again for the life of a trapper, but through her influence, the beavers he trapped came increasingly to represent the vanishing wilderness he wished to defend. Anahareo and Grey Owl started to adopt orphan beavers ('the little people') rather than trap them and now he started to write about his experiences in books and articles. This led to him being approached and recruited by the Ranger Service of the National Parks. By the time his fame had reached Hastings, he decided to return to Britain to lecture, where he became a figurehead for the environmental movement.

Belaney died aged 50 on 13 April 1938 of pneumonia. His legacy as one of the great conservationists was originally obscured by the search for his 'true' identity. He represents that mixture of late Victorian and Edwardian daring and eccentricity that, turning against itself and its age, formed the foundations of the future.

The cult of the body natural and in nature was another offshoot of those who believed in the wild. Free of artificial clothing, the body would once more become a sepulchre, alone or in company with nature. The movement took some of its sensibility from romanticism and some from the cult of Pan and the growing humanism of the period. It had a remarkable and bathetic beginning in the countryside of Essex. The movement had already had an abortive beginning in India during 1891 when Charles Crawford, a district judge, caught the bug from a certain type of ascetic Hinduism. The club he formed had three less than enthusiastic members and shut in 1892.

That might have been the end of the idea if the Germans hadn't begun developing their theories of the body beautiful, the outdoor life and natural health. First came Dr Heinrich Pudor, who began to develop a philosophy of naked healthy living, sport and co-education of the sexes. His book *Nachtkultur*, written under the pseudonym Heinrich Scam, was followed by those of Richard Ungewitter, who in the early years of the twentieth century advocated a series of ideas including physical health, open-air bathing, nudism and sunshine in order to improve moral and mental well-being. This amounted to a new philosophy of life and it was enthusiastically adopted by those who wished to throw off the mental 'tweeds' of a Victorian age that had gone on too long. Fresh air, health, sunlight and nudity were the watchwords of those who were born at the very end of the nineteenth century and formed the centre of that 'Grecian' cult of beauty that fascinated the young things who hovered around Rupert Brooke and his circle in the decade before 1914.

The first official nudist club was set up by Paul Zimmerman near Hamburg in 1903. The Freilichtpark or Free Light Park actually pre-dated Ungewitter's bestselling book *Die Nacktheit* or *Nakedness*, a book successful for its impact as much as for its suggestive title. Not until 1912 did the British begin to really embrace the new philosophy as a philosophy and not just as eccentricity. Encouraged by his reading of Marguerite Le Fur's *Le Bonheir d'etre Nu* in 1912, which described nudism in Germany, Harold Clare Booth began proselytising in Britain and America through the magazine *Physical Culture*, but his initial success was cut short by hostilities, the German idea falling finally out of favour by the time of the sinking of the *Lusitania* in 1915. Nevertheless, there was a revival after the war encouraged by papers such as *The New Statesman* and journals such as *Health and Efficiency*.

By 1922, Booth and others were able to advocate the philosophy of their Gymnosophist Society at public meetings in the Minerva Café in Holborn, London. The meetings were attended mostly by men. By 1926, the Society had moved to bigger premises in Cheapside, where the renamed New Gymnosophy Society grew in influence. By 1924, others were keen to be involved. A Dr Saleeby founded the Sunlight League to advocate sunbathing, something that had been anathema during the previous century. In the same year, the Moonella Group formed out of members of the Gymnosophy Society had begun meeting on a farm in

Witham in Essex, but building next to the land spoiled the activities, which had to stop.

The Society had a colourful leader. Harold Hubert Vincent was born in 1881 to a respectable family; he married in 1916 and enlisted in the same year in the newly formed tank division, but was cashiered for mistakenly firing on his own men. So far, Vincent, who remains a shadowy figure, had shown no signs of the eccentricities that would take him to nudism and jail. Apparently earning his living as an engineer, living off the Edgware Road in the West End of London, he seems to have seen or read the philosophy being advocated in *Sunlight*, the magazine of the Moonella Group, and *The New Statesman*. Either way, he now openly advocated nudism and tried to organise a nudist march on Hyde Park, whilst himself cavorting naked in public places. In 1918 he founded the Sun Ray Club. Nevertheless, in 1932 he finally went from being a nuisance to a criminal when he pushed a female policewoman into the Serpentine in Hyde Park. He was sentenced to three months in jail, his previous convictions for 'indecency', soliciting donations and being insulting in a public place having been taken into account.

Despite the bad press, the nudism movement continued, with offshoots of the Moonella Club and the newly formed Sunbathing Society helping to make nudity and skimpy bathing fashions respectable, and by 1927 even the Dean of St Paul's would claim that 'the new freedom which is sweeping Europe is a splendid omen of increasing health' – a most ill-timed prediction for the future. The Sun Ray and New Health Society was formed in 1930, later becoming the National Sun and Air Association. Nudism continued to grow up to, and partially beyond, the Second World War, but now the ideals of British nudist practice became uncomfortably tangled up with the same practices in Nazi Germany and the body beautiful became more and more associated with the athletic Aryan.

The 'environmentalist' back-to-the-land ideology of the late Victorian period came to its logical conclusion in the early twentieth century in that offshoot of the 'scouting' movement known as Kibbo Kift. Kibbo Kift was the creation of John Gordon Hargrave, a Quaker by birth and by inclination an inventor, author, Boy Scout commissioner and psychic healer, who took the name White Fox and created a non-political 'camping handicraft and world peace movement' in the 1920s, later to transform it into the Green Shirts: 'the green clad shock-troops of the people's fighting front'.

Hargrave was born on 6 June 1894 in the Lake District to parents who took little care of his schooling, but were interested in all things countryside, both anthropological and sociological. By 1906, he was illustrating books for John Buchan although only 12, and by 14, he had read Ernest Thompson Seton's accounts of Native American culture and formed a posse of like-minded boys to roam the woods. His young antics may well have influenced Buchan, Arthur Ransome and Richmal Crompton in their depictions of childish adventures.

Hargrave's family moved to Buckinghamshire after the death of his brother, but by this point Hargrave had become a successful commercial artist and regular contributor on woodcraft to the Scout Movement magazine *The Trail*. As White Fox, he gained a ready readership and rose through the ranks of the scouting movement. At the age of 17, he had a reputation for the outdoors life which even attracted royalty, who made a trip to visit his encampment. The First World War caused him to reaffirm his Quakerism, but not to refuse the colours. He joined the Royal Army Medical Corps, was sent to the Dardanelles and was invalided out in 1916 with a bout of malaria.

After the war, he was appointed Boy Scout Commissioner for Woodcraft and Camping, but his experiences at the front reinforced his pacifism in the face of the growing militarisation of the Scout movement, which had become a sort of territorial army for young people. This dissatisfaction with the movement's new sense of purpose simply strengthened his own resolve and in 1920 he split with the Scouts to form Kibbo Kift, the rather strange name supposedly being archaic Kentish for 'proof of great strength'. In the endeavour he was joined by other pacifist Scout leaders.

The Kibbo Kift was to be not merely a youth organisation but was to involve old and young, male and female. Hargrave called for outdoor education, physical training, the learning of handcrafts, the reintroduction of ritual into modern life, world peace and the regeneration of urban man through the open-air life. The new movement was to be nothing less than the 'human instrument' that would create a new world civilisation:

> It must be an idea clothed with flesh and blood.
> It must show itself healthful, dynamic, capable ...
> It must inspire and direct. It must be mobile
> and rapid in action; able to respond and resist ...
> It must look to the young first ...
> It must develop a technique of life in the midst
> of a chaotic civilisation.

His new organisation would require a type of idealistic dedication which was half 'red Indian' and half Robin Hood. This was a movement that, despite its dislike of militarism, was highly organised, 'uniformed' and trained. It arose at precisely the time of the appearance of the Communist Party of Great Britain and the National Fascisti and, despite being a non-sectarian and pacifist organisation, must be seen in the light of other organisations arising out of the personal, social and cultural destruction of the war, which had left a vacuum from which ideas based on leadership appealed. D.H. Lawrence wrote of him:

> I respect him as a straightforward fighter. But he knows there's no hope, his way en masse. And therefore, underneath, he's full of hate. He's ambitious: and his ambition isn't practical ... he's overweening and he's cold. But, for all that, on the whole, he's right, and I respect him for it.

The whole movement was swathed in a type of freemasonry of signs and activities and was clothed in suitably medieval flimflam. Their curious reactionary garb and deep pantheistic love of the outdoors were not a return to 'Merrie old England' but a very real and direct response to modern life and how to deal with it and its corrupt values. Indeed, it was one stimulus to J.R.R. Tolkien's own expression of the division between the schizoid man of modernity embodied in Gollum and the life of the little contented man of the masses living in the 'shire'. The Kibbo Kift

Foundation still exists; the original mission of the organisation and its rather complicated structure can be explained as follows:

> Kinsmen were organised in clans and tribes, and each individual was given a red-Indian-style woodcraft name by his fellows. The correct costume had to be hand-made by each individual or 'rooftree' (family group) and while the everyday 'habit' of Saxon hood, jerkin, shorts and long cloak must have seemed outlandish enough in the English countryside of the early 1920s; for ceremonial occasions, brilliantly coloured surcoats or silk-embroidered robes were worn by the various office-holders such as the Tallykeeper, Campswarden and Ritesmaster, Hargrave himself was 'Head Man' and his leadership was dynamic, inspirational and frankly autocratic.

Kibbo Kift was never a mass organisation, but its charismatic leader was able to persuade famous people to endorse its aims: H.G. Wells, Julian Huxley, Havelock Ellis, Maurice Maeterlinck and the Indian poet Rabindranath Tagore were on its advisory board and former suffragette Mrs Pethick Lawrence was a 'Kinswoman'. The German outdoors and youth movement were also courted and the 'Wandervogel' acknowledged Kibbo Kift as fellows and translated Hargrave's books. Many followers believed that Hargrave had a solution to their personal and spiritual needs, but continued to commit themselves to socialism or even communism.

A split by the socialist wing of the organisation led to the creation of Leslie Paul's Woodcraft Folk, which was associated with the cooperative movement. The social and personal aspects of the movement were starting to become a cult divorced from society. Many Kibbo Kift 'Kinsfolk' were socialists, Fabians and internationalists, and all were pacifists. The problem was one of political direction. In 1923, Hargrave met Major C.H. Douglas. Douglas had written a series of books which argued that the root of all social ills was economic, and could be defined as a basic and universal shortage of purchasing power. This was hardly revolutionary, but it gave Hargrave more than just the key to the personal development of his followers. Here he found the 'key' to poverty, war and exploitation that was neither right wing nor 'red'. Douglas' idea was that the shortage of wealth was the result of a fundamental flaw in the modern cost-accountancy system; this flaw meant that there was not enough money to consume what was produced.

Douglas proposed radical and simple technical solutions to the 'money problem' and postulated a society where a 'birthright' payment or a type of 'unearned' income designed to combat the inequality of family inheritance would be paid by the state to each individual, rich or poor. An automatic 'Scientific Price Adjustment' linked to national prosperity and lowering retail prices to the consumer (working rather like VAT in reverse) would further increase the purchasing power of the individual while preventing any inflation. Industry, unhindered by the social necessity to 'create jobs', would institute rapid technological development financed by interest-free credits. The result, argued Douglas, would be a 'Leisure State', where the compulsion to work merely in order to live decently simply did not exist.

By 1925, 'Social Credit' was already central to Hargrave's vision for his movement. The great work of salvation that he now knew he had to undertake to regenerate mankind crystallised around these economic ideas and was to galvanise his rather middle-class followers, who already considered that they were a vanguard of social regeneration: 'Half our problem is psychological and the other half is economic. The psychological complex of industrial mankind can only be released by solving the economic impasse.' Only in Douglas' Leisure State could the Kindred's ultimate aims be achieved. By 1927, social credit formed the central plank of an increasingly messianic political movement.

The movement was to be converted to one of a more militant nature. This was enough to alienate many, causing them to leave, and it alienated those who had no interest in politics or the message of social credit which could only be delivered in the towns they abhorred. The Kindred were now uniformed in green and marched to the beat of a drum corps with flags flying. This was enough display to warrant the attention of Oswald Mosley and to jog his memory when it came to the organisation of the Blackshirts.

Colour coding and uniforms identify every group who wanted power once the old world of the Edwardians had passed. Hargrave understood that the urban poor needed organising, so a 'Legion of the Unemployed' was set up in Coventry in 1930, and in 1934 they were uniformed in a green shirt and beret. The Legion were affiliated as 'Green Shirts of the Kibbo Kift', whilst in 1932 the Kibbo Kift itself wore the new uniform. In 1933 (surely not coincidentally) Kibbo Kift became the Green Shirts. 'That is going to be the popular name of this movement – the Green Shirts: Kibbo Kift is too difficult and the Legion of the Unemployed is too much of a mouthful. We've been misnamed Green Shirts, that name will stick to us – let's stick to it!', argued Hargrave against growing disquiet.

In the years that followed, attempts were made to convert Hargrave's social credit ideas into legislation in Canada, but failed, and his Green Shirts lost their uniforms alongside the Blackshirts. Yet a fertile mind kicks against its limitations. He wrote a 'breakthrough' novel, but it was left unread and he also developed a clever and complex navigation system that did succeed and would be developed much later in the 1960s and be used on Concorde. Like many messianic figures before him, he discovered that he could psychically heal. As for his economic ideas, they eventually filtered into the policies of the modern Liberal Party. Nevertheless, he died on 21 November 1982, largely forgotten.

EIGHTEEN

THE LIFTING OF THE FOG

When Victoria died on 22 January 1901, the empire may have mourned, but there were some who felt that the age had grown vicious and that viciousness was exemplified by the small woman in black who had ruled for too long. She saw much, did nothing and said nothing, choosing, when convenient, to interfere in matters of lifestyle or of state, and to record her impressions of her subjects in private journals. Of one visit to the Black Country in 1852, she had written:

> It is like another world. In the midst of so much wealth, there seems to be nothing but ruin. As far as the eye can reach, one sees nothing but chimneys, flaming furnaces, many deserted but not pulled down, with wretched cottages around them … And to this a thick and black atmosphere … and you have but a faint impression of the life … which a third of a million of my poor subjects are forced to lead. It makes me sad!

She was not cruel, but her charity was personal, not social, aimed at the individual symptom rather than the cause. She rarely lobbied her prime ministers, but when she did, it was mostly negatively, either to stop legislation she disapproved of or for her own personal gain.

Victoria's most famous epithet and the one by which she is most remembered was not even recorded in her lifetime, but appeared in a single memoir of a lady in waiting, hidden in a passage otherwise meant to be admiring. There is a tale of the unfortunate equerry who ventured during dinner at Windsor to tell a story with a spice of scandal or impropriety in it. 'We are not amused', said the Queen when he had finished.

That such a comment could be raised to the status of something that epitomised a reign of over 60 years (and may not have actually been said at all) suggests a wave of relief that the enervating symbol of an age had finally passed and that the world could begin anew. Certainly, this was the attitude of Aleister Crowley, who, whilst on holiday in Mexico, was brought the news of the passing of the mother of the empire. Crowley started to laugh and dance a jig, exclaiming to the shocked hotel porter that '[Victoria] was a huge and heavy fog ... we could not see; we could not breathe'. He also saw the Queen in the same light as he saw his dislikeable hidebound mother. 'I cannot imagine', he mused, 'why, at this very early age, I cultivated a profound aversion to and contempt for Queen Victoria. Merely, perhaps, the clean and decent instincts of a child!' More than anything, Crowley felt that 'a sovereign of suet, a parliament of putty, an aristocracy of alabaster, an intelligentsia of india rubber [and] a proletariat of pulp' would finally be swept away and the 'smug, sleek, superficial, servile, snobbish, sentimental [world of English] shopkeeping' could finally be destroyed.

To some like Ezra Pound, Victoria was 'an old bitch gone in the teeth', symbolic of a worn-out and stifling age, something the Irish thought when Edward VII unveiled a statue to his mother outside Leinster House in 1904. The statue was intensely disliked. Nicknamed the 'Auld Bitch', it was discreetly removed in 1947 and was not re-erected until the late 1980s in Sydney, Australia.

The death of Victoria brought about accelerated change and new times. Despite appearances, the age of deference had passed. T.E. Lawrence, recalling the death of Victoria's daughter-in-law Queen Alexandra in *The Mint*, gives voice to a world more harsh, more begrudging and less accepting of authority. Lawrence was now a recruit in the Royal Air Force and he and his fellow squaddies had been forced to parade to listen to a vacuous sermon on the virtues of the royal family after the death of Alexandra:

It was an odd morning, that on which we heard Queen Alexandra was dead ... Our distrusted chaplain preached one of his questionable sermons. He spoke of the dead queen as a Saint, a Paragon: not as an unfortunate. A long-suffering doll ... The body should not be kept alive after the lamp of sense has gone out ... Balls! hissed someone savagely, from behind me ... Not even a half-holiday for the old girl.

These were not the words of a 'gentleman' or of a royalist; they were bitter, disillusioned and weary. Here in the tight prose of modernistic language was the new relationship of subjects to royalty. Respect was now to be withheld unless earned and not dressed in the Christian propaganda of a 'distrusted chaplain'. Victoria's age was one of increasing disturbance, much of which had gathered pace in the last 20 years of her reign and spilled over into the new century. Henry James, musing on her passing, was worried and saw only the spectre of chaos in the place where there had once been order; the death of 'the motherly old middle-class Queen' who had hibernated under her 'big, hideous, Scotch-plaid shawl' would give vent to terrible forebodings. 'I fear her death much more than I should have expected', mused James; Victoria was a 'sustaining symbol' after whose demise 'the wild waters [would be] upon us'. James spoke for many when he heard of her death. 'We all feel a bit motherless today', he mused, for 'mysterious little Victoria is dead.' For him, the age of indecency had now commenced with 'fat vulgar Edward' on the throne, overweight and over-age.

It would not be until 1921, when Lytton Strachey wrote his biography, that Victoria was returned from being a sour symbol of all that was bad about the past to being a woman with feelings, fears and hope. Victoria may have been stubborn and aloof, but she was also a mother and a caring wife and queen, mysteriously wrapped in the silence of monarchy. What was less well understood, though radicals guessed at it easily enough, were her political machinations. Indeed, it would not be until 1932, with the publication of her letters, that the extent of her hidden influence and curb on government decisions was fully exposed. It was a secret well hidden from her subjects and appeared to distinctly hamper the progress of democratic institutions.

Victoria had come to the throne an aristocratic, oligarchical Whig under the influence of men like Lord Melbourne. Although not a Hanoverian Tory, she was of the opinion that whilst individual charity was admirable for the relief of society's ills, constitutional change was harmful. The Glorious Revolution had settled the constitution once and for all, and only the absolute pressure of events would change her mind on the issue. She was all her life a Whiggish type of conservative (with a small 'c') who disliked the radical Liberals and a conservative who disliked the new dynamic Conservatives that opposed them; in this respect, her political outlook remained much as it had been on her accession. Individual sympathies, which occasionally clouded her belief system, never permitted her to see the bigger picture. Victoria never waivered in her implicit belief in her divine appointment, although she never pressed the point. She was 'chosen' to rule and that was enough; it was an essentially static system that she favoured, while change was opposed for reasons that slowly and quietly led to stagnation. An absolutist 'Jacobite' at heart, as she reminded her ministers, Victoria was jealous of foreign monarchs with titles and power, being finally elevated to Empress of India on 1 May 1876 by her favourite flatterer, Benjamin Disraeli. Nevertheless, she often displayed enlightened views far ahead of her time towards her subjects, mixing with Muslim servants and Jewish prime ministers and disavowing derogatory remarks as to colour and race, but when opposed on imperial policy by views she could not stomach, like Home Rule for Ireland or votes for women, she was inclined towards aggressive self-pity, threatening to 'lay down her crown' and 'abdicate' – fits of pique so impetuous and imperious that politicians invariably were scared into humiliating submission.

Victoria's political ambitions, dreamed with Prince Albert, were far worse. The dynamics of the royal marriage and the frustrations of the Prince Consort at the difference between German and British ideas of monarchy presaged a disastrous clash of ideology averted only by his death on 14 December 1861. The married couple's imagination was fixed firmly on the past, something made quite explicit since the days of their medieval Bal Masque on 12 May 1842. According to Disraeli, the royal spouses longed for nothing less than a reversal of the democratic tendencies of the reign and the return to 'German' autocratic rule. When Albert was buried, Disraeli mooted a hypothetical outcome to Albert's 'rule', a rule Disraeli saw as explicit in the marriage and implicit in the country:

We have buried our sovereign. This German Prince has governed England for twenty-one years with a wisdom and energy such as none of our kings have ever shown … If he had out-lived some of our old stagers, he would have given us the blessings of absolute government.

With Albert dead, Victoria retired into the caricature in which she has largely remained in the public mind ever since, and to some extent the public mind is more acute than revisionist historians. For Victoria, all change smelled of radicalism or, much worse, revolution. This was an idea she shared with those who were the aristocratic backbone of a Britain that had refused to take cognisance of 1832 or of any parliamentary voting reform. Palmerston was described by Lord Derby in the 1860s as a 'Conservative Minister working with Radical tools and keeping up a show of Liberalism' for appearance's sake. The words 'radical' and 'democracy' were to Victoria a curse and whoever uttered radical ideas wore the mark of Cain, a mark both of shame and of personal moral collapse. Why oh why should her subjects increasingly turn to radicalism and democracy as solutions to economic or social concerns? She simply could not understand democracy at all:

> These are trying moments and it seems to me a defect in our famed Constitution, to have to part with an admirable Government like Lord Salisbury's for no question of any importance, or any particular reason, merely on account of the number of votes.

Change would be fought all the way. Radicalism made Victoria feel morally unclean. One of her ministers, W.E. Forster, remembered a conversation with the Queen in 1874:

> No one can be more truly liberal at heart than the Queen is, but she also thinks that the great principles of the Constitution of this great country ought to be maintained, and that too many alterations (and there have been so many) should be avoided.

To her Private Secretary, Henry Ponsonby, Victoria confided that she was inherently 'Liberal but never Radical or democratic'. It was, nevertheless, a strange liberalism detached from the Liberal Party, whose policies she did not care for. Historian Frank Hardie summed up her interference in politics as 'a clog on the activity of every Liberal Government after 1841, and a stimulus to every Conservative Government after 1868'.

The Liberals, the radical party for 50 years, had been washed away with the First World War as their old base in working-class non-conformist evangelism and middle-class business was eroded by the slow inroads of Conservatives and the Labour Party (after 1910). The Whig aristocracy had slowly but surely abandoned its own particular version of politics and had merged into the new Liberal Party or had joined the Conservatives or Unionists, or slipped from patrician leadership of the newly enfranchised into the oblivion brought about by the rise of democratic demands. The old aristocratic Whigs:

> Clung to the sort of superiority that only land and blood can buy ... Manu-facturers, non conformists and Jews ... plainly required the leadership of a patrician class trained in the mysteries of government and the Whig-Liberal party spoke their language. Yet after mid century ... the Whigs diminished into a band of isolated potentates ... by 1886 only five of the great Whig families still belonged to the Gladstonian Liberal party: the rest had slid across to Tory or Liberal unionist benches or withdrawn to their town houses.

Yet to many observers, the revenant Whigs still threw a gigantic shadow over the politics of Edwardian Britain. Reactionaries seemed dressed up in the fashionable clothes of revolutionaries. To Wilfred Blunt, Henry Campbell-Bannerman – elected in December 1905 (the 'first Radical Prime Minister' so people thought) – was not the upholder of that 'violent democratic change' so many had hoped for, but the same again from last century: 'the new Cabinet is a Whig Cabinet', Blunt lamented.

Gradualism, not cataclysmic change was the order of the new century as of the old. To most people, of course, the Liberal Party and its 'left' wing was the epitome of radicalism, a sentiment summed up by John Morley in a speech of 1889:

> The name of Radical is good enough for me ... do not let us quarrel about nicknames ... If we are agreed upon certain definite ends for today, that is enough for me. Let us achieve the task which is assigned to us: do not let us endeavour to settle millennial problems, let us do what we have to do.

Doing what had to be done and doing it stoically was the mark of radicalism and the spirit of reform. To be a radical required an infinite capacity for disappointment and defeat, but an equal belief in the inevitability of slow progress and a final unshakeable optimism that right was enshrined in the people and that that right would, given time, prevail. It was, nevertheless, a sort of humourless optimism based on 'peace, retrenchment and reform', where patience had to be infinite and whose adherents amongst working-class non-conformists were used to standing around in God's waiting room. That the programme of the radicals might have been successful during the turbulent year of Campbell-Bannerman's election was a hope soon dashed, as Arthur Balfour realised:

> If I read the signs aright ... C[ampbell]-B[annerman] is a mere cork, dancing on a torrent which he cannot control, and what is going on here is the faint echo of the same movement which has produced massacres in St. Petersburg, riots in Vienna and Socialist processions in Berlin.

Indeed, the radical voice was often one whose message lost its way in compromises. This was not helped by radicals attempting to square the circle of orthodoxy, where socialists might be Liberals or Tories socialists. Hence, Lloyd George could campaign as a Welsh nationalist and an imperialist:

> As Welsh Liberals we are Imperialists because we are nationalists, and we are also Liberals for the same reason. We know ... that by the sum of the success, prosperity and happiness attained by little Wales, the greater Empire of which she is a part will be the more glorious.

The fact that radicals were rarely willing to break the rules, make a fuss or get into 'dirty' political infighting meant their cause was doomed to fall to other more rigorous and adventurous voices where revolution was not considered 'barbarism' or, if it was, where that same barbarism was seen as a wholly good thing in the face of a corrupt civilisation.

William Morris certainly felt in his growing frustration with industrial capital that the destructiveness of barbarism might finally bring about the revolutionary future by a return to the past, a 'past' recreated in the guild socialism world that he so desired. In a letter to Mrs Burne-Jones sent in May 1885, he vented his annoyance: 'I am in low spirits', he complained, 'about the prospects for our "party" [socialism] … You see we are such a few … I have [no] more faith than a grain of mustard seed in the future of "civilization" which I know now is doomed to destruction, and probably before long: what a joy it is to think of! And how it consoles me to think of barbarism once more flooding the world.'

This was a sentiment that would echo throughout the period and would become more visionary and more biblical as it went. By 1919, it was the fully formed vision of apocalypse and of the Antichrist in W.B. Yeat's poem *The Second Coming*: 'and what rough beast', wondered Yeats, 'Its hour come round at last/Slouches towards Bethlehem to be born?' It was a question asked by a number of radicals awaiting the collapse of all values, lined up in anticipation of being the saved at the end of time.

Victoria lived a long time. She was 81 in 1900, empress of peoples that stretched around half the globe, whose industry seemed impervious to market forces, whose navy was the glory of world arms and whose capital was the greatest ever seen. She enjoyed her jubilees with cheering confident crowds. At her Golden Jubilee in 1887, she smiled and her expression was caught on camera, a fleeting moment, a strange false-toothed grin captured on film as proof that the Queen was a human being and not a mere mask whose gaze watched over her people and their travails.

When Victoria died, her eyes were closed by her grandson, Kaiser Wilhelm, and her funeral courtege was filled with the crowned heads of Europe, a grand and magnificent occasion recorded on early film. The pomp was hollow, the grandeur short-lived. Her son, Albert Edward, was himself crowned Edward VII on 9 August 1902. He was an old man with a playboy's eye and a love of the nouveaux riches, with whom he could go sailing and womanising, and the landed aristocracy, with whom he could hunt and fish. It was the last hurrah for an aristocracy more entrenched and more in control than when Victoria had come to the throne.

The Whig aristocracy (always conservative and sometimes downright Tory in disguise) had metamorphosised into that Tory 'conservatism' which was to define those entrenched attitudes that, with all of their modernity, still stood somehow for permanence and unending power before 1914. 'When we served the [sixth] Duke and Duchess of Portland', wrote the footman John Gorst, 'there were always three men in attendance; two footmen and either the wine butler or the groom of the chambers. There was no butler on the staff because [there] was the chief steward or major-domo and unlike smaller establishments this great house required departmental heads and assistants.' There were a bevvy of servants in the household, from the wine butler to the valet and from the head coachman to the ten grooms, 15 chauffeurs, window cleaners, golf course attendants and the Japanese trainer for the private gymnasium amongst 100 others. The Earls of Derby spent £50,000 a year before the war, while the Earl of Lowther greeted the arrival of the Kaiser with a squadron of his own yeomanry to escort his imperial majesty the nine-mile ride along his drive; Lowther also had a privately maintained orchestra to entertain in the evening.

Despite their great wealth, which was greater than ever before, even the aristocracy was forced to reinvent itself several times before and after the First World War in order to maintain its position of dominance. It did this amidst the unstoppable rise of that working-class solidarity, trade unionism and socialism, that would challenge social hierarchy, first through the Liberals and later through the Labour Party, to overwhelm and defeat the forces of the old order, still tenaciously holding on to power through an admittedly diminished House of Lords, its land holdings now tied to its involvement with the new men of money and of industry, its wives chosen from wealthy Jewish heiresses and the daughters of American plutocrats.

While the sale of assets enabled economic survival for some, it was also a blow for the aristocracy's identity and self-confidence. 'A man does not like to go down to posterity as the alienator of old family possessions', Lord Aylesbury ruefully remarked in 1911. Some peers unwilling to go this way married themselves out of trouble by hitching their old names to new, often American wealth. Lord Roseberry married Hanna de Rothschild, the Duke of Marlborough married Consuelo Vanderbilt, while Lord Randolph Churchill famously married Jenny Jerome, the daughter of a New York financier.

Renewed through the infusion of money and trade, old aristocratic families had to rub along with the William Levers of this world, a manufacturer of soap who rose by degrees to become Lord Leverhulme, who already owned Scottish islands and, by 1910, when he was a mere Viscount, had purchased the home of the Marquess of Stafford. Jewish bankers and manufacturers, tea importers and grocers were to infiltrate the ranks and dilute the stock. However, privilege still persisted and the upper classes were as capable of revolutionary or reactionary action as their workers and servants when it suited them. Philipp Blom points out that:

> It was true that the value of land had evaporated and had become a burden rather than a blessing, but one that still had to be shouldered, even though 'the political power of the state' which once was 'in the hands of those who had property' had now apparently passed to 'the hands of the multitude', as the Duke Of Northumberland complained in 1908. By 1900, some 14,000 estates had been mortgaged, with only 2,800 of their owners managing to keep up their repayments. Between 1903 and 1909 alone, Britain's aristocrats sold nine million acres of land.

The Victorian age was defined not so much by a queen's reign but by a series of developing sentiments and ideologies beginning at the fag end of the Georgian era and culminating in the middle of the twentieth century. Beyond Victoria, the Victorian age seemed to never end, and yet in its beginnings was its end, for such change came not only in the political or social dimension but also in the personal, where revolution was not merely for the greater good, but was a revolt into that self-made salvation of sheer bloody willpower that would, it was believed, usher in a new cleaner world stripped of old values, a final valid substitute for religious belief in an age of growing cynicism, secularism and atheism. This was the dream of Jacobins, anarchists, communists, imperial adventurers, town planners, advocates of nudism and even fascists: that the old world must be blown up to be born anew. It was the only way out of that industrial, ecological, political and personal hell that imprisoned and emasculated the mass of British people and the peoples of their empire and held them within the conformity of the stifling propriety of orthodox political, social and personal imagination.

Should this new world be one of machines, technology and collectivism or of the handmade, the communitarian and the local? Should it have the one leader or the many: had the democratic experiment finally failed in war and unemployment, to be replaced by the dictatorship of the proletariat or of the Superman? What role should the individual play in the new world order: anarchy or socialism or a reconciliation of both? Either way, the old was washed up, a heap of rubbish in an overheated and overwrought culture; 'our society is a cemetery', exploded Wyndham Lewis in *The Apes of God* in 1930, but the end had been heralded long before in the *Weltschmerz* of existential disappointment and ennui attending the last clash of beauty and ugliness in the pages of Oscar Wilde and the early pronouncements of Lenin. For the Fabian Beatrice Webb:

> this conflict [of interests] was harboured in a type of self wherein there was a conflict between the 'Ego that affirms' and the 'Ego that denies', the unresolvable nature of this primarily inner conflict being either suicidal tendencies or the destruction and reconstruction of society.

The conflict was symbolically incubated deep within Webb's own little family 'secret', which was enlarged and expanded to explain her world:

> I hear that a brother and sister of [grandmother] committed suicide, and two or three of the family have been threatened with suicidal mania. Perhaps it is from that quarter that we get our 'Weltschmerz'.

The urge to self-destruction and the feeling of ultimate futility and 'melancholy for the race' was in essence a type, first and foremost, of self-hatred stemming from a sense of helplessness in the face of social problems. Webb believed that she had inherited the 'suicidal constitution' of her family, coupled with her own 'melancholy' and 'mental strain', and this set her about turning those negative enervating attitudes into something socially positive. Yet this new-found energy for hard work and social investigation was precisely designed to bring the old structures tumbling around her ears. Sociology and socialism would destroy the Victorian complacency of liberalism and philanthropy. The old regime had had its day and had failed.

NINETEEN

THE CRUSADE

B y 1900, English radical traditions seemed to have petered out and yet there appeared the possibility of at least a challenge to the Liberal monopoly of the working-class and radical vote. This was to come from the slow and painful evolution of an independent 'labour party' which had grown from an alliance of new unionism and intellectual 'socialist' and 'labour' clubs and associations. That it would prove a disappointment to revolutionaries did not mean that it might not come to power by legitimate means and still inveigle revolutionary socialist ideas into Parliament.

Nevertheless, the Labour Party, when it emerged, was always gradualist and conservative in its politics. In his presidential address to the Labour Party Congress, Sidney Webb had talked of 'the inevitability of gradualness'. George Bernard Shaw also saw gradualness as the solution to social ills and looked with pleasure at the lack of revolutionaries or 'impossibilists' in the Fabians. C.F.G. Mastermen, writing in *The Nation* in 1907, could see only 'a mixture of old-fashioned Trade Unionists with a sprinkling of well behaved and pleasant Socialists' in the ranks of the labour movement. To his rather faux surprise, he could see 'no wild revolutionaries, harbingers of the uprising of the lower orders'. A.K. Chesterton acerbically noted that no aristocrat had yet been lynched: 'From his hour, in his expensive cot/He never saw the tiniest viscount shot', he chuckled. R. Cunningham Graham, at least, expected a few fireworks from the new party, but found only a crawling conformism and certain obsequiousness in the place of power:

When Labour members get into Parliament they are at once bitten with the absurd idea that they are no longer working men, but statesmen, and they try to behave as such. I tell them … that they would do more good if they came to the House in a body drunk and tumbling about the floor.

It was the old story of radicalism tamed. 'Before the Queen made me a Cabinet Minister', lamented the Liberal, W.E. Foster, 'I was much more of a Radical. After that I did what I could and not what I would.'

Alternative (and revolutionary) parties of the left, such as the SDF, the Socialist League, the Independent Labour Party, the Scottish Labour Party and the Communist Party of Great Britain, or of the right, such as the British Union of Fascists, seemed unable to raise any effective challenge to parliamentary inertia and, although highly effective at a local level in communities and trade unions, were unable to mount real action at a national level. It seemed that the only action available to millions was to ballot and hope, the only concession in 100 years of any importance being the right to vote in secret, the valuelessness of the gesture being driven home as late as 8 December 1944 by Winston Churchill in a speech during a Commons debate:

How is the word 'democracy' to be interpreted? My idea of it is that the plain, humble, common man, just the ordinary man who keeps a wife and family, and goes off to fight for his country when it is in trouble, goes to the poll at the appropriate time, and puts his cross on the ballot-paper showing the candidate he wishes to be elected to Parliament – that is the foundation of democracy … He marks his ballot paper in secrecy, and then elected representatives meet together and decide what government, or even, in times of stress, what form of government, they wish to have in their country. If that is democracy, I salute it. I espouse it.

If the old parliamentary system was so inelastic in defending rigid class positions that it could appear to change only to reconfigure itself so completely, then other measures, whose impulse was personal but whose outcomes would be political, would have to be tried.

This closed political and social world was to be severely challenged (but not entirely broken) in the early years of the twentieth century by the middle classes in revolutionary temper, by militant suffragettes, by intellectuals in artistic, Fabian and philosophical circles, by town planners, by adventurers in the dust of Empire, by those questing in the realms of the occult, by revolutionary British Bolsheviks and by the working classes now banded together in strong trade unions willing to fight for pay and conditions that raised them above paid slaves and gave them the new dignity of labour (as opposed to the dignity of heredity), taken from a lifetime education in the new socialism which demanded collectivisation, republicanism and shared wealth; it would even reach the aristocracy, reborn in the black uniform of a very British version of fascism.

By the 1930s, it was out and out class war, not deference, that defined politics. In 1934 Giles Romilly, nephew of Winston Churchill and leading an ambivalent left-wing revolt of public schoolboys, attended the fascist rally at Olympia in order to heckle:

> One of the things which most disgusted [me] was the attitude of certain sections of the audience. Coming in evening dress and Rolls-Royce cars, they gave every sign of enjoying the spectacle of the brutal ejection of the interrupters. Their spirit, indeed, I felt, was very much that of the Roman aristocracy watching the early Christians being thrown to the lions ... During the fighting I recognized a boy I had known slightly at Wellington. He was wearing a black shirt ... so as he came towards me I punched hard with my fist into his face. Recalling the incident half an hour later, I had an idea that perhaps he might have been trying to shake hands with me.

For the first time since the Chartist riots almost a century earlier, the years just before and just after the First World War as well as the first half of 1934 saw a possibility of fast, revolutionary changes in the British constitution and social system, and the end of the ancient regime of Victorian values. The situation was summed up by proto-fascist, aeronaut and MP Anthony, Viscount Knebworth, great-grandson of Edward Bulwer-Lytton. Writing in his diary, he noted that:

> The world appears to be shaking off the yoke of democracy ... the hour is so ripe everywhere for a man, and a drive and a policy. I hope the great National Government is the last of the ancient regime.

Perhaps the most significant radical shift in thinking came with women like Sylvia Pankhurst, whose revolutionary position was a rejection of her mother's authoritarianism and her sister's born-again religiosity. Instead, she embraced the causes of feminism, atheism, rationalism, anti-imperialism, socialism, internationalism and anti-fascism that would be a ticket of all progressivism in the twentieth century, but which emerged from the households of late Victorian progressives. In this, she was able to understand the ideologies which would command the future, whilst her sister and mother retreated into that reactionary conservatism which would see both the emergence of the cult of the leader and of that pseudo-religious sensibility which would worship him. Thus, the suffragette movement summed up perfectly both sides of the revolutionary struggle.

Pankhurst's belief that there was 'too much suffering in the world', but that it would be cured by human effort alone and her dream of a better world in this world was for a future 'Golden Age when plenty and joy should be the gift of all'. Such idealism could no longer be comforted by revived sentimentalities which would now appear retrogressive and outmoded.

Sylvia Pankhurst was born on 5 May 1882 to Emmeline and Richard Pankhurst in Old Trafford, Manchester. Richard Pankhurst was a doctor, freethinker and radical who was a friend of the Chartist Ernest Jones and of John Stuart Mill, a supporter of the Liberals under Gladstone, of independence for Ireland and an early women's advocate, drafting the first suffrage bill in the late 1860s. He was also an atheist who told his daughter in no uncertain terms that 'if you ever go back into religion you will not have been worth the upbringing'. He was, Sylvia recalled, 'a standard-bearer of every forlorn hope, every unpopular cause then conceived for the uplifting of oppressed and suffering humanity'. Emmeline also came from a radical background, whose own mother had been influenced by Morris and whose uncle had met Marx. Richard Pankhurst, Sylvia's only son, recalled that after his family had emigrated down to London's Russell Square, the house became a centre for radical discussion. His mother would later regale him with tales of their many distinguished (or notorious) visitors:

[These] included politicians and political thinkers of many 'advanced' hues: Socialists, Anarchists, Radicals, Republicans, Nationalists, suffragists, free thinkers, agnostics, atheists and humanitarians of all kinds. Among them were the Italian Anarchist Malatesta, the Russian refugees Kropotkin, Stepniak, and Nicholas Tchaykovsky, Henri Rochefort (whose daughter was still in close contact with young mrs. Pankhurst), the American apostle of negro freedom William Lloyd Garrison, and Dadabhai Naoroji, the first Indian member of the British House of Commons. Other callers included William Morris, Herbert Borrows – the enthusiastic organiser of the matchgirls' strike of 1888 – and the feminist Annie Besant. Perhaps the person who most struck the youthful Sylvia was, however, the French woman Louise Michel who had been active in the Paris Commune almost a generation earlier.

Sylvia proved to be an artistic child, inspired by the arts and crafts movement, and by Morris and Walter Crane, as had been her mother, who had opened a small arts and craft emporium; moreover, her mother had also been inspired, for a while, by the socialist sentiments behind the movement. Never a great or inspired artist, Sylvia nevertheless was a follower of the 'cult of beauty' (as was her mother) and gained access to the best art schools and won prizes for pictures of working-class women at work in the factories.

Sylvia's artistic pursuits were at one with her political interests. She joined the Independent Labour Party when it was formed, became a friend and helper of James Keir Hardie and even whilst at school had opposed the Boer War, to the annoyance of the school authorities. Not yet a confirmed supporter of women's suffrage, it was, nevertheless, the combination of the pursuit of beauty and the compassion for the plight of the downtrodden worker that gave her politics the sentiment it required and the idealism that looked to a more equitable society where things might be beautiful.

Sylvia was commissioned to decorate the new Independent Labour Party hall in Salford with murals in the style of Walter Crane. The hall was dedicated to the memory of her father, who had died in 1896. The mural scrolls would read 'England arise!' and a quotation from Shelley's *The Revolt of Islam*, which read 'Hope will make thee young, for Hope and Youth are children of one mother, even Love' and would be decorated variously with lilies, sunflowers, bees, roses, apple trees, doves, butterflies and allegorical symbols of plenty, honesty, industry and purity. The interior decorations would be influenced by the arts and crafts movement and early Owenite socialism, and the spirit of Christian socialist evangelism. The hall was dedicated to philosophically progressive ideals and the cult of a future not yet realised; the litany of industrious ideas that followed, the summation of the future realised in the present, recalled by the words of Shelley, the poet of revolution, the poet much loved by Eleanor Marx and by the socialist movement.

Interestingly, Sylvia was always a traditional painter, influenced by Crane and Morris and unworried by the inventions of abstraction or Soviet Constructivism, her socialism firmly grounded in a solid type of British common sense. Her art was essentially conservative and certainly not in step with her vision of a future society.

On 10 October 1903, Sylvia's mother Emmeline formed the Women's Labour Representative Committee with six other Independent Labour Party women, but changed the name shortly afterwards to the Women's Social and Political Union (WPSU). The group originally wanted equality within the Independent Labour Party, but soon changed direction. All the family were involved; Sylvia, Christabel and their sister Adela were expected to form ranks with their autocratic matriach for the fight ahead. Sylvia, meanwhile, preferred painting and at the Royal College of Art met and befriended the occultist and artist Austin Osman Spare.

The WSPU began its campaign for the vote in the autumn of 1905, a time of movement in politics when the old Conservatives were about to finally leave the stage for the more progressive Liberals. Many believed that a new era of progressive thinking, which had built up in the previous decades, would now come to fruition. One of these new ideas was the simple equality of women in politics. The atmosphere surrounding this new sense of political will as embodied in progressive politics liberated hopes which, when dashed, were all the more bitterly felt.

The enfranchisement of women was to turn from a mere political battle to one of extreme existential struggle, so strong was the disappointment of its advocates in the face of such determined opposition. The violence of women's responses to the continued crisis was one of the great shocks of the age. Young middle-class women had joined forces with their working-class sisters and were gathering stones on Brighton beach to throw at the windows in Whitehall, were making bonfires to burn down the houses of their opponents and were willing to go to jail and be force-fed for a principle. Such things were unheard of and unthinkable; the very heart of Edwardian stability was being rocked. Sylvia herself, who was rather distant from the political centre of the movement but was happy to make banners and rosettes for it, was nevertheless first arrested on 24 October 1906. Her reaction to being imprisoned is notable for its astonishment and incredulity. Two worlds had collided which should never have mixed:

How long the way seemed to Holloway, as the springless van rattled over the stones and constantly bumped us against the narrow wooden pens in which we sat! As it passed down the poor streets the people cheered – they always cheer the prison van. It was evening when we arrived at our destination, and the darkness was closing in. As we passed in a single file through the great gates, we found ourselves at the end of a long corridor with cubicles on either side. A woman officer in a Holland dress, with a dark blue bonnet with hanging strings on her head, and with a bundle of keys and chins dangling at her waist, called out our names and the length of our sentences and locked us separately into one of the cubicles, which were about four feet square and quite dark. In the door of each cubicle was a little round glass spy-hole, which might be closed by a metal flap on the outside. Mine had been left open by mistake, and through it I could see a little of what was going on outside.

Once we had been locked away, the wardress came from door to door, taking down further particulars as to the profession, religion, and so on, of each prisoner … The prisoners called to each other over the topes of the cubicles in loud, high pitched voices. Every now and then the officer protested, but still the noise continued. Soon another van load of prisoners arrived and the cubicles being filled, several women together were put into the same compartment – sometimes as many as five in one of those tiny places! It was very cold, and the stone floor made one's feet colder still, yet for a long time until I was so tired that I no longer stand – I was afraid to sit down because, in the darkness, one could not see whether, as one feared, everything might be covered with vermin.

The first 'Women's Parliament' met at Caxton Hall on 12 February 1907 after the King's speech made no mention of women's suffrage. The 'Parliament' met a further nine times, each time attempting to lobby the Commons and each time meeting the resistance of authority:

> Still we strove to reach our destination, and returned again and again. Those of us who rushed from the roadway on to the pavement were pressed by the [police] horses closer and closer against the walls and railings until at last we retreated or were forced away by the constables on foot. Those of us who took refuse in doorways were dragged roughly down the steps and hurled back in front of the horses. When even this failed to banish us, the foot constables rushed at us, catching us fiercely by the shoulders, turned us round again and then seizing us by the back of the neck and thumping us cruelly between the shoulders forced us at a running pace along the streets until we were far from the House of Commons. They had been told to drive us away and to make as few arrests as possible. Still we returned again, until the last five women and two men, all of them bruised and dishevelled, had been taken to the police station, and those who had not been arrested were almost fainting from fatigue. Then, after ten o'clock, the police succeeded in clearing all the approaches to the House of Commons, and the mounted men were left galloping about in the empty square till midnight, when the House rose.

Frustrated with the progress and with the will of her fellow women, Emmeline declared herself dictator of the movement in 1907. The decision split the organisation and alienated Sylvia.

The fight went on, seemingly getting nowhere, whilst all the time intensifying. Imprisonments in 1906 to 1907, which stood at 191 weeks, had increased to 350 weeks by 1907 to 1908. A rally at the Albert Hall in 1908 drew huge numbers, but only resulted in more arrests. Sylvia worked tirelessly to create banners, posters and emblems. The WSPU was now a single-issue political party and its policies were becoming more extreme and more violent. On 16 February 1912, Emmeline declared that 'the argument of the broken window pane [was] the valuable argument in modern politics'. At the same time, Christabel, frustrated with the level of progress, initiated a campaign of large-scale arson attacks. They were the first homegrown 'terrorist' attacks in Britain, as Sylvia realised, the unacknowledged inheritors of the work of the previous century's Irish bombers and anarchists. The decision to destroy property was a signal for the authorities to act more harshly; hunger strikes were met with the brutalised and brutalising practice of force-feeding and the horrors of Emily Wilding Davison's (perhaps unintended) suicidal jump in front of the King's horse on Derby Day, 4 June 1913. Although Sylvia was against such increased extremism, she was reluctant to oppose it, considering her qualms to be too traitorous to utter:

> I would rather have died at the stake than say one word against the actions of those who were in the throes of the fight. I knew but too surely that the militant women would be made to suffer renewed hardships for each act of more serious damage. Yet in the spate of that impetuous movement, they would rush enthusiastically to their martyrdom, and bless, as their truest saviours, the leaders who summoned them to each new ordeal. I realised how supremely difficult is the holding of calm thought and the sense of perspective at such a time, how readily one daring enthusiast influences another, and in the gathering momentum of numbers all are swept along. Posterity, I knew, would see the heroism of the militants and forget their damage, but in the present they would pay dearly.

Such tactics created yet more fissures in the movement, with a decisive break with old comrades such as Lawrence and Emmeline Pethick-Lawrence, who had campaigned alongside the Pankhursts from the beginning, but were ruthlessly expelled from the suffagettes by Emmeline and Christabel Pankhurst when they expressed qualms about the new strategy of violence. Sylvia's own followers now moved to the East End of London, where she hoped to attach working-class militancy to the interests of the women's movement. The first thing that had to change was the class bias of the suffragettes – no more 'Votes for Ladies', but votes for women, a significant change of emphasis. Sylvia had begun to realise that the struggle for women's rights was the struggle for all human rights. The basis of human rights was the equitable distribution of wealth and opportunity, and only socialism offered that.

The movement, of course, really proved to be a special lobby group and once it had attained its goal, its members fell away in order to join the rising fascist parties, rejoin the old Conservatives or, as Sylvia realised, create a new party for the liberation of everyone. That being said, in 1909 these differences were still to come, even if Sylvia, who was essentially a pacifist, realised the contradictions, contradictions she could not yet escape. The struggle for women's rights changed the orientation of political demands from those of radical women working within a lobby group to those of both women and men who sought universal revolution.

The suffragettes supported the Allied cause during the First World War and suspended activities; Sylvia, opposing 'capitalist' war, increased hers. In 1917 she supported the Bolshevik Revolution and Lenin; she changed the name of her paper from *The Women's Dreadnought* to *The Workers' Dreadnought*; she illegally attended the first congress of the Third International in Russia and was imprisoned on her return to Britain; she fought fascism in Italy and the invasion of Ethiopia; and she supported the Irish and the Indians in their fights for independence. In doing so, she had moved from being the daughter of visionary Victorian parents to becoming an embodiment of the promise of the future.

The Pankhursts led what was only one of a number of crusades. As the nineteenth century came to its end, there was a growing sense that the nation had become effete and corrupt. Immigrants, prostitution and lax morals had all been to blame for this. There seemed to be a hidden enemy within that only a robust Christian muscularity could combat. An air of hysteria fuelled neuroses. Christianity gathered forces for the fight against Satan. Societies like the White Cross Army, the National Purity Crusade, the National Vigilance Association and the Women's Social and Political Union all adopted a language of fundamentalism with talk of 'crusades', 'holy war' and 'martyrdom' in the fight against 'Oriental' and 'Eastern' corruption. This Christian jihad was fired by the Church and aimed at moral 'regeneration'. The Bishop of Durham in 1883, for instance, told his male listeners in Gateshead to enlist in the crusade for purity that '[they were] an Army of God … enlisted in a holy campaign … called to do battle with the most malignant and insidious of foes ... [to] fight shoulder to shoulder in this glorious crusade', while W.T. Stead, as editor of the *Pall Mall Gazette*, campaigned 'to enlist in this army those who would wage war against the men and women who, for greed or gain, seek victims to satisfy the insatiable lust of men'.

To crusade for purity and rebirth, one had to become mired in the dirt of depravity and spiritual death. This was a heady mixture, where the idea of beauty became inseparable from the idea of destruction, which in itself was seen as the ultimate expression of beauty; to die young and beautiful was better than to die old and decayed. To the poet-priest Gerard Manley Hopkins, the idea of destruction was the self-fulfilment of the beautiful.

In Hopkins' *The Windhover*, a poem he wrote in May 1877 whilst watching a kestrel, the destructive explosion of 'gold-vermillion' is far more significant than the 'sheer plod' of labouring in the field, the 'windhover' (the kestrel) itself a symbol of Christ's sacrifice:

Brute beauty and valour and act, oh, air, pride, plume, here
Buckle! And the fire that breaks from thee then, a billion
Times told lovelier, more dangerous, O my chevalier!

No wonder of it: shéer plód makes plough down sillion
Shine, and blue-bleak embers, ah my dear,
Fall, gall themselves, and gash gold-vermilion.

Such ideas fed into the mental landscape of war exemplified by the sacrificial poetry of A.E. Housman and the war sonnets of Rupert Brooke, as well as the 'blood sacrifice' of the rebels in the Dublin Post Office during the rising of 1916, but it also fed another vision: that of a whole new way of living, combining the individual quest for beauty with a communal quest for harmony. This heated rhetoric reached its apotheosis in 1915.

Arthur Foley, the Bishop of London, exhorted his congregation in language that would not have been out of place during the Crusades of the feudal period, but here directed at 'Huns' and 'Teutons' and the secret cabals on international 'Oriental bankers' fuelling the war. 'I think', he suggested, that 'the Church can best help the nation ... by making it realise that is engaged in a Holy War ... You ask my advice as to what the church is to do. I answer MOBILIZE THE NATION FOR A HOLY WAR [sic].'

Although criticised for his overblown rhetoric, Foley was back in vituperative mode in a sermon delivered in December 1915, where he told his congregation that they were 'banded in a great crusade ... to kill Germans: to kill them, not for the sake of killing, but to save the world ... and to kill them lest the civilisation of the world should be destroyed'. Such heated language was always on the brink of hysteria, hiding sexual wish-fulfilment even as it spoke of military self-sacrifice. Thus, Basil Bourchier of St Jude's in Hampstead could tell his parish quite straightfaced that 'to die for England ... [was] to taste the sweetest vintage of death that can be offered to English lips ... and to pass to that which is to come in a veritable ecstasy'.

Against such unconsciously sado-erotic imagery and such sexualised sentiments, there was little defence. The psychic make-up of the times betrayed the real nature of what had been taken for peaceful progress in the past. Belligerent sentiments were a psychic betrayal, an unmasking of the real in the illusionary. The whole set-up was one gigantic sham, or so Henry James thought on the day that the First World War was declared:

> The plunge of civilization into this abyss of blood and darkness by the wanton feat of those two infamous autocrats is a thing that so gives away the whole long age during which we have supposed the world to be, with whatever abatement, gradually bettering, that to have to take it all now for what the treacherous years were all the while really making for and meaning is too tragic for any words.

However, there was another broader but less obvious tendency hovering over late Victorian Britain. The politics of anarchism had not faded with the Greenwich bomb, but had grown in strength. Anarchism took hold of advanced thinking from the 1880s onwards, its belief in cooperation between communities, the withering of the state, the destruction of capital and imperialism and the elevation of individuality proving a heady counterblast to Labour inertia and mainstream socialist posturing.

British anarchists dreamt of bombs but did little, but this was not the case with the more ruthless terrorists who came to Britain from the Russian Empire (especially Latvia and Lithuania) between 1909 and 1911 and settled temporarily amongst the Jewish immigrants in the East End of London. These dedicated revolutionaries were social democrats of various creeds, including Mensheviks and Bolsheviks, as well as nationalists and anarchists. Entry into Britain was easy and the import of weapons or even bomb-making equipment was virtually ignored. Escaping the harsh regime of the Tsar's secret police, revolutionaries from the Baltic had found a welcome in London where socialist groups supported those dedicated to democratising Russia after the failed uprisings in 1905.

These hardened men and women, already used to extreme violence, adhered to the doctrine of 'expropriation' by which robbery (in order to finance further revolutionary activity) was dressed up as reappropriating the already 'stolen' profits of the capitalists. Theft was the chosen method of income for such groups, who moved between Britain and Eastern Europe in a number of disguises and under a variety of names. For the most part, these desperados went about armed with the latest machine pistols, expecting no mercy from the British police, whose methods they mistakenly took to be the same as those of the Tsar's Ochrana.

The waves of bombings and assassinations that had terrified Europeans in the 1880s and 1890s had merely made newspaper headlines in Britain until then, but in 1909 there was a warning of what was to come. Earlier, in 1907, an abortive attempt to assassinate the President of France killed the bomber, 'Strygia'. His brother, 'Jacob Lepidus', and his fellow accomplice, 'Paul Hefeld', fled to Britain; both disguised their identity through multiple aliases. In January 1909, the two plotted the armed robbery of the wages of Schnurmann's Rubber Factory in Tottenham. The raid was badly bungled and both men found themselves pursued by police and civilians across the Tottenham Marshes towards Walthamstow and then Chingford, at that time one of London's countryside villages.

During the pursuit, the revolutionaries commandeered a milk cart and even a tram, shooting at anybody and everything that threatened them. Exhausted and cornered, the two fought it out. Hefeld shot himself and was captured (he later died); Lepidus committed suicide. The day turned into a bloodbath. A policeman was murdered, a stray bullet killed a young boy and 15 others were wounded. Anarchists in France gloried in the 'heroes' of 'the Tottenham Outrage'. The anarchist paper *Le Retif* reported the deaths of 'our audacious comrades' whom it saw as victims 'under attack' from 'citizens, believers in the State and authority'.

Hefeld and Lepidus were both armed with sophisticated weapons, but the authorities were wilfully oblivious to both the consequences and the implications of this. Britain was an open country and there was no interference with privately held arms. British members of the SDF were, however, actively involved with gun running to European socialist colleagues and European arms were smuggled to Britain. S.G. Hobson, an SDF member, recalled how he provided fake passports to revolutionaries and helped smuggle 6,000 Browning automatics into Russia via the docks in East Ham during 1904; in 1907 a cache of arms was discovered in Newcastle; the SDF also smuggled arms through Glasgow and Edinburgh to Russia. Maxim Litvinoff, a Russian closely attached to Lenin and expelled from Europe for gun running, remained in London after the 1903 Congress, re-emerged as Maxim Harrison and continued to organise the smuggling of arms to the Bolsheviks.

A year after the Tottenham Outrage, an even more violent confrontation occurred after a bungled robbery at H.S. Harris the Jewellers in Houndsditch, in a run-down warren of old shops which backed immediately onto a set of tenements known as Exchange Buildings. It was inevitably in the East End of London that the last apocalyptic scenes of the 'anarchist' drama were to be acted out. A number of Bolshevik expropriators had planned the robbery and had rented part of numbers 9 and 11 immediately behind Harris' shop, from whence they had attempted to break through the wall using cutting equipment to get to the safe. Unfortunately, in streets that were silent because of the Jewish Sabbath, their handiwork made too much noise and attracted the attention of the neighbours, who alerted the local policeman on the beat, Constable Piper.

Piper now told his colleagues and gathered a little group of two plain clothes and five uniformed men to go and investigate. They were armed only with truncheons, but, suspecting nothing but ordinary burglars, knocked at the door of number 11 Exchange Buildings only to be greeted by the leader of the gang, 'George Garstein', who tried to get rid of them. They then knocked again, but this time they were met with a hail of gunshots. One policeman was killed outright, two others were fatally wounded and died later and another two were badly wounded. Gardstein was also wounded in the melee, shot perhaps by mistake and then dragged off by his colleagues, later to bleed to death in a pokey bedroom in a nearby lodging house.

The gang were all seasoned in revolutionary warfare, all members of the 'the Flame' (a front organisation for Lenin and the Bolsheviks) and all heavily armed with the latest weapons: Mauser and Dreyse automatic pistols. It was determined that if caught, its members would fight to the death. The leader of the gang was later identified as 'Peter the Painter', who soon became the most famous East End bogeyman since Jack the Ripper.

The 'Houndsditch Murders' were shocking because of their cold-blooded indifference to authority and a massive hunt soon got under way. Gardstein's body was discovered with ammunition and papers linking him to the Lettish Anarchist Communists and with guides on how to make bombs. In one letter to his brother, he asked mysteriously: 'Have you written to the finger of God in Libau?' His passport called him 'Schafshi Khan', but all the expropriators had numerous aliases.

An immediate round-up of suspects started and posters showed the main culprits. The police seemed to be making progress, especially with the help of Charles Perelman, the former landlord of the gang who had come forward to give evidence. Two or three of the gang were now holed up at 100 Sidney Street, a three-floor tenement near a brewery. It was a 15-minute walk along Whitechapel Road from where the robbery had gone wrong. 'Peter the Painter' was also allegedly hiding out there. There were, however, only two men inside, Fritz Svaars and a man called 'Joseph' or 'Yosef' Marx or 'William Sokolow', who were both armed with large amounts of ammunition and automatic weapons that had a range of 1,000 yards. The police on the other hand had out-of-date rifles, shotguns and Bulldog pistols with a range of only 100 yards.

Taking no chances, the police began to surround the area with 200 officers and evacuate those who lived there. This took some time, as some residents who spoke only Yiddish in this predominantly Jewish area were frightened and disturbed. Amazingly, the head of the Whitechapel Division, Inspector Wensley, then sent a number of his officers to knock on the door of the besieged house and throw pebbles at the window, but unexpected gunfire wounded a policeman and his party were forced to withdraw.

Unable to make any headway, the police asked the Home Secretary, Winston Churchill, for military reinforcements. A detachment of Scots Guards duly arrived, as did Churchill, who brought his Purdey shotgun, the whole thing being 'so extremely interesting'. As he arrived, the chant of 'Oo let 'em in?' came from onlookers, who disliked the lenient government policy towards immigrants. The 'siege' played out its tragic story for over five hours. Eventually, the besieged house caught fire. Svaars and 'Joseph', unable to escape, kept up a rapid and deadly barrage until one was finally shot dead and the other died in the burning building. When the roof collapsed, it trapped and killed one of the firemen sent to put out the fire.

A vast amount of ammunition had been used on both sides. The artillery was even on their way. An over-enthusiastic Churchill had been caught on newsreel. When it was shown in cinemas, the audience catcalled: 'Shoot 'im!' The French press thought the episode amusing. The Russians said too bad for harbouring their enemies and the Germans offered to show the British how to run a proper police state.

As for those still held in custody, little could be proved and it was convenient to blame the dead for everything that had occurred. The accused were all acquitted. One, Nina Vassilleva, worked for the Russian trade organisation in London (and spy 'front') Arcos; she died in 1963, having lived all her life near Brick Lane, only a few hundred yards from the tragedy of 1911. Another of the accused was Jakob (or Jacob) Peters, a cousin of Fritz Svaars, the man who had actually killed the policemen at Houndsditch and later had planted his gun on Gardstein. He too operated under a series of alter egos, including Jacob Colven or Kolnin. In Russia he was known as Svornoff. Acquitted for lack of evidence, he journeyed back to Russia to take part in the Revolution of 1917, rising to become Deputy Chairman of the Cheka, the Bolshevik secret police. He finally vanished in 1939 or 1944, purged by Stalin. Foreign revolution had come for the first time to the streets of London.

The deaths of the main protagonists drew a line under the affair. The government, embarrassed by the incident, by the actions of its own Home Secretary and its own inadequacy to deal with the threat of foreign terrorists, was not looking for explanations, only closure.

For many onlookers at the start of the Edwardian era, it was not only foreigners who seemed to have lost their collective mind; for others on the brink of the First World War, the entire ruling class seemed to have lost its collective brains as well as its nerve.

The Curragh 'Mutiny', as it became known, was potentially the greatest challenge to 'Edwardianism'. Indeed, although George V was on the throne by now, military complacency was a far greater threat than scientific controversy or anarchist bombs. The 'Mutiny' threatened the very fabric of the Empire. It began on 20 March 1914 with the proposal by the Liberal government to accept John Redmond's assurances about Irish loyalties and grant limited Home Rule to the South, thus splitting Ireland in two. Irish unity had become a plank of the new-style Conservatives and the party had recently added 'Unionist' to its name.

The army's officer cadre, who were expected to maintain order in the likelihood that Ulster would rebel and demand reunification, were predominantly Protestant, some even had families in Ireland, but all were temperamentally conservative. Moreover, the army, which had had a bad press after the Crimean War, had gained a reputation for loyalty and discipline, which was reflected in the numerous highly patriotic poems of the period often written by public school poets who expressed their brand of loyalty through images of sports such as cricket in far-off dusty lands. If the navy was the supreme branch of the armed forces, it was the army that was apostrophised. It was therefore unthinkable that the army would be disloyal or under what circumstances that this might occur.

The difficulty was Ireland itself, to which there was a sort of fanatical loyalism, more specifically to the myth of Ulster as a bastion of imperial loyalty. Although of little actual imperial importance, Ireland represented the cornerstone of Empire and Ulster had come to represent the cornerstone of Protestant loyalty to the throne. In anticipation of the passing of a Home Rule Act, Ulster volunteers had started arming at an alarming rate. Sir Edward Carson, a dedicated Orangeman since the age of 19 (and incidentally the barrister engaged by the Marquess of Queensberry to prosecute Oscar Wilde) and now a highly influential Irish politician, was busy stirring up emotions that were tantamount to rebellion, the agitators coming seriously close to being seen as traitors. Yet they were not seen as such because they argued that they opposed a traitorous Liberal government under Herbert Asquith, a radicalised Prime Minister voted in by traitorous elements who would bring the Empire to its knees by backdoor legislation. It was the government that therefore actually opposed king and country and was unpatriotic, not those who were arming Ulster. To the Conservatives, the government had lost its head, had been mistakenly voted in by the 'unlettered' and ignorant, and was about to pass a law that was itself an attack on the King/Emperor George V, who would literally have to be mad to sign it into law.

Meanwhile, the army was rallying to Ulster, contact being made very quickly between officers, politicians and members of the Ulster Volunteer Force in a way that was not only highly patriotic and deeply conservative but also highly subversive and divisive. The army might not, it appeared, be willing to coerce Ulster's acquiescence in a split country. It was the revolt of 'society' against the rest argued as the ultimate sacrificial stand on behalf of the King/Emperor. The fear was that by refusing orders, the Liberals might reform the armed forces by arguing for a 'democratic' army or campaign on a ticket of 'the people versus the army'. Such a position would revive the recent raw class antagonisms that had seen numerous strikes since 1911. The old stable world of clear values and definite moral positions was forced to understand its own contradiction. The world was mad indeed. Letters to *The Times* spelt out the conundrum facing the army: to obey an unacceptable order or to mutiny.

The consequences of choosing whose orders to obey were obvious to everyone. Private correspondence clearly showed the extent to which Ulster politics confused the situation for men who were meant to have the custodianship of the Empire. One letter of the time noted 'that the first duty of the corps of officers [was] the maintenance of discipline' and showed an awareness that '[we] not admit politics to the Army [sic]', a deeply held but disingenuous position as the army was deeply traditionalist. Once such restraints were removed, 'it might be the end of us', lamented the writer.

The storm centred on Brigadier-General J.E. Hough (who believed the elected government to be 'a crowd of disloyal agitators'), whose position was central to the loyalty of soldiers in Ulster. He committed his position to paper in a memorandum written between September and December 1913:

If Ulster had put herself in the wrong by a popular outburst in the form of rioting or attacks on convents etc., then many officers would no doubt obey any orders that the government might issue. If, however, Ulster maintained a fairly correct attitude, & her leaders kept their men in control – then I thought many officers would refuse to serve against Ulster & a certain number would actually join the Ulster forces. At the same time, I added, much depended upon the lead given by senior officers, & my impression was that the lead would be forthcoming and I thought that perhaps as many as 40% to 60% of the Officers would refuse to serve … The possible attitude of the Army as it was terrible even to think that the Army might refuse to obey orders & what the ultimate result might be.

… the blame could not be attached to the Army, but must be borne by the government which could issue orders so repugnant to the feelings of the Officers. The Officers & the Army were more loyal to the King & were prepared to sacrifice more for the Empire than any other body of men in the British Empire. People like myself felt strongly on the question of Ulster, and speaking for myself my reasons were three.

(1) I wanted a loyal government. Loyal to King and Empire. But the Nationalist party would not be loyal. We know what they had said &

done as regards the King & late Queen – and what their attitude had always been to England's enemies & specially during the S[outh] A[frican] war. The idea of these disloyal men becoming our rulers was an outrage to every decent feeling I possessed.

(2)   I wanted to clean government – one which would rule for the good of the country & in which the government officials would be upright & honest. I was firmly convinced that the Nationalist party would not give us a clean government, but instead we would have corruption & graft, & probably the country would be inundated with unscrupulous Irish American low class politicians.

(3)   I could not tolerate the possibility of having a priest-ridden government. No matter whether the priest were Roman Catholic – Protestant – Mahomedans or Hindus. Knowing the Irish priesthood as I do I had little doubt that religious beliefs would enter into politics and administration…

I pointed out that the objection was not that officers objected to Home Rule qua Home Rule, if there was a reasonable prospect of an Irish government being loyal, honest & not priest-ridden then Ireland might have Home Rule tomorrow for all I cared.

The memorandum reads as the swansong of Victorian ideals and Edwardian certainties. A new world was forming.

Field Marshall Sir John French, commander of the British army, had a number of meetings with the King's equerries, but was unable to resolve his own loyalties. Major General Henry Wilson, himself later to be gunned down by the IRA, noted in his diary a conversation he had had with French on 4 November 1913, in which:

I told him that I could not fire on the North at the dictation of Redmond, and this is what the whole thing means. England qua England is opposed to Home Rule, and England must agree to it before it is carried out … I cannot bring myself to believe that Asquith will be so mad as to employ force. It will split the Army and the colonies, as well as the country and the Empire.

In the end, French wrote directly to Asquith on 20 March 1914, pointing out that there would be 'civil war' in England, uprisings in major cities, agitation in India and a possible invasion of the Empire by foreign powers, and no guarantee of a disciplined army or navy to oppose the break-up of the Empire if the Home Rule Bill was passed. This was an apocalyptic warning if ever there was one and one that suggested how thin the social fabric actually might be and how the lower orders were kept in their subordinate position simply because they had not noticed the fragility of their rulers or the veneer of their civilisation.

The whole affair eventually came to nothing, as it was agreed that Home Rule would be shelved during the war and the discipline of the old army held until it was decimated during 1915 and 1916. The officers at the centre of the agitation watched as the old order apparently changed. After the war, the Bill passed without event, but so did the old ideas of the army, of patriotism and empire, king and the Protestant cause. Sir George McMann later observed:

> I often wonder if General Seely and Winston Churchill ever offer little candles to the memory of William Hohenzollern [Kaiser Wilhelm II] for restoring the officer cadre of the British Army and Navy, even though it died in the process.

The call to imperial loyalty from now on would have to be predicated on the possibility of the future, one in which the betrayals might be healed and the non-cynical Englishman resurrected. And yet the debate was undercut by a constant undertone of pessimism just surfacing before the war. The project of the future would somehow have to overcome the cynicism of its advocates over the possibility of ever achieving anything against the inertia of the present.

TWENTY

THE SOUND OF DISTANT DRUMS

By 1913, the idea of violent insurrection and war (both personal and national) would be the rhetorical position of almost all advanced thinkers, their imaginative metaphors filled with crusades, apocalyptic violence and images of heroic death. Paradoxically, the old world now had to be swept away in order to save it; blood would bring a cleaner future. Every branch of art and letters reeked of the charnel house: Emmeline Pankhurst in 1913 talked of an endless 'woman's war' and during a period of unprecedented strike action, Lloyd George struck an even more apocalyptic note:

> I should not be doing my duty here as Finance Minister if I did not utter this word of solemn warning – that the prospect of an equitable settlement of these dangerous disputes is complicated and darkened, undoubtedly, by the situation in Ireland. Should there be civil strife in that land, and Heaven avert it, in the course of the next few weeks, when that industrial trouble which I have referred to is maturing, the situation will be the gravest with which any Government in this country has had to deal for centuries.

Foremost of the young men of blood was Percy Wyndham Lewis. Lewis was a follower of F.T. Marinetti, the Italian founder of Futurism, who had come to Britain in 1914 to advertise his movement to British artists lagging behind in their provincial backwater. Marinetti's movement, which would later align itself with fascism as an aesthetic ideal, preached a nihilist cocktail of impossible demands. 'We wish to glorify War', the first Futurist manifesto proclaimed, 'the only health-giver of the world – militarism, patriotism, the destructive arm of the Anarchist, the beautiful

Ideas that kill, the contempt for women'. Lewis embraced Marinetti's views and gave them an English name, Vorticism. Lewis became, as Ezra Pound called him, 'a man of war', and the war was against everything that could be smashed in the old culture. God, religion, politeness, reason, manners, good taste – all were consigned to the bonfire:

> Mr Lewis has got into his work something which I recognise as the voice of my own age, an age which has not come into its own, which is different from any other age which has yet expressed itself intensely ... And we have in Mr Lewis our most articulate voice. And we will sweep out the past century as surely as Attila swept across Europe.

Nevertheless, it was the impulse of the barbarians, not the Romans that was the taste of the new, and it was the barbarians (in this confused rhetorical soup) that would cleanse civilisation even as they swept it away. It was civilisation that had grown decadent and flabby, so away with it and good riddance.

Edmund Gosse saw war both as an astringent and as an 'awakener from the idleness of opium dreams':

> War is the great scavenger of thought. It is the sovereign disinfectant, and its red stream of blood is the Condy's Fluid that cleans out the stagnant pools and clotted channels of the intellect. I suppose that hardly any Englishman who is capable of a renovation of the mind has failed to feel during the last few weeks a certain solemn refreshment of the spirit, a humble and mournful consciousness that his ideals, his aims, his hopes during our late past years of luxury and peace have been founded on a misconception of our aims as a nation, of our right of possess a leading place in the sunlighted spaces of the world. We have awakened from an opium-dream of comfort.

Indeed, war would even renew art itself, as Sir Charles Stanford, Professor of Music at Cambridge, sincerely believed:

> The unmistakable influence which natural convulsions and inter-national wars have had at all times in awakening the highest forces of musical art is one of the most interesting problems of the historian and the psychologist.

The evidence is convincing and cumulative. At no time has a great country failed to produce great composers when its resources have been put to the supreme test of war ... Hence it is as common to find a great artistic movement rising at moments of gravest peril, and even of disaster, as at a period of triumphant success.

Such views were the commonplace of intellectual and drawing-room life, even being repeated when war became a reality. Against them were ranged internationalism and pacifism, branches of secular socialism and socialist Christianity respectively. The Universal Peace Congress of 1908 was even attended by George V, but the idea of peace had withered by 1914. The women's movement and the socialist movement split over the coming war; Henry Hyndman and Emmeline Pankhurst both took an ultra-patriotic line, whilst the internationalists of the socialist left, led by Theodore Rothstein and the internationalists of the women's movement under Sylvia Pankhurst, turned to the class struggle in place of the national struggle.

Nevertheless, the antagonists were not lined up as pure pacifists against war per se, but against this particular dirty war led by 'capitalists', 'plutocrats' and arms dealers; class war was the only clean war and as such socialists and left-wing feminists would sit out the conflagration. A debased Darwinism stood at the heart of the debate over war: were humans developing towards greater cooperation or towards the survival of the fittest?

Even as the nineteenth century waned, there was concern over the direction of those democratic tendencies that had begun in the 1832 Reform Bill. Collectivism had taken hold, but democracy still seemed a long way off. Causes such as the women's movement and the socialist movement had become frustrated with progress and internal division; democracy seemed indefinitely postponed. On the other hand, the sense of individualism and self-expression seemed squeezed. The result was growing frustration with the politics of the period and the successes of the Victorian age. In their place grew a new sense of purpose determined by collective action directed from a singular head. Thus, Henry Hyndman became more wilful and more authoritarian as the new century progressed, Emmeline Pankhurst, frustrated with the progress of women's rights, became 'dictator' of her movement, and Oscar Wilde took to the 'dictatorship' of the martyred Christian self, as did the born-again Christabel Pankhurst and the new-minted messiah Octavia. The radical authoritarianism of British fascism was not therefore merely a result of the enervation following the First World War, but had gestated much earlier in the latter years of the nineteenth century and the early years of the twentieth. In many ways, the revolutionary nature of fascism lay before the war, the ideology being itself the last incarnation of the Victorian spirit and a motivating spirit of the new, combining the dictatorship of the proletariat under the dictatorship of the supreme self.

That supreme self, defined against the masses but leading them on to victory against the forces of the old and reactionary, was to be embodied in the Byronic Oswald Mosley, who, although born late in the century on 16 November 1896, was to incarnate many of the tensions discussed up to now. On the one hand, he was an aristocrat of the old school, the son of Sir Oswald Mosley senior, fifth Baron of Ancoats, whose silver-spoon first marriage to Lady Cynthia Curzon was attended by three kings and two queens. On the other hand, he was a supremely self-made man who was defined by his own self-image. The aristocracy who flocked to his cause in the early years was never able to recognise the ultimate deception, because his self-image led him to move restlessly between the Conservatives (1918–22), Labour and the Independent Labour Party (1924–31) until he settled on a party of 'one', the New Party (1931–2), which turned into the British Union and (before the war) the British Union of Fascists (1932–8). Such apparent wavering was simply a journey through the democratic process and out into the rejection of the parliamentary process and towards an age of collectivism directed under technocrats. The last swashbuckling individual, good at fencing and womanising, would be Mosley himself.

Mosley represented all the elan and anxiety that characterised the aristocracy at the time, but he also represented a rejection of the aristocratic and conservative values of conservation, continuity and tradition. Instead, he attempted to give voice to a different set of anxieties – those of the 'common' man bereft of natural leadership. In this, his solution was an ideology of the future defined by collectivism (but not by Bolshevism or communism) under a supreme leader. Thus, his approach combined the collectivism of the past with a belief in the new 'great' man, whose inner vision gave him supreme individualism and whose role was that of messiah of the new age; in this case, an age not of tolerance but of authoritarianism, defined as an era of perpetual struggle for a fascist future. Ultimately, he appealed to very few, as did those countervailing forces that preached internationalism and class war. Nevertheless, between them, the two ideologies of fascism and communism, with their messianic belief in collective action and far-off utopias, came to define the most aggressive ends of the democratic spectrum and each was dedicated to destroying it.

Mosley's innovation with British fascism was to turn a post-war reactionary movement which appealed to retired army colonels living in Eastbourne and eccentric imperialists into a dynamic force with a revolutionary message. In some ways, of course, he had no other option if he wished to distance himself from the National Fascisti and the old-style reactionary politics of his predecessors, but he also understood that all political movements following the Bolshevik takeover would, of necessity, have to prove revolutionary in order to suggest the energy and drive that would distance them from the old corrupt world they wished to replace.

In creating a revolutionary fascism designed for British consumption, Mosley understood that older reactionary views would have to be aligned with new ideas of change and the future. Unlike labourism, socialism and communism, from which he heavily borrowed ideas of economic management and change, Mosley cleverly aligned economic regeneration with moral and national regeneration, thus creating a personal psychic landscape that mirrored the national scene. Before the turn towards anti-semitism, British fascism was a movement that borrowed the clothes of revolution as a distancing device from other political movements even as it copied them.

Mosley set down his creed as early as 1932 in a little pamphlet called '10 Points of Fascism', in which he explained his ideas for new adherents. He opened his call to arms with an apparent contradiction – one that had caused argument since the French Revolution – that is, how may one reconcile conformity and patriotism with revolution and disruption? It was a question that had been asked throughout the nineteenth century and was now supposedly answered in a fascist ideology that was no longer tied to earlier fascist movements. Fascism was the creed of patriotism *and* revolution. For the first time, a movement emerged which, on the one hand, was loyal to king and country and, on the other hand, stood for far-reaching and revolutionary changes in government, in economics and in life itself:

Hitherto, patriotism has been associated with those who wished to keep things as they were … We love our country, but we are determined to build a country worthy of that love. Things cannot remain as they are: we must have great changes to adapt modern Britain to modern fact. True patriotism finds expression for the first time in the revolution of Fascism.

No longer related to that 'flabby internationalism' of old, those Britons who had been 'betrayed' by the system could now prepare for the 'day of action' when the 'state' would be challenged on behalf of those whose interests were truly 'British'. It was a message that appealed to many sections of society fearful of Bolshevism, terrified by unemployment and annoyed at government lassitude. It appealed to all those who longed for a new world order where cooperation and regularity would rise above either selfish individual desire or big business bullying. Mosley therefore represented himself as the fulfilment of egalitarianism in a mirror image of communism in which the myth of 'team-work' and the sportsmanship of the Eton Boating Song would be the abiding framework. The very use of uniforms was itself the outward sign of the new-style equality:

Fascists bind themselves together to serve their country in a voluntary discipline, because without discipline they realise that nothing can be done. The black shirts which they wear symbolise their determination to save the nation. They are not afraid to stand out from their fellows as men dedicated to the service and revival of their country. The wearing of the black shirt by our more active members breaks down all barriers of class within our ranks, for all are dressed alike. The salute is the recognition of a brother Fascist who is inspired by the same passionate ideal of national service. Fascism, like every political creed this country has ever known, is common to all great countries, but Fascism is more in keeping with the British character than any other political faith. For the essence of Fascism is team-work, the power to pull together and to sink individual interests in the service of the nation. This we claim has been the leading characteristic of the British people at every great moment of our history.

To solve the crisis in capitalism, a result of the inability to match purchase power to productive capacity, fascism would also invoke collectivism in the form of a centralised or 'corporate' state run effectively by nominated 'soviets', but preserving, where necessary, individual ownership regulated by national state-led control, control which would also apply to agriculture:

Fascism solves the problem of unemployment and poverty by establishing the Corporate State. Industry will be divided into national Corporations governed by representatives of employers, workers and consumers, operating under Fascist government. The State will not attempt to conduct industry as it would under Socialism. Instead, the State will lay down the limits within which industry may operate, and those limits will be the national welfare. Private ownership will be permitted and encouraged, provided such activity enriches the nation as well as the individual. All interests which operate against the nation will be rigorously suppressed. The function of the Corporations will be to raise wages and salaries over the whole field of industry as science, rationalisation and industrial technique increase the power to produce. Consumption will be adjusted to production, and a Home Market will be provided by the higher purchasing power of our own people.

Mosley also wholeheartedly took up the challenge of that machine society proposed by Italian Futurism and by British Vorticism and aligned it to H.G. Wells' Fabian vision of a new group of 'Samurai' supermen who would be the technical experts of the age of automatism. Fascism explicitly argued for a 'technical' rather than a 'political' parliament to end division, 'chaos' and 'class war', and the world of 'old men'.

To support these ideas, Mosley called for a rigid and controlled empire (an autarchic empire) federated with the British in the 'New British Union', which would be as far as possible isolated from global economic friction and therefore the vicissitudes of global market forces. The 'virile manhood' of Britain would join the happy sweat of colonials in providing all that would be needed. The global market would be tamed by isolation and removing the 'alien menace' of the 'financiers of the City of London'.

Under the heading 'Leadership–Parliament–Liberty', Mosley's Britain was to be one regulated and controlled by the 'democratic will' of the people whose aim would be to replace democracy with a new style of dictatorship, bearing much in common with the universe of Plato's Republic: authentic democracy would be now be restored by abolishing those current democratic processes which were just a smokescreen for exploitation. What would replace the sham of British democracy would be a fascist government elected in the name of the whole people, a political idea as old as the French Revolution and one put into practice more recently by Lenin's Bolsheviks. The will of the people would replace the will of the representatives of the people in Parliament and, in so doing, would effectively end political differences and the party system. What would replace it would be a party dedicated to leading and directing the will of the people as the vanguard of the future. This was nothing less than the will to dominate the processes of the future by abolishing the conflicts of historical process; the intention was effectively to abolish the very idea of the future as a process of change and replace it with the concept of permanence:

Fascism is a leadership of the nation. It is not dictatorship in the old sense of the word, which implies government against the will of the people. It is dictatorship in the modern sense of that word, which implies government armed by the people with complete power of action to overcome problems which must be solved if the nation is to live. We seek to achieve our aims by peaceful, legal and constitutional means with the willing consent of the nation declared at a General Election. Fascist Government, however, will at once take power to act by securing from the first Fascist parliament complete power of action for the Government … Women who are not in industry will vote as wives and mothers, and will thus be represented for the first time by people competent to speak for the great national interest which they represent … Government will no longer depend on the intrigues and manoeuvres of conflicting parties, but on the will of the nation directly expressed. Thus the people will retain full liberty to approve or reject the policy of the Government, but a Government so approved and supported will have power to act and to end economic chaos.

This version of the Blackshirt life looked backwards to earlier decades and an equally decadent time where the soul was required to rise above the 'posturing' of the 'flaneur' and the 'pampered ego', whose only existence was a 'riot of self-exhibition', a phrase more appropriate for the days of Oscar Wilde than the 1930s. The 'Leadership Principle' now being openly espoused by Mosley's followers was one that had to rise above the 'redundant soul's decay' and pull mankind upwards 'above all cosmic fears'.

Mosley, we are told in his pamphlets, was in the great regenerative tradition of the nineteenth century calling upon Britons to renew their 'soul' in a great 'crusade'. Yet this crusade was dedicated to the appearance of a totalitarian state whose function would be to subsume the individual within its grasp in order to guarantee that individual's freedom, because for fascism, the state embodies the needs of all citizens, just as 'the people' did in the French Revolution. The state would effectively be the new religion, defeating the crass commercial and 'pagan' religion that then existed.

This fascist crusade was, in effect, a revolutionary swerve calling us back to 'Merrie England' cured of that social 'progress' that was 'inherent in the social scheme of things', but which tended towards 'disintegration'. Again there is the appeal above 'class war', above the do-nothing attitude of Toryism and the blandishments of the 'red flag', as well as Labour's 'inevitability of gradualness'. Procrastination was to be replaced by revolutionary action, but revolutionary action that was peculiarly British rather than the antics of revolutionary France or Russia. A.K. Chesterton, cousin to the author G.K. Chesterton, long-time supporter of Mosley and founder of the National Front in 1967, wrote another pamphlet during 1935 setting out 'The Creed of a Fascist Revolutionary':

The people of Britain are not adepts in the use of anger. That is why our politicians sleep so peacefully at night, and why no nocturnal terrors hover around the pillows of our Press magnates, or disturb the beatific slumbers of our money-jugglers. The indignation which melts before newspaper blandishments or is conveniently side-tracked by newspaper lies, is not the kind to draw tumbrils through the street in the glow of a blood-red sunset.

Fascism came upon the scene to insist that anger, far from being akin to madness and the peculiar vice of the barbarian, was indispensable to the ordered progress of mankind:

Tempered and disciplined [fascism] becomes perhaps the chief of all the social virtues which shall redeem the world. Not that the streets of Merrie England shall flow red with blood; not that heads will roll in the sand. The Fascist revolutionary refuses to regard the lives of the quacks and jugglers as sufficiently valuable to destroy. What shall be destroyed is the toleration which is their breeding ground, together with the political and economic systems which they have shaped so deftly to their heart's desire.

As British fascism moved towards what it believed to be its ultimate triumph, it became more revolutionary and more strident. Fascist revolution was not merely a change in government but a change in the self so that 'before transforming society', the budding fascist had to 'transform his own life'. Fascist revolutionaries, like revolutionaries before and since, had to renounce the world for the cause and had to renounce the present for the future in their unswerving duty to the supreme leader:

It shall be said of the Fascist revolutionary that before transforming society he transformed his own lie ... Those who serve Fascism as revolutionaries must lay aside creature-comforts and security. That is the least of the demands made upon them. Night after night shall they go forth to speak, or to protect those who speak from the argument of broken bottles. Week after week shall they surrender themselves to routine long after the novelty has worn thin.

If there is to be discerned in the Blackshirts an immeasurable confidence, it is because we know that such a leader has already come among us; because we have looked for him in the eye and fear no more for the future of our race.

It appeared that the Vril superman had arrived just in time. Chesterton's final appeal was to the 'lost generation' and to the 'Warrior Dead of the Empire' watching:

> The vision of a future that held no place for the sordid futilities of the past – a future sanctified by the blood-caked agony of the fields of France and dedicated for all time to the noblest aspirations of your race.

> Looking back upon the wreckage of the years we contemplate, not alone the organised betrayal of your cause, but the hideous, calculated cynicism by means of which it is encompassed. To your memory they raised the Cenotaph, but the FUTURE [sic] of your vision they did not build.

What would compose this vision of futurity rising over the ruins of the past, and who would own it and inhabit the new Jerusalem? Here, then, are the mystic symbols of a century decaying even as it imagines it is in the rudest health: a splash of red paint and the colour green; a balanced hazelnut and a rag of ectoplasm; a manifesto in the hands of a shivering peddler; Eastern European voices talking of revolution; a laboratory full of chemicals; a green carnation; a beaver pelt and an eagle's feather; an encounter in a Cairo hotel; angels and electrics; opium and a striptease; a Martian attack and London destroyed; three dead policemen in Houndsditch and a shoot-out in Stepney; a feeding tube; a lightning-bolt lapel badge and an Arab headdress – all come into focus as the age progresses, as strange as the man on the moon.

In one sense, this story is about the tatters of a century or those marginal scribblings formed out of the fog of peripheral vision, swirling slowly into recognisable patterns and slowly becoming intelligible, these scribblings being the hidden forces of a period, marginal notes little recognised or ignored for what they were and what they meant at the time, coming quietly to define an age, to make it what it was and is to become.

Images from a scrapbook of 'defeats' and defeated individuals, where hopes were often dashed and expectations ridiculed, until unfaded and yet brighter, the personal desires of rebellious outsiders came finally to resurrection, dreams and ideologies lived in utopian times. In the mutterings of marginalised people, which the nineteenth century heard only as a distant undifferentiated murmur, but through which the Edwardian twilight and beyond was to become the cacophony of the twentieth century, arose the unmistakable voices of revolutions shaking both the stability of society and the meaning of the self.

Here were the revolutionary voices of the margins which spoke against the centre, a centre seemingly so powerful as to be unshakeable, but nurturing, deep in its heart, a fear of imminent collapse and a growing entropic sense of its own unsustainable progress. Collapse and entropy, the godless landscape of barbed wire and bombs from which a new world was born, but which had gestated in the darkness of the margins for 100 years. Every century produces its outcasts, whether ideas or people. It is in this disregarded jetsam that future worlds emerge and future tragedy and triumph are finally born.

The Victorian and Edwardian periods saw the fermentation of ideas regarding the state of the self and the meaning of the state that had far-reaching consequences; whether they came from Oscar Wilde's 'invention' of celebrity or T.E. Lawrence's work for Arab nationalism, from Aleister Crowley's Temple of Thelema or from the forgotten anarchists whose incendiary methods punctured the century, the age was dedicated to an ideology of the realisation of the future which would be realised in deed and thought of as the *only* future. This ideological discourse would provide the trajectory in which history finally would stop its narrative meanderings: it would be a place of dreams, lofty ambitions and death; it is what sent Dadd mad and Chatterton howling. It is the project of the unrealised future that unites the self to its political realisation. The appearance of this future state would be brought about by constant revolutionary change and the appearance of a 'future race', one not yet determined as communist, anarchist, libertarian, feminist, spiritualist, environmentalist or even fascist, for this was for generations as yet unborn to decide.

BIBLIOGRAPHY

Adams, Jad, *Gandhi: Naked Ambition* (London: Quercus, 2011).

Barkas, Janet, *The Vegetable Passion: A History of The Vegetarian State of Mind* (London: Routledge & Kegan Paul, 1975).

Barrow, Logie and Bullock, Ian (eds), *Democratic Ideas and the British Labour Movement: 1880–1914* (Cambridge University Press, 1996).

Beckett, Ian F.W., *The Army and the Currragh Incident, 1914* (London: Bodley Head, 1986).

Bentley, Michael, *The Climax of Liberal Politics: British Liberalism in Theory and Practice: 1868–1918* (London: Edward Arnold, 1987).

Blom, Philipp, *The Vertigo Years: Europe, 1900–1914* (New York: Basic Books, 2008).

Bondeson, Jan, *Queen Victoria's Stalker: The Strange Story of the Boy Jones* (Stroud: Amberley, 2010).

Boorstin, Daniel J., *The Americans: The Democratic Experience* (New York: Vintage, 1974).

Booth, Martin, *A Magick Life: A Biography of Aleister Crowley* (London: Hodder & Stoughton, 2000).

Camus, Albert, *The Rebel*, Anthony Bower (trans.) (Harmondsworth: Penguin, 1953).

Charlton, John, *It Just Went Like Tinder: The Mass Movement & New Unionism in Britain, 1889* (London: Redwords, 1999).

Chesterton, A.K., *Creed of a Fascist Revolutionary* (Ramsgate: European Action, 2010).

Colloms, Brenda, *Victorian Visionaries* (London: Constable, 1982).

Conrad, Joseph, *The Secret Agent* (London: Methuen, 1946).

Cornish, Kimberley, *The Jew of Linz: Wittgenstein, Hitler and the Secret Battle for the Mind* (New York: Century Books, 1998).

Cross, Colin, *The Fascists in Britain* (London: Barrie & Rockliff, 1961).

Crowley, Aleister, *The Heart of the Master* (London: OTO, 1938).

Crowley, Aleister, *The Book of Lies* (York Beach, ME: Samuel Weiser Inc., 1952).

Crowley, Aleister, *The Book of the Law* (York Beach, ME: Samuel Weiser Inc., 1976).

Dicey, A.V., *Lectures on the Relation between Law & Public Opinion in England During the Nineteenth Century* (London: Macmillan, 1948).

Dickson, Lovat, *Half-Breed: The Story of Grey Owl* (London: Peter Davies, 1947).

Doyle, Sir Arthur Conan, *The Lost World and Other Stories* (Ware: Wordsworth Classics, 1995).

Fishman, William J., *East End Jewish Radicals, 1875–1914* (London: Five Leaves, 2004).

Foote, G.W., *Reminiscences of Charles Bradlaugh* (London: The Freethought History Research Group, 2009).

Freitag, Sabine, *Exiles from European Revolutions: Refugees in Mid-Victorian England* (New York: Berghahn Books, 2003).

Fussell, Paul, *The Great War and Modern Memory* (Oxford University Press, 1975).

Garner, Les, *Stepping Stones to Women's Liberty* (London: Heineman, 1984).

Gittings, John, *The Glorious Art of Peace: From the Iliad to Iraq* (Oxford University Press, 2012).

Gould, Gerald, *The Coming Revolution in Great Britain* (London: W. Collins & Sons, 1920).

Hardie, Frank, *The Political Influence of the British Monarchy, 1868–1952* (New York: Harper & Row, 1970).

Hattersley, Owen, *Militant Modernism* (Ropley: Zero Books, 2008).

Himmelfarb, Gertrude (ed.), *The Spirit of the Age: Victorian Essays* (New Haven: Yale University Press, 2007).

Hoare, Philip, *Oscar Wilde's Last Stand* (New York: Arcade Publishing, 1997).

Holland, Caroline, *The Notebooks of a Spinster Lady: 1878–1903* (London: Cassell, 1919).

Hopkirk, Peter, *On Secret Service East of Constantinople* (London: John Murray, 1994).

Hopkirk, Peter, *The Great Game: On Secret Service in High Asia* (London: John Murray, 2006).

Hyde, H. Montgomery, *Famous Trials 7: Oscar Wilde* (Harmondsworth: Penguin, 1948).

Hynes, Samuel, *A War Imagined: The First World War and English Culture* (London: Bodley Head, 1990).

James, Lawrence, *The Golden Warrior: The Life and Legend of Lawrence of Arabia* (New York: Skyhorse Publishing, 2008).

Jefferys, Kevin, *Politics & The People: A History of British Democracy since 1918* (London: Atlantic Books, 2007).

Kapp, Yvonne, *Eleanor Marx: The Crowded Years: 1884–1898* (London: Virago, 1976).

Kapp, Yvonne, *Eleanor Marx: Family Life 1855–1883* (London: Virago, 1979).

Katanka, Michael (ed.), *Radicals, Reformers & Socialists* (London: Charles Knight, 1973).

Kendall, Walter, *The Revolutionary Movement in Britain 1900–21* (London: Weidenfeld & Nicolson, 1969).

Lamont, Peter, *The First Psychic: The Peculiar Mystery of a Notorious Victorian Wizard* (London: Abacus, 2006).

Lavin, Deborah, *Bradlaugh Contra Marx* (London: Socialist History Society, 2011).

Lawrence, T.E., *The Mint* (London: Jonathan Cape, 1955).

Lawrence, T.E., *Seven Pillars of Wisdom* (Ware: Wordsworth Classics, 1997).

Lewis, Wyndham, *The Apes of God* (London: Nash & Grayson, n.d.).

Litvinoff, Barnet, *Weizmann: Last of the Patriarchs* (London: Hodder & Stoughton, 1976).

Longford, Elizabeth, *Queen Victoria* (Stroud: Sutton Publishing, 1999).

Machen, Arthur, *The Great God Pan* (London: Creation Books, 1996).

Maeterlinck, Maurice, *The Life of the Bee* (London: George Allen & Unwin, 1935).

Manvell, Roger, *The Trial of Annie Besant and Charles Bradlaugh* (London: Elek/Pemberton, 1976).

Marsh, Jan, *Back to the Land* (London: Quartet Books, 1982).

Martin, Stoddard, *Art, Messianism and Crime: Sade, Wilde, Hitler, Manson and Others* (London: Macmillan, 1986).

Marx, Karl and Engels, Freidrich, *On the Paris Commune* (Moscow: Progress Publishers, 1971).

McClellan, Woodford, *Revolutionary Exiles: The Russians in the First International and the Paris Commune* (London: Frank Cass, 1979).

McKay, George, *Radical Gardening: Politics, Idealism & Rebellion in the Garden* (London: Frances Lincoln, 2011).

Miller, Russell, *The Adventures of Arthur Conan Doyle* (New York: St Martin's Press, 2008).

Milton, Nan, *John Maclean* (London: Pluto Press, 1973).

Morris, A.J.A., *Edwardian Radicalism: 1900–1914* (London: Routledge & Kegan Paul, 1974).

Morris, William, *News from Nowhere* (Oxford University Press, 2009).

Morrison, Robert, *The English Opium Eater: A Biography of Thomas De Quincey* (London: Phoenix, 2009).

Mosley, Oswald, *10 Points of Fascist Policy* (Ramsgate: European Action, 2008).

Muggeridge, Kitty and Adam, Ruth, *Beatrice Webb: A Life 1858–1943* (London: Secker & Warburg, 1967).

Murphy, Paul Thomas, *Shooting Victoria: Madness, Mayhem and the Modernisation of the Monarchy* (London: Head Zeus, 2012).

Newman, Paul, *Aleister Crowley and the Cult of Pan* (London: Greenwich Exchange, 2004).

Niblett, Bryan, *Dare to Stand Alone: The Story of Charles Bradlaugh* (Oxford: Kramedart Press, 2010).

Pankhurst, Richard, *Sylvia Pankhurst: Artist and Crusader* (New York: Paddington Press, 1979).

Parrinder, Patrick and Gasiorek, Andrzej (eds), *The Oxford History of the Novel in English, Volume 4, The Reinvention of the British and Irish Novel 1880–1940* (Oxford University Press, 2011).

Pater, Walter, *The Renaissance* (London: Macmillan, 1912).

Pearsall, Ronald, *The Table-Rappers* (London: Michael Joseph, 1972).

Pellew, Jill, *The Home Office: 1848–1914: From Clerks to Bureaucrats* (London: Heinemann Educational Books, 1982).

Pelling, Henry, *Origins of the Labour Party* (Oxford: Oxford University Press, 1965).

Pendlebury, Alyson, *Portraying 'the Jew' in First World War Britain* (London: Valentine Mitchell, 2006).

Poe, Edgar Allan, *Tales of Mystery and Imagination* (London: J.M. Dent & Sons, 1931).

Pugh, Martin, *The Pankhursts: The History of One Radical Family* (London: Vintage, 2008).

Purkiss, Diane, *Troublesome Things: A History of Fairies and Fairy Stories* (London: Penguin, 2000).

Rappaport, Helen, *Conspirator: Lenin in Exile* (London: Windmill Books, 2010).

Reay, Barry, 'The Last Rising of the Agricultural Labourers', *History Workshop Journal* 26 (1988), 86.

Reay, Barry, *The Last Rising of the Agricultural Labourers: Rural Life and Protest in Nineteenth-Century England* (London: Breviary Stuff Publications, 2010).

Rogers, P.G., *The Sixth Trumpeter: The Story of Jezreel and His Tower* (Oxford: Oxford University Press, 1963).

Rose, Paul Lawrence, *Wagner: Race and Revolution* (New Haven: Yale University Press, 1992).

Rosenberg, Chanie, *1919: Britain on the Brink of Revolution* (London: Bookmarks, 1987).

Rothstein, Andrew, *Lenin in Britain* (London: Central Books, n.d.).

Ruskin, John, *The Lamp of Memory* (Harmondsworth: Penguin, 2008).

Saklatvala, Sehri, *The Fifth Commandment: Biography of Shapurji Saklatvala* (Salford: Miranda Press, 1991).

Shaw, Jane, *Octavia, Daughter of God: The Story of a Female Messiah and Her Followers* (London: Jonathan Cape, 2011).

Sinnot, Nigel, *The Reverend Stuart Headlam and Friends: Anglo Catholics, Atheists, Actors, Aesthetes and Radicals* (Melbourne: The Existential Society, 1 August 2006).

Stack, David, *Queen Victoria's Skull* (London: Continuum, 2008).

Stirner, Max, *The Ego & His Own*, Steven T. Byington (trans.) (New York: Dover, 1973).

Strachey, Lytton, *Queen Victoria* (Harmondsworth, Penguin, [1921] 1971).

Sweet, Matthew, *Inventing the Victorians* (London: Faber & Faber, 2001).

Tromans, Nicholas, *Richard Dadd: The Artist and the Asylum* (London: Tate Publishing, 2011).

Turner, Michael J., *The Age of Unease: Government and Reform in Britain, 1782–1832* (Stroud: Sutton Publishing, 2000).

Walpole, Horace, *The Castle of Otranto*, in Peter Fairclough (ed.), *Three Gothic Novels* (Harmondsworth: Penguin, 1986).

Washington, Peter, *Madame Blavatsky's Baboon* (New York: Schocken, 1995).

Watson, Ben, *Art, Class & Cleavage* (London: Quartet Books, 1998).

Webb, Beatrice, *My Apprenticeship* (London: Longmans, Green & Co., 1926).

Wilde, Oscar, *De Profundis* (London: Methuen, 1943).

Wilde, Oscar, *Plays* (Harmondsworth: Penguin, 1977).

Wilson, Ben, *The Making of Victorian Values: Decency & Dissent in Britain: 1789–1837* (New York: Penguin, 2007).

Wilson, Colin, *The Outsider* (London: Victor Gollancz, 1957).

Wistrich, Robert S., *Anti-Semitism: The Longest Hatred* (New York: Pantheon Books,1989).

Woodcock, George, *Oscar Wilde: The Double Image* (New York: Blackrose Books, 1989).

Websites

www.andrewwhitehead.net/dan-chatterton.html
www.kibbokift.org/jhbio.html
www.srgw.demon.co.uk/CremSoc
www.thaxted.co.uk/content/conrad-noel

INDEX